HARVARD ECONOMIC STUDIES

VOLUME LXXVI

THE STRUCTURE OF
SOVIET WAGES

A STUDY IN SOCIALIST ECONOMICS

BY

ABRAM BERGSON

ASSISTANT PROFESSOR OF ECONOMICS, UNIVERSITY OF TEXAS

CAMBRIDGE, MASSACHUSETTS
HARVARD UNIVERSITY PRESS
1954

PRINTED AT THE HARVARD UNIVERSITY PRINTING OFFICE
CAMBRIDGE, MASSACHUSETTS, U.S.A.

To

F. W. T.

PREFACE

THE PRESENT STUDY deals mainly with wage statistics for 1928 and 1934, but an effort has been made to trace the course of Soviet wage policy up to 1937, which is the year when the work was initiated, and certain related subjects are followed for brief periods to roughly the same date.

The scattered information available for more recent years reveals no notable shift in wage policy, but mention ought to be made here of a decree of November 1937, boosting the wages of low-paid workers in industry and transport. A similar decree, enacted in May 1934, is referred to in the text; the promulgation of a second such measure, however, suggests that equalitarianism has not been as completely expunged from Soviet wage policy as the discussion in the text might imply.

Of events that took place prior to Russia's entry into the war, perhaps the most important, in spheres on which this study touches, are a series of decrees promulgated in 1940. Reference is to the October decree restoring fees for secondary and higher education in the U.S.S.R., the June edict providing for the criminal prosecution of workers leaving their employment without permission of the director of the employing establishment, the edict of October providing for the drafting of youths by local officials for training and employment in industry and transport, and finally the edict of the same month providing for the obligatory transfer, subject to certain compensation, of skilled workers, engineers, and other technical personnel from one employment to another. All these measures represent a substantial change in Soviet law and practice in the spheres affected, though the first is not as novel as might be supposed. Whether these measures are only a product of stringent emergency, or betoken a long-run shift in Soviet policy, it is not now possible to say. The texts of these statutes and of the November 1937 decree on the wages of low-paid workers are inserted in Appendix F.

Since the present investigation makes large use of Soviet statistics and other Soviet materials, it is desirable to anticipate a usual question: To what extent can such data inspire confidence? This question has confronted other writers, and in part my confidence in the reliability of the data used here is based on the favorable answer which careful students of Soviet economics have given it.

But independent considerations also lead me to regard the Soviet materials as trustworthy. The data which are studied here are used and discussed in Soviet economic journals, and in other Soviet publications. It seems clear that these materials are also the facts on which Soviet administrators base their decisions. On this score alone "double bookkeeping" is not remotely probable. It has been found also that the data used in the present study, when taken together with other Soviet factual materials, exhibit a broad consistency in widely diverse fields and in very different vehicles of expression. An "external" consistency, too, if the term may be used, is apparent. The comparisons which are undertaken between the inequality of wages in the U.S.S.R. and in capitalist countries reveal a striking uniformity in results, with respect to both the relative inequality in different industries and the general level of inequality in the different countries. Such consistency, of course, could hardly be demanded of the data. But it could not have been realized if the Soviet statistics were distorted or if in important degree they were inaccurate.

These remarks are not to constitute a blanket endorsement of "Soviet facts." As elsewhere, perhaps to a greater extent, attention must be given to the source of the data and the manner of their presentation. I should have less confidence, for example, in data obtained from popular literature in the U.S.S.R. than from a publication by a government statistical bureau. The data used in the present investigation are largely from the latter source, or sources comparable to it. The wage statistics are described in detail in the text.

The present work was initiated in the summer of 1937 when the writer was in the U.S.S.R. on a Sheldon Traveling Fellowship from Harvard University. A later grant from the same fund made possible a largely undistracted year's study of the rich collection of Soviet materials at the Library of Congress in Washington. Mr. N. Rodionoff and his colleagues at the Library were most helpful in making these materials accessible to me.

I am happy to acknowledge my indebtedness also, for critical comments on various parts of the manuscript, to Professor Wassily W. Leontief, Professor Paul A. Samuelson, Dr. Theodore Norman, Dr. Everett Hagen, and Mr. Paul Baran. My wife has been a most patient and encouraging listener and critic and has cheerfully assumed much of the onerous work involved in putting the manuscript through the press. Computations were performed largely by William B. Saunders.

The University of Chicago Press has kindly permitted me to make extensive use of my "Distribution of the Earnings Bill among Industrial Workers in the Soviet Union," which appeared in the *Journal of Political Economy* for April 1942.

A. B.

WASHINGTON, D. C.
January 1943

CONTENTS

TABLES IN TEXT

CHARTS

THE STRUCTURE OF SOVIET WAGES

CHAPTER I

SOCIALIST ECONOMICS

THE PRESENT WORK investigates the inequality of wages in the Soviet Union and the principles according to which the inequality is determined. To add that this is a study in socialist economics, perhaps, should not be controversial. But a note as to the basis for the designation will at the same time introduce the subsequent discussion.

By 1928, which is the first year for which detailed wage statistics will be presented, the role of private enterprise in the non-agricultural economy of the U.S.S.R. was limited mainly to domestic trade and small-scale industry. In retail trade the position of the petty capitalist was still important, but no longer the dominating one of the early years of the New Economic Policy.[1] Apparently his existence hung only on the receding physical and economic limits to the development of an administrative apparatus to replace him. The quarter of the retail sales conducted by the private trader in 1928 was in three years replaced by a *nul* in the state reports. In small-scale industry, — that is, according to Soviet terminology, in all industrial establishments producing goods for more than one household but employing 30 wage earners or less or, if motive power were used, 15 wage earners or less — three-quarters of the personnel in 1929 worked in establishments administered by private individuals and organizations. This sphere was an important one in the economy, but because of its handicraft character, and the sporadic employment furnished by it, its role was far less significant than would appear from the number of personnel: in 1929, 4.5 million persons (including independent artisans and

---

[1] The New Economic Policy is usually dated from March 1921, when the policy of requisitioning peasant grain surpluses was replaced by a fixed government tax in kind.

domestic producers) as compared with the 3.2 million employees in large-scale industry.[2]

The bulk of the non-agricultural economy of the U.S.S.R. in 1928, and the strategic sectors in it, were conducted in establishments and institutions owned and administered by the state. In railway transportation, and with minor qualifications, in banking, foreign trade, and shipping, private individuals and organizations were excluded as they had been since shortly after the October revolution.[3] In large-scale industry, establishments administered, and either owned or leased from the government by private individuals and organizations, employed but 1.3 per cent of the total number of workers. Even in the years following shortly after the introduction of the New Economic Policy the private sector of large-scale industry was little larger. The share of private enterprise in construction work was likewise small.

The state sector did not comprise all non-private enterprise. Between the two spheres a segment of the economy was administered by various coöperative organizations, such as the consumers' coöperatives, the industrial coöperatives, and the mutual credit societies. These organizations possessed various degrees of autonomy. In some cases they did not differ substantially from private organizations, and in others, in important respects, resembled state organs.[4] But, like private enterprise,

---

[2] The worker in small-scale industry on the average was engaged in this sector only one-third as long a time in the course of a year as a worker in large-scale industry. The total number of *employees* including domestic workers in all small-scale industry was 356.2 thousand.

[3] For a period the government monopoly of foreign trade was relaxed to permit private organizations to trade directly with foreign countries in those cases where they could obtain better terms than the state trading organizations. However, a state license for each transaction was required. In the banking sphere, semi-autonomous mutual credit organizations were permitted after 1922, but these never occupied a significant place in the economy.

Over two-thirds of the Russian railway mileage was in the hands of the state before the war.

[4] Larin ("Chastnyi Kapital v Promyshlennosti," *Ekonomicheskoe Obozrenie*, June 1927, pp. 109 ff.) refers to industrial coöperatives which served as a disguise for capitalists working with hired labor. The mutual credit societies also seem

they were significant mainly in small-scale industry and, in the case of the consumers' coöperatives, in retail trade. With respect to the latter, it should be noted, price policy and for a large number of commodities specific prices or price limits were determined directly or controlled by the government departments.

Soviet agriculture in 1928 was in the hands of the peasant farmer, as it had been since shortly after the revolution. All but 3 per cent of the land was tilled by nearly 25 million peasant producing units.[5] In no small measure the persistence of this multitude of individual farm holdings affected the success of the government in administering its own sector of the economy. Nevertheless, in the years prior to 1928 a foundation was laid for the planning technique, which since has been identified as a Soviet institution. Partial plans for the direction of particular divisions of the state economy were already familiar in the early twenties. Control figures for the whole state sector were drawn up for the first time by the State Planning Commission for the fiscal year 1925–26, and thereafter appeared regularly. The fiscal year chosen, beginning with October, enabled the government to project its activities on the basis of estimates of the incoming harvests. At first the control figures served at best only to orient the work of the various commissariats. Despite the State Planning Commission's pleas, the plans were not made obligatory upon the commissars, who, the Commission complained, regarded the concept of economic equilibrium somewhat cavalierly as an "abstraction." [6] In the period 1925–27

---

to me to have differed in no important respect from private organizations. On the other hand, S. and B. Webb (*Soviet Communism*, New York, 1936, I, 309) point out that after the replacement of the old leadership of the consumers' coöperatives by "well disposed" coöperators, "The Central Board . . . has ever since been in complete accord with the 'General Line.'"

[5] Private property in the land (the right of sale and lease) was abolished in the early days of the revolution, but control over the use of the land was vested in the hands of those who tilled it, and there it remained.

[6] "Dokladnaia Zapiska Gosplana SSSR Sovetu Truda i Oborony, Peresmotr Kontrol'nykh Tsifra Narodnogo Khoziaistva na 1925/26 g.," *Planovoe Khoziaistvo*, 1926, no. 2, pp. 44 ff.

only the plans of the individual commissariats were confirmed by the higher state organs. The framework of the plan for 1927–28, however, was confirmed by the government, and the control figures, with some latitude, were directives for the various state departments. The plan for 1928–29 was confirmed in its entirety by the government and all plans of individual departments had to be subordinated to it.

In concentrating on the characteristics of the Soviet economy in 1928, it is not intended to minimize the importance of changes which occurred after that time. In the sphere of planning, the most spectacular of the Soviet achievements was a product of a later period. Not until 1929, after much controversy, and after at least five different projects had been considered, was the first five-year plan for the social and economic development of the U.S.S.R. confirmed by the government. The period of operation was to end with the third quarter of 1933. The socialist transformation of the agricultural economy likewise was an accomplishment of the years following 1928. In the four-year period 1928–32 over two-thirds of the sown area was collectivized.

It will be of much interest, then, in the course of our statistical investigation to examine wage data for a post-1928 year to see whether the later Soviet developments were accompanied by a change in wage policy. Nevertheless — to return to the point from which we embarked earlier — it is quite clear that in the earlier year the Soviet economy already exhibited peculiarities which would justify labeling distinctly a study of the wage principles applicable to it. The characteristics which have led the writer to call the present investigation a study in *socialist* economics are several: first, the ownership and administration of the bulk of the community's industrial resources by the government; second, the direction and integration of this sector, though it is true with varying effectiveness, by a system of planning; and finally, the differential wage system, which is described in the following chapters. The last characteristic, it will appear, distinguishes the Soviet economy from the ideal, communism, rather than from competing systems. This usage, it is believed, does not depart from the customary one; in any case, the characteristics rather than the label are of primary interest here.

CHAPTER II

PRINCIPLES OF SOCIALIST WAGES

THE ATTEMPT to illumine Soviet wage principles made in the present study will consist primarily of squaring one particular set of wage principles against the available Soviet facts. The principles studied should sound no new note to the reader, for they are none other than the principles usually applied to capitalist wages. This fact, of course, is no bar to their application to socialist wages as well. Indeed there is strong support for the view that Marx among others foresaw just such an eventuality.[1] But before plunging into the complex Soviet world it is well to inquire whether, in general, there is any reason for focusing attention on capitalist wage principles rather than on any others.

2

Accounting Wages. The administrators of the socialist economy are confronted not only with the task of distributing wealth, but of producing it. The results realized in the second sphere are by no means independent of the principles applied in the first. The failure to recognize this fact is the utopian signature of more than one well-meaning solution to the problem of socialist distribution. Certain elements of the problem of production, it is true, may be attacked without necessarily prejudicing the solution of the problem of distribution. But, so far as the utilization of labor resources is concerned, even these aspects of socialist calculation are not likely to be without practical significance for the solution of the problem of distribution.

The socialist administrators, it is to be expected, will seek to extract as high a value product as possible from the resources at their command. Just what administrative procedure

---

[1] Marx's treatment of the problem of socialist distribution is discussed in section 5, below.

will be resorted to in order to attain this objective is not a ready subject for generalization. An omniscient planning board with the powers of Superman could arrive at an optimum allocation of resources without more ado. Administrators who are not Jovian will be greatly aided in their task, however, if a system of accounting records is maintained by the various production units into which the community is organized. Such records not only serve to record the past, but also aid the administrators to form decisions as to the future and to delegate authority and to fix responsibility. To be useful the accounting records must be kept in some unit of account, the output of each enterprise being valued at an established price, and the in-puts of labor as well as of other resources recorded at predetermined wages and prices. These practices, at least, have a counterpart in the administrative procedure of the Soviet Union. The incidental result is that socialist wages, at least as an accounting category, can claim an existence outside the minds of non-Jovian administrators.

It is an easy step to formulate in terms of the accounting-category wages a socialist production policy designed to realize the objective of utilizing labor resources as effectively as possible. It may be supposed, though it need not be inquired here how such a result is accomplished, that the prices at which the outputs of various products are valued in the state's books indicate the rates at which the socialist administrators would be willing to substitute one product for another in the community's real income, if a choice had to be made. The satisfaction of two conditions, then, will assure that the community's labor resources are used effectively. First, for any given set of accounting wages, the total wage bill required to produce any given value product must be a minimum. Thus wages are regarded as costs to be economized. Second, the actual wage rates must be such that, for some given value product, the numbers of the different kinds of workers required to operate at a minimum cost equal respectively the numbers of the different kinds of workers available for employment. In other words, at the given wage rates there must be full employment of the available labor resources.

To formulate these conditions, needless to say, is a much easier task than to realize them. The socialist "leap into plenty" is hardly automatic. Even able administrators cannot hope to more than approximate an effective utilization of the resources of an entire community. But, to whatever extent the conditions for an optimum utilization of resources are approximated, it should be clear, wages are to that degree restricted. For the optimum conditions also determine the accounting wages of different types of labor. Though nothing is implied as to the administrative or market procedure through which the conditions are approached in practice, they are logically equivalent to the conditions of supply and demand which determine capitalist wages in a competitive market. To the extent that the conditions are satisfied, furthermore, the accounting wages of the different types of labor in the socialist state must be proportionate to or within limits set by the productivity — in technical language, the "marginal value productivity" [2] — of the different types of labor. This familiar principle of capitalist wages follows directly from the fact that wage costs are minimized. For, if wages were not proportional to productivity, the substitution of workers whose wages were low relative to productivity for workers whose wages were high relative to productivity would always reduce costs. More of the low-paid and fewer of the high-paid workers would be required than were actually employed.[3]

[2] The marginal productivity of any particular type of labor employed in a particular production unit is the increment of product associated with the employment of the last worker of that type in the production unit in question. Marginal value productivity is simply the value of the increment of product. It is usually understood that both before and after the addition of another worker all resources in the production unit are employed as efficiently as possible.

[3] Strictly, in a position of minimum cost, wages will only be proportional to productivity if the production process is highly flexible, so that with the employment of additional workers in a particular occupation, the corresponding increments of output do not differ sharply, each from its predecessor. Ordinarily this is probably not the case, and relative wages are only determined within limits set

It is of more logical than practical significance to observe that in a position in which the available resources are fully employed the optimum position could be attained, too, if wages were not proportional to productivity — *provided* the disproportion for any particular type of labor were the same in every use.[4] Socialist administrators, enamored of the beauties of logic, doubtless would find it pleasant to devise administrative rules to make possible an approximation to this elegant result. But in view of the manifest simplicity of the administrative rule of equating supply and demand, it is justifiable to regard it as a highly likely, if not necessary, element in a rational socialist production policy.

But workers do not eat accounting categories, and so far it is only to accounting wages that capitalist wage principles appear to apply. Once having determined accounting wages it is not unlikely that both administrative convenience and political pressure would impel the socialist administrators to keep one set of books rather than two, and to distribute to consumers claims against goods corresponding to their accounting wages. But the effective utilization of the available labor resources implies nothing as to the economics of such a distribution. In the case of land and machinery, clearly, no personal claims against real income are established in the socialist state by the sums recorded in the state's books for their employment. Though interest and rent may continue as accounting categories, they need not be categories of consumers' income. Whether or not this is likely to be so in the case of labor, too, is a matter to be determined.[5]

---

by marginal value productivity. If such limits are wide, of course, the value of this condition as a determinant of wages is much reduced. But it may be hazarded that if a whole industry or a whole economy are taken into account the limits are quite restrictive.

[4] The essential requirement is that in a position in which all resources are employed the productivity of a particular type of labor is the same in every use.

[5] The conclusion stated in this section as to the determination of accounting wages in the socialist state is contained in the more general conclusions as to the determination of prices of the factors of production which have been advanced in the recent studies of O. Lange ("On the Economic Theory of Socialism," *Review of Economic Studies*, October 1936, February 1937, particularly pp. 60 ff.

3

Wages: Consumers' Claims. If, as was implicitly assumed in the preceding section, the supply of different types of labor were fixed, the problem of distribution under socialism would be a quite distinct problem economically from that of production. Indeed, distribution would not be an economic problem at all. The same would be true if the supply of the different types of labor were variable, but the variation were not subject to administrative control, or if the supply could be varied by administrative action, but without the incurrence of any social cost that would otherwise be avoided.

In fact, however, with respect to but few workers might these conditions be said to have a counterpart in reality. Artists, musicians, and poets, it is often said, are called to their occupation at an early age and would serve in no other. This view may be only romanticism, but to the extent that it is fact the supply of these workers is not subject to administrative control. Their reward is akin to an economic rent, and its magnitude is to be determined solely by considerations of ethics, politics, and administrative convenience.

But for most types of labor the situation confronting the socialist administrators is otherwise: the supply of workers can be influenced by administrative action. The overzealous administrator whose ethos blinds him to this fact would err gravely. The Just Shares distributed to the populace by such an official would turn out, at least in the long run, to be woefully shrunken shares. Socialist distribution is very much a problem for the tarnished abacus.

In the solution of the problem, however, much depends on the manner in which the costs of varying the supply of the different types of labor are determined. The most obvious procedure, and one which the socialist administrators would find as politic as it is simple, is to determine these costs from the work-

in the October issue) and H. D. Dickinson (*Economics of Socialism*, Oxford, 1939, particularly chapter iii). The argument supporting the conclusion, however, differs somewhat from those of Lange and Dickinson.

ers' own preferences for the different types of work. If this is done, the cost of shifting a worker from one occupation to another, which he is able to perform, is simply the additional claim on consumers' goods necessary to compensate the worker for any additional risk, responsibility, training, and physical and mental hardship or disagreeableness involved in the change. The cost of employing a new worker in one occupation rather than another is established similarly.

In determining costs in this manner, of course, the socialist administrators would not break new ground. Under capitalism costs are determined thus wherever workers have freedom of choice and the labor market is competitive — probably now a quite limited sphere. Freedom of choice and the determination of costs from a consideration of individual preference, however, are not one and the same thing. Conceivably, if the socialist administrators were sufficiently cognizant of the preferences of different workers, a free labor market in which the workers could express their preferences would be unnecessary so far as the determination of costs is concerned. Or vice versa the workers might be allowed to express their preferences in a free market and these preferences be disregarded in administrative calculation.[6] In practice, however, it is certainly questionable whether, if there were any large and continued inroads on freedom of choice, costs would continue to correspond with individual preference in the socialist state. The possibility is not to be tested, in any case, by a study of Soviet experience. The militarization of labor which characterized the early post-revolutionary years appears to have been a unique chapter in Soviet history.[7]

---

[6] The analogous possibility in the case of the market for consumers' goods has been discussed by O. Lange. (*Review of Economic Studies*, October 1936, pp. 68 ff.)

[7] These were the years of so-called War Communism. For the purpose of reducing the labor turnover, certain penalties were imposed in the period of the five-year plans on workers who shifted their employment from plant to plant. Judged by the turnover itself, however, the measures must not have been a serious deterrent to the worker's movement. See below, Chapter XI, section 3.

No principle is certain to prevail, but an approximation of the labor costs reckoned with by the socialist administrators to the workers' own evaluations of alternative employments, it is believed, has a good claim to be regarded as an integral feature of a socialist society.[8] But whether or not this view is correct, the prevalence of the principle of evaluation is very plausible. Even a supremely egocentric administrator might well quail at the administrative task of establishing and applying other values of alternative occupations than those of the workers actually engaged in them. And this is to say nothing of the political opposition which such a course might arouse.

If labor costs under socialism are determined in the manner described, socialist distribution policy is immediately restricted. For it follows that the community would gain by any shift in labor from one occupation to another for which the additional claims necessary to compensate the workers for the shift were less than the addition to the community's value product due to the change. Shifts in employment for which the added value product were less than the additional claims, *pari passu*, would result in a loss. Thus, if the claims paid workers in the different occupations differ by more or less than the productivity[9] of labor in those occupations, a change in claims up to the point where the two correspond always will result in a social gain as long as the supply of labor in the different occupations is altered by the change.[10] Should the consumers' claims differ by more or less than productivity, the supply of labor will not adjust itself fully to the opportunities which the economy affords to acquire income.

Thus, the effective utilization of resources in the socialist com-

---

[8] Compare O. Lange, *Review of Economic Studies*, October 1936, p. 70.

[9] Strictly it is "marginal value productivity" which is in point. See above, footnotes 2 and 3.

[10] It is implicitly assumed in this argument that "freedom of choice" prevails in the socialist labor market. The conclusions as to socialist distribution which are derived, however, would still be valid in the unlikely case that the administrators accept the workers' evaluations of alternative occupations as indicating differences in labor cost, but do not grant the workers freedom of choice.

munity requires that differences in the claims paid workers for different types of work equal differences in the contribution of the different types of work to the community's value product. Again the socialist principle is also a capitalist principle.

It is clear also that if the wages recorded in the socialist books are to measure labor costs correctly, accounting wages must differ from a worker's claim against consumer's goods, if at all, only by a fixed lump sum — the worker's "tax," or "dividend," as the case may be —, which is the same for all workers. Hence wages — they are no longer simply accounting wages — must be not only proportional but equal to productivity, if the resources of the community are to be utilized as effectively as possible.[11]

4

Inequality of Wages under Socialism. The morrow of the revolution, it appears, must prove profoundly disappointing to those among the socialists — and there have been and doubtless still are many — who regard equality of reward as a prime revolutionary objective. Socialist wages, the equalitarians should long ago have learned from Marx, are unlikely to be equal wages. A convinced equalitarian who by chance found himself in the saddle after the revolution and who attempted immediately to equalize the rewards of labor soon would find that in consequence both the community's income and his political power were much deflated.

The determination of socialist wages in accord with capitalist principles, however, does not imply that socialist differentials must be the *same* as capitalist differentials. Even an equali-

[11] The principles of socialist wages stated in this section are the same as those advanced by O. Lange (*Review of Economic Studies*, February 1937, pp. 123 ff.) and which Dickinson supports (*op. cit.*, chapter iv). However, it is believed that the argument supporting the principles here states more clearly than has been done heretofore the value content of the principles. The argument is stated more exactly, with respect to the general problem of attaining an optimum utilization of all resources, in my "Reformulation of . . . Welfare Economics," *Quarterly Journal of Economics*, February 1938.

tarian, if a patient one, might become reconciled to operating within a capitalist framework.

For, first of all, if the socialist administrators succeed in relaxing the monopolistic restrictions on the supply of skilled labor established by unions under capitalism, the wage differentials corresponding to productivity will be reduced. The vested interests of specially privileged workers are a political rather than an economic force in the socialist state. Also it might be expected that under socialism general and vocational education would be made more accessible to able citizens than is the case under capitalism, where the costs of education are an important obstacle to the acquisition of the higher skills. One important barrier between the non-competing groups of economic theory thus would be broken down, and in the long-run wage differentials could be reduced on this account.

To be reckoned with, too, is the possibility that socialist workers of ability might be stimulated to produce more, to undergo special training, or to assume responsibility by other incentives than an increased supply of material goods for their own use. The desire for power and the desire for a position of prestige and honor in the community undoubtedly are at least partial motives for the performance of numerous tasks in a capitalist society. It is a prevalent belief that the so-called non-pecuniary incentives will be even more influential in a socialist society. The common ownership of the means of production, the knowledge that every value created by the worker "ultimately redounds to the benefit of himself, his own kind and class" has been presented specifically as the basis for a far-reaching change in the worker's atittude towards labor. This view perhaps assumes a greater plasticity in human nature than is justified, but to the extent that workers can be stimulated by non-pecuniary incentives the pecuniary differentials prevailing under socialism may be reduced.

Wages and the Disutility of Labor. It is an oft-noted paradox of capitalist wage differentials that many occupations which seem in all other respects unattractive are also poorly remunerative, and that many occupations which seem highly attractive are also highly remunerative. Heavy dirty labor rather than light clean labor, monotonous labor rather than varied labor, disciplined labor rather than autonomous labor, often draw the blanks in the capitalist lottery. Righteous critics of the inequality of reward prevailing under capitalism doubtless are chiefly indignant at this anomaly. Differences in remuneration which merely correspond to differences in the disutility of labor are, if at all, not nearly so provoking.

The paradox of capitalist remuneration is largely resolved, of course, by the fact that under capitalism the disutility of different types of labor is not the only factor which limits the supply of workers in the different occupations. The cost of education, trade union and professional restrictions on the labor supply, and finally ability are also limiting factors.

The application of capitalist wage principles under socialism, thus, does not imply that the anomalous differentials of capitalism must remain intact. If education is supplied free, and the monopoly power of unions and professional organizations is broken, and wage differentials are reduced on this basis, the resulting differences in reward will approximate more nearly the differences in the disutility of labor. The equalitarian socialist might derive much comfort from this fact.

But that the socialist wage structure will continue to be encrusted with anomalous disparities is not unlikely. Though many workers who are incompetent for the task might be delighted to shift to a more remunerative occupation for less than the prevailing differential, the differential cannot be reduced on this account. Furthermore, the disutilities of a particular type of work are not the same for all workers who can be employed productively at a particular task. Among the workers able to accept responsibility and to undergo training for more skilled work, for example, some will relish these tasks more than others. It is to workers on the margin of choice between occupations that wage differentials are directed under capitalism, and so they must continue to be under socialism, if labor resources are to be used as effectively as possible.[12]

The possibility is not to be excluded that the socialist administrators will discriminate in fixing the wages of different workers in the same occupation, paying more to workers on the margin of choice than to other workers. In this manner the large value products of specially endowed citizens might be extracted in some measure for the benefit of the community as a whole. The administrative burden of such a wage policy, however, is obviously imposing and the chances of success are by no means clear. The discrimination, too, doubtless would arouse such political opposition as even a relatively secure administrator could not afford to ignore.

For the persistence of anomalous rewards under socialism is an economic rather than a political paradox. The principle of rewarding labor in accord with its contribution to the social product will have all the support under socialism that its long prevalence in the capitalist era has given it.

Social Services. The wage received by the socialist citizen derives its significance for him from the fact that he may acquire goods by expending it. In exchange for his wage commodities and services will be made available to him at established prices. It might be expected that in the consumers' goods market, as in the labor market, the citizen would be permitted freedom of choice, though alternative distributive procedures, such as rationing, are quite conceivable.

The goods and services obtained by the worker in this manner, however, will not comprise his entire real income. Some goods and services will be made available to him as social services, without charge. In any modern community certain services, owing to their physical nature, must be distributed in this

[12] Lange argues that in the optimum position wage differentials must correspond to differences in the disutility of different occupations as well as to differences in productivity (*Review of Economic Studies*, February 1937, p. 124). It should be clear, however, that this applies only to workers who are on the margin of choice between occupations. It does not apply to the bulk of the workers, who are intra-marginal.

manner. In the case of police protection, national defense, and to an extent, sidewalks, roadways, parks and sanitary measures, it is either impossible or impracticable to determine the extent to which individual citizens avail themselves of these services, and to charge them accordingly. Further, if freedom of choice prevails in the socialist consumers' goods market, it will be undesirable to distribute in this market goods which have a very high social value, but a low, or zero value to a sizeable minority of the citizens. As is the case in caiptalist communities, infectious diseases should be treated without charge. And if many parents do not give the education of their children nearly the value consonant with its importance to the community, a free distribution of this service, or a compulsory distribution of it, or both may be desirable.

The distribution of goods and services without charge necessarily equalizes real incomes beyond what they would be in the absence of such a distribution. A prevailing ethic in favor of greater equality within the framework of a private property system, indeed, is probably one of the motives for the distribution of goods and services as social services under capitalism. An equalitarian ethic doubtless will also prevail, and perhaps will have more political weight, under socialism. But it is well to recognize that here large property incomes are no longer an influencing factor. The scope of the social services may well be expanded in a socialist community, but the force of the equalitarian argument for such a distribution is largely dissipated. Indeed, an attempt on the part of the socialist administrators to substantially equalize real incomes through an expansion of the social services is more than likely to be self-defeating. The inequality in the distribution of the remaining goods purchased in the consumers' goods market would have to be all the greater to attract workers in the different occupations in the proper proportions.

The Tax, or Dividend. While social services, like other goods, require the payment of wages for their production, they realize no values for the state in the consumers' goods market. This is likewise true for any investment goods production undertaken by the administrators. To finance these wage payments the socialist administrators will have available the rent, interest and depreciation reserves on the state's resources — these items, it should be expected, will appear as accounting categories in the state's books — and any voluntary saving undertaken by members of the community. But it is unlikely that these two sums will coincide, and the administrators will have to finance the difference.[13]

One course open to the socialist administrators is simply to adjust the prices of marketable consumers' goods, upward if the wage payments for the social services and new investment are in excess, and downward if the converse. There is little danger that this procedure will entail the alarming consequences that some economists have predicted in similar circumstances for a capitalist economy. Once having engaged in, say, a new investment program, and having adjusted the prices of consumers' goods upward, it is unlikely that the large consumers' goods profit will rouse the administrators to abandon their investments, and rush again to the production of consumers' goods, with a cumulative contraction process following.[14] Nevertheless this tempting course is objectionable. If the system is administered in accord with individual evaluations of consumers' goods as well as of work done, it can be shown, the prices of consumers' goods should equal costs.[15] If some other value principle were followed prices would have to be adjusted

[13] While I speak of "finance," I do not regard this word as appropriate for socialist economics. Here the problem of finance is purely one of consistently arranging the state's accounts. It should be noted that the balance struck in the text does not include all the items it should: the agricultural balance of payments should also be included.

[14] Cf. F. A. Hayek, *Prices and Production* (New York, 1932).

[15] More accurately, marginal costs. This is equivalent to the requirement that wages equal marginal value productivity. Where workers are producing goods for future rather than present consumption, the marginal value productivity must be discounted, but the insertion of this element does not affect the argument of the text. The discount should be determined by an independent appraisal of the values of present and future income.

according to this principle. The arbitrary adjustment of consumers' goods prices upward to allow for investment and social
service costs, if substantial, would imply a long-run departure
from the optimum utilization of resources. Differences in wages
would not correspond to differences in value productivity, and
not as many workers as is socially desirable would be attracted
into the more arduous, the more responsible, and the more
skilled occupations.

While price manipulation is an economically objectionable
means of financing the investment program, it has all the advantages of indirection possessed by a sales tax under capitalism. Consequently it might prove an irresistible political
expedient even for socialist administrators. If the administrators were unaware of the economic consequences of their
acts they would only be following in the footsteps of more than
one economist who has carefully studied the problem.[16]

The alternative to an over-all price increase which first suggests itself is a proportionate income tax. But in a socialist
state such a tax, too, is likely to be objectionable. To whatever
extent that marginal workers take account of the tax in weighing the merits of alternative occupations, the wages recorded as
costs no longer correspond to social costs, and an insufficient
amount of labor will be attracted to the more remunerative occupations.[17] The effect of a progressive income tax on the utiliza-

---

[16] Lange has advocated that the socialist administrators levy a proportionate
income tax (or pay a proportionate dividend) to balance the state's outlays and
revenues (*Review of Economic Studies*, October 1936, pp. 64, 65). This procedure
is undesirable, however, as is indicated in the text of the present study. The
objectionable character of Lange's solution was first pointed out by A. P. Lerner,
in a note appended to Lange's article (pp. 72 ff.). But Lerner himself regards
the over-all level of prices relatively to costs as arbitrary, and thus implicitly
admits the possibility of a proportionate adjustment of prices as a means of
financing the state's investment program (*Review of Economic Studies*, October
1926, pp. 75, 76; October 1938, p. 71). More recently Dickinson (*op. cit.*, pp. 136,
137) has fallen into Lange's original error.

[17] This assumes that freedom of choice prevails in the socialist labor market.
But even if it does not the income tax is inconsistent with the acceptance of individual preference as a measure of social cost.

tion of resources would be more adverse than that of a proportionate tax. The progressive tax has the redeeming quality, however, that it expropriates part of the economically unnecessary gain accruing to workers who are not on the margin of choice between occupations.[18] In view of the political and administrative obstacles to the adoption of a discriminatory wage policy, this may be a consideration of no little import.

The only method of adjusting the state's financial position which is economically unobjectionable is through the lump-sum tax or dividend that was referred to earlier. This share might prove politically unpalatable, but its allocation would in no way bar attainment of an optimum use of resources. Despite the tax, differences in wages still would correspond to the marginal workers' evaluations of alternative employments, and the adjustment of wages to equal value productivity would be favorable to the attainment of an optimum utilization of resources.

The use of a lump-sum tax to finance the state's investment and social service program does not preclude its use also to redistribute income. Such a redistribution, however, is limited by the nature of the share. As a means of recouping the larger incomes paid to skilled workers, for example, the tax could not serve in the stead of a progressive tax. But other things being equal it would be quite consistent for a worker with a small family to be taxed more heavily than a worker with a large one. The levying of heavy taxes on individuals with special native abilities also would not be precluded, provided it were possible and practicable to distinguish these individuals from others who acquired a similar position through special training. In the case that, within wide limits of wages, these individuals were bent on entering one occupation only (artists are the usual example), their wage would in fact be indeterminate within this range, and if their product were automatically (through the administrative procedure used) imputed to them as a wage, the tax might extract a considerable amount of the "rental" return on their abilities for distribution among the members of the community.

[18] See above, p. 17.

5

Marx on Socialist Distribution. The conscientious reader will find in the scattered references fringing the text of the preceding sections a brief statement of the relation of the present study of socialist distribution to other recent ones. It will be desirable before proceeding, however, to dwell in some detail on one early contribution to the subject which has had a vast influence on the wage policy of the lone modern state where socialist symbols are the accepted political symbols.

A theory of the distribution of income in a socialist state was developed by Karl Marx as early as 1875 in a criticism of the draft program of the congress of the German Workers' Party held at Gotha in that year.[19] The passages which relate to distribution are short, and the essentials can be set forth briefly.

Marx argued that, contrary to the view implied in the Gotha program, inequality of income would persist in the socialist state. As in a capitalist community, the relative shares of the workers in the consumers' goods (aside from the products reserved for communal satisfaction of needs) will be proportionate to the quantity of labor supplied by them. Marx regarded this principle of distribution simply as an expression of the "bourgeois right," which would still prevail in the socialist society, that each producer should receive back from society the value equivalent of what he contributed to it. The equivalents are determined simply by an extension to labor of Marx's theory of commodity values:

Here obviously the same principle prevails as that which regulates the exchange of commodities, as far as this is an exchange of equal values. . . . So much of labor in one form is exchanged for an equal amount of labor in another form.

But quantity of labor was not to be measured simply by labor time. Differences in intensity, and differences "in individual en-

---

[19] Karl Marx, *Critique of the Gotha Programme.* Quotations are from the International Publishers' edition (New York, 1938), pp. 6 ff.

dowment and thus productive capacity," Marx was careful to add, were also to be recognized.

Inequality of reward, according to Marx, could be liquidated only with the higher development of the socialist economy.

In a higher phase of a communist society, after the enslaving subordination of individuals under division of labor, and therewith also the antithesis between mental and physical labor, has vanished; after labor from a mere means of life, has itself become a prime necessity of life; after the productive forces have also increased with the all round development of the individual, and all the springs of coöperative wealth flow more abundantly — only then can the narrow horizon of bourgeois right be fully left behind, and society inscribe on its banners: from each according to his ability to each according to his needs.

To those who continue to identify equalitarianism with Marxism this argument should be conclusive evidence of their error. But it must be acknowledged that Marx's brief analysis of socialist distribution leaves much to be desired. The relative rewards of different workers in a capitalist society, and in a socialist society, cannot be explained simply in terms of the quantity of labor they supply; this is not the *bourgeois* right. It is true and important that for Marx the quantity of labor depended on intensity and individual capacity as well as on duration. But the gap between the Ricardian labor theory of value that Marx used and the modern theory that relative rewards are determined by the productivity of labor — and more generally, by value productivity — could be bridged only by applying sufficient patches to the definition of quantity of labor for the concept to contain implicitly the latter theory. In this case the labor theory would indeed be redundant. Without such patching the essential difference between the two theories is clear: in one case relative rewards are determined by the characteristics of the workers, while in the other case they depend as well on the state of technique, and on the demand for the various commodities produced.

Furthermore, the reason for the persistence of capitalist principles of distribution in the socialist state is left obscure by Marx. Is the explanation, as the expression "bourgeois right" might imply, simply that there is an ethical lag in the socialist community? Do capitalist principles continue to prevail simply because of the pressure of the vested interests of privileged workers? Or, as the passage on the conditions for full communism implies, are there economic forces at work? These questions are raised but not resolved by a reading of Marx's discussion.

But whatever the shortcomings of his analysis, the fact that Marx attacked the spinning of utopias and proceeded himself to develop a concrete theory of socialist distribution attests once again to his grasp of the scientific approach to social phenomena. Whether it is a tribute to his analytic power or to his intuition, his conclusion that inequality will persist in a socialist state has gained rather than lost support in the thought and events of the ensuing years. The weight of Marx's authority has served the Soviet administration in good stead to support their wage policy, even if conditions affecting the demand for and supply of labor obtrude in their considerations.

CHAPTER III

MONEY WAGES IN THE SOVIET UNION

It is inevitable that in studying the inequality of wages in the U.S.S.R. one be confronted with the question: But what do the money wages mean? A partial answer, of course, is that these wages, like the wages discussed in Chapter II, are the costs incurred when a Soviet enterprise hires additional labor. But a larger problem remains: to what extent does the inequality in money wages also connote an inequality in command over goods? An answer to this question is not so easily forthcoming, but it is well to seek it at the outset. Of chief concern here is the significance of money earnings in the two years, 1928 and 1934, to which our basic wage statistics relate.

The position of clerical workers, engineers and technical workers, and foremen and administrative workers has been subjected to a number of special regulations in the U.S.S.R. Certain of the qualifications required for these workers in the present discussion will be deferred to Chapter IX, which is devoted to salaries in the Soviet Union.

2

The Soviet worker, like the citizen of the hypothetical community discussed in Chapter II, receives certain services from the state free of charge, and is called upon to pay certain direct taxes in return. Neither the social services nor the taxes, however, are an exact counterpart of the simple categories that have been discussed.

Education. A free primary education of three or four years in length already had been supplied in Russia long before the rise of the Soviets to power. The main contribution of the Soviet regime in this sphere was a great increase in the student body, and concomitantly a near approach to universality. The total number of students in the first four school grades in the school year 1934/35 was 2.5 times the 7.3 million students in the area of the U.S.S.R. at the outbreak of the first World War. By the following year approximately 95 per cent of the children in the Russian Republic between eight and eleven years of age attended school.[1] Four-fifths of the increase in the student body occurred after the inauguration of the first five-year plan.

For secondary and higher education in the pre-war school system, tuition payments were required, but there were scholarships and some stipends. According to one estimate, the fees paid by students covered but one-fourth of the total costs of education in the Tsarist secondary schools, and but one-tenth of the total costs in the universities.[2]

In both these spheres tuition was at first abolished by the Soviet government, but, surprisingly, payments were reintroduced in 1923; and for a short period tuition was charged by the Soviet authorities for primary as well as advanced education. The reversal in policy, however, bore lightly on the mass of workers. As the tuition policy was formulated in the Russian Republic in 1927, the local authorities in rural districts were permitted to charge fees for the secondary education of those living on unearned income — tradespeople and capitalists — and payments were required generally in the secondary *vocational* schools, or technicums, and in the higher educational institutions.[3] For wage earners, salaried workers, and their fam-

---

[1] The Russian Republic, or the Russian Socialist Federated Soviet Republic, is the largest of the republics forming the Soviet Union. In 1926 it contained two-thirds of the total population.

[2] N. Hans, *The History of Russian Educational Policy, 1701–1917* (London, 1931), p. 227. See also P. N. Ignatiev et al., *Russian Schools and Universities in the World War* (New Haven, 1929), p. 141.

[3] Postanovlenie VTSIK i SNK RSFSR, February 18, 1927, *S.U.R. RSFSR*, 1927, part I, no. 13, section 88, pp. 127 ff. By a later decree individuals deprived of election rights could be charged fees for secondary education in rural districts.

The decree is ambiguous on payment for secondary education by other members of the community than tradespeople and capitalists. Articles 2 and 3 could be interpreted as giving local authorities permission to charge workers also in

ilies, the university and college fee for the dependents of those having an income of more than 75 to 100 rubles a month, according to the region, varied progressively from 3 to 5 per cent of income, with a maximum annual tuition of 225 rubles a year. The dependents of workers earning less than the 75 to 100 rubles minimum, and students receiving stipends, were exempt from tuition payments. Since average monthly earnings of Soviet industrial workers in 1928 were but slightly over 70 rubles, and over 70 per cent of the workers earned less than 90 rubles a month, the exemptions were quite important. The 1927 decree required in any case that at least 50 per cent of the students receive free tuition. The tuition rates charged in the secondary vocational schools were lower than those charged in the universities, but the incomes exempted were the same.

Under this system of fees the proportion of the costs of higher education borne by students, the families of non-workers included, was considerably less than that indicated above for pre-war Russia. In 1925–26, when the fees in the higher educational institutions were little different from those of 1927, the tuition payments were 3.2 per cent of the total expenditure.[4]

It came to this writer as a surprise for which studies of Soviet education had left him unprepared to discover that the decree of 1927, with minor changes, was still in effect as late as July 1936.[5] Apparently tuition was abolished only by the new Soviet constitution promulgated in December 1936.[6] To what extent fees had been charged in the interim is uncertain. But despite

---

this sphere. It has not been possible to determine how the decree was applied in this respect. But from the exemptions listed in the text such fees in any case would not have been important for workers.

[4] TSU, *Narodnoe Prosveshchenie v SSSR, 1926–1927* (Moscow, 1929), pp. 188–189.

[5] For a list of changes see *Khronologicheskii Perechen' Zakonov RSFSR deistvuiushchikh na 1 Iiulia 1936 g.*, p. 16.

[6] In Article 121 it is stated that: "Citizens of the U.S.S.R. have the right to an education. This right is assured by the universal compulsory primary education, by the fact that education, including higher education, is free, by the government stipends paid to the overwhelming majority of students in the higher schools."

the general rise of wages and the constancy of the income exemption limits, the number of non-tuition paying students, it would appear, increased. Students receiving stipends alone composed three-fourths of the student body in 1934, as compared with two-fifths in 1926.[7]

The Soviet tuition policy was only one of the factors making secondary and higher education accessible to the masses of workers. The geographic distribution of the schools, particularly the primary and secondary schools, was of course a factor of more importance to the rural population. But in addition a reorganization of the educational system to facilitate movement from lower to higher schools was important. In all, the number of students in the fifth through the tenth school grades and in the technicums, universities, and specialized institutes in 1934/35 was nearly ten times larger than the 1914/15 figure of 673 thousand. Again the bulk of the increase occurred after 1928. For other spheres of Soviet education such as pre-school education, factory schools, adult workers' secondary schools ("workers' faculties"), and party schools there seems to have been no developed Tsarist counterpart.

Health Care. In the industrial law of pre-war Russia there was a requirement that employers should maintain hospital facilities, to the extent of one hospital bed per 100 wage earners, for the care of their employees, and that any medical services supplied should be at the employer's expense.[8] The medical care of the workers was also a subject of orders issued by provincial factory commissions. As this system of regulation was applied, the bulk of the smaller Russian establishments by 1907 provided at most facilities for first aid and treatment of light illnesses. But the larger factories employing 44 per cent of the 1.8 million wage earners in industry subject to factory inspec-

---

[7] TSU, *op. cit.*, p. 186; TSUNKHU, *Kul'turnoe Stroitel'stvo SSSR 1930–1934* (Moscow, 1935), p. 68.

[8] V. P. Litvinov-Falinskii, *Novye Zakony o Strakhovanii Rabochikh* (St. Petersburg, 1912).

tion supplied to the employees hospital care of varying sort, either separately, or jointly with other establishments, or by special arrangement with outside health services.[9]

A considerable extension of employee medical care was required by the Russian social insurance laws of June 1912. Under their provisions workers in all large-scale factories and mining establishments were to be supplied with free medical services, including hospitalization for illness of up to four months duration (industrial accidents disabling the worker were separately provided for).[10] To what extent in the period before the war these requirements led to a redistribution of medical care in favor of the workers is uncertain. But in that short interval, as might be expected, there was not an unusual expansion of medical personnel and hospital facilities.

Besides the precedent for free care of the worker, pre-war Russia developed also for the rural population a system of medical care which was a notable forerunner of socialized medicine.[11] But so far as its total medical resources are concerned, it provided but a meager endowment for the public-health policy embarked on by the Soviet Union. At approximately the beginning of 1914 there were, in all the area now occupied by the U.S.S.R., 3.3 doctors and assistant doctors, or *feldshers*, and between 12.6 and 14.2 hospital beds per ten thousand inhabitants.[12] The feldshers, in addition to their work as assist-

[9] Litvinov-Falinskii, *op. cit.*, pp. 30 ff. The scope of factory inspection corresponds roughly to that of the manufacturing sector of present-day Soviet large-scale industry.

[10] Vysochaishe Utverzhdennyi Odobrennyi Gosudarstvennym Sovetom i Gosudarstvennoi Dumoiu Zakon, ob Obezpechenii Rabochikh na Sluchai Bolezni, June 23, 1912, articles 1 and 44 ff., *Polnoe Sobranie Zakonov Rossiiskoi Imperii, Sobranie Tretie*, vol. XXXII, 1912, part 1, section 57446, pp. 855 ff. (Petrograd, 1915). The requirements also applied to railway, internal water transport, and tramway companies.

[11] For a description of the system of rural medical care — *zemstvo* medicine — see E. H. Gantt, *Russian Medicine* (New York, 1937); and C. E. A. Winslow, *Public Health Administration in Russia in 1917*, U. S. Public Health Reports, December 28, 1917.

[12] NKZdrav RSFSR, *Statisticheskie Materialy . . . za 1913–1923 gg.* (Moscow, 1926), p. 108; TSUNKHU, *Zdorov'e i Zdravookhranenie Trudiashchikhsia SSSR*

ants, themselves headed many rural medical stations in lieu of physicians because of the scarcity of the latter.

Under the Soviet regime the right to medical care without charge was extended to all persons who were entitled to receive social insurance benefits; with minor qualifications, to all wage earners, salaried workers, and their families. But with the medical facilities available after the world war, revolution, civil war, and famine, the first fruits of this right were severely limited. Despite a large expansion in the number of doctors in the recovery years, the total resources were overburdened. Private practice continued, and it is likely that not only capitalists and tradesmen, but to some extent workers who could afford it, paid fees rather than wait their turn at state medicine.[13]

During the period of the five-year program, medical personnel and hospital facilities expanded considerably. By 1936 the number of doctors and feldshers per ten thousand inhabitants had risen to 7.7, and the corresponding number of hospital beds to 29.8.[14] Private practice during the same period declined. It has been estimated that by 1933 it composed but 10 per cent of the total (this mainly in the after hours of state-employed physicians), and that by 1936 it was insignificant.[15] In addition to the increase in the resources enumerated, there was in the U.S.S.R. an expansion of sanatoria, health resorts, and creches, and also a considerable extension of prophylactic measures. Sanitary and other general health measures became a vital element in Soviet health care.

It might be expected, and medical observers are of this view, that the rapid expansion of medical resources cost a reduction

---

(Moscow, 1936), pp. 53, 60. The hospital beds include those in maternity homes, but not those in health resorts and sanatoria. The population figure used in the calculation in the text is 139 million.

[13] Cf. A. J. Haines, *Health Work in Soviet Russia* (New York, 1928), p. 19.

[14] TSUNKHU, *Zdorov'e i Zdravookhranenie Trudiashchikhsia SSSR*, pp. 53, 60, 164, 174, 175. The figures relate to the beginning of the year. The estimate of the 1936 population which I have used in the calculation is 170 million.

[15] A. Newsholme and J. A. Kingsbury, *Red Medicine* (New York, 1933), pp. 54, 55, 218, 220.

in the quality of personnel and of service.[16] But so far as changes in the death rate are indicative of health care (there are of course other factors, such as food and housing conditions), the net result of the qualitative and quantitative changes in Soviet medical resources would appear to be clearly positive.[17]

Besides education and health care the social services in the U.S.S.R. include only those which are physically determined. Charges are made for the use of tramways, the subway, electricity, and water. As to the importance of the supply of education and health services in the Soviet economy, some notion may be obtained from the sums expended on them. In 1935 the total expenditures on these two services for the entire U.S.S.R. were respectively 8.9 and 5.0 billion rubles. Of these sums 4.6 and 3.2 billion rubles may be taken as generous estimates of the amounts expended on the education and care of all wage earners, salaried workers, and their families. The total for the two services is 14 per cent of the 1935 wage and salary bill of 56.7 billion rubles.

The social services certainly should be taken into account in any consideration of real income in the U.S.S.R. The direct result of supplying services without charge, of course, is that real income is to some extent equalized. The scope and extent of the social services in the U.S.S.R., however, is not such as to vitiate interest in the distribution of the real income purchased in the consumers' goods market. The discriminatory Soviet tuition policy, to the extent that it was applied, resulted in a greater equalization of real income than would have occurred if education had been distributed free to all workers. It appears, however, that at no time after 1927 were the bulk of the Soviet workers subject to the tuition charges.

[16] Newsholme and Kingsbury, *op. cit.*, pp. 209, 211–212; E. H. Gantt, *op. cit.*, pp. 189–190.

[17] See the rates for Moscow and Leningrad in Upravlenie Glavnago Vrachebnago Inspektora M. V. D., *Otchet o Sostoianii Narodnago Zdraviia . . . za 1907 god* (St. Petersburg, 1909), pp. 7 ff.; the 1935 rates from TSUNKHU, *Zdorov'e i Zdravookhranenie Trudiashchikhsia SSSR*, p. 43.

Taxation. The direct taxes levied in the U.S.S.R. vary with the number of dependents of the payee; also with his social position (e.g., there are special taxes for capitalists and tradesmen); and there are separate schedules for artists and authors. But, unlike the lump-sum taxes discussed in Chapter II, Soviet direct taxes also vary with income. In 1928 there was one such tax on wage earners and salaried workers, the so-called Income Tax. The amount of the tax for different levels of income is shown in Table 1. Workers earning less than a minimum

TABLE 1

PARTIAL SCHEDULE OF DIRECT TAXES LEVIED ON WAGE EARNERS AND SALARIED WORKERS IN THE U.S.S.R. IN 1928 AND 1934

Monthly Income (rubles)	1928 Income Tax (%)	1934 Income Tax (%)	1934 Tax for Cultural and Housing Construction (%)
Less than 85	.60	..	..
100	.65	.80	.75
200	1.15	1.43	2.00
300	1.73	2.05	2.50
400	2.14	2.71	2.50
500	2.77	3.50	2.50
1000	8.80	3.50	3.00
2000	17.69	3.50	3.00
Excess over 2000	30.00	3.50	3.00

Sources: Postanovlenie TSIK i SNK SSSR, December 14, 1927, *S.Z.R. SSSR*, 1928, part I, no. 1, sections 1–2, pp. 1 ff.; Postanovleniia TSIK i SNK SSSR, January 23, 1934, May 17, 1934, June 11, 1934, *S.Z.R. SSSR*, 1934, part I, no. 5, section 38, pp. 78 ff.; no. 27, section 211, pp. 365 ff.; no. 33, section 249, p. 458.
Aside from the all over and all under classes, the taxes relate to the specific incomes listed. Varying tax and surtax income classes as between the different taxes make it impracticable to present here the taxes for all income levels.

amount, varying according to the region of employment from 75 to 100 rubles a month, were exempted from the tax. The deductions for dependents, granted to all workers who earned less than 350 rubles a month, were one-quarter of the tax if there were three dependents, and one-third if there were more.

The income tax rates in 1934 (Table 1) were higher than in 1928 except that the progressive increase in the rate stopped at 500 rubles instead of 2000 rubles. Minimum taxable income was unchanged until June 1934, but at that time the exemption limits in the different regions were raised by 15 rubles. The exemptions for dependents were altered only slightly as compared with 1928. But besides the income tax another direct tax, designated the Tax for Cultural and Housing Construction, was levied. In all respects, except the use of funds collected, this tax is simply an additional income tax. As to its use, it is uncertain whether there is any other or more specific restriction than is contained in its title. The schedule is shown in Table 1. The minimum taxable income in the different regions is the same as that for the income tax, and the deductions for dependents are also.

The Soviet direct taxes had the effect of reducing both absolutely and relatively the real income differential corresponding to any given money-earnings differential. For the bulk of the Soviet industrial workers, however, the equalization was slight. Over 75 per cent of Soviet industrial workers in March 1928 earned less than 100 rubles a month, so that the tax on these workers was either 65 kopeks or nil. The tax on an income of 134 rubles, which income was exceeded by the earnings of only 10 per cent of the workers, amounted to 1.09 rubles, or 82 kopeks if the income recipient had three dependents. In October 1934, 25 per cent of the industrial workers earned 107 rubles a month or less, 75 per cent earned 220 rubles or less, and 90 per cent earned 321 rubles or less. The direct taxes on these incomes, for workers having three dependents, were respectively 1.71 rubles, 7.89 rubles, and 15.13 rubles. Only the 1934 taxes, evidently, would result in any significant equalization of real incomes.

Social Insurance Payments. In 1935, 2.5 billion rubles or 4.4 per cent of the Soviet wage and salary bill was paid to wage earners, salaried workers, and their families, in the form of funeral and maternity benefits, temporary disability payments, old-age and invalid pensions, and pensions for the dependents of deceased workers.[18] The security thus offered represents a siza-

---

[18] Unemployment benefits were ended in 1930.

ble addition to the real income which the worker purchased with money wages. But for our purposes this addition is only formally distinct from wages. Logically regarded, the Soviet social insurance payments represent a redistribution of earnings over time undertaken by the state, rather than an addition to earnings. The premium paid, it is true, is called a payroll tax, and is listed in the enterprise's books as a cost item *separate* from wages. But since the tax is a percentage of the payroll the distinction is purely formal so far as the cost of hiring labor is concerned. From the point of view of the insured persons the correspondence of the benefit to the premium paid is assured by the fact that the benefits also are proportionate to earnings.[19] Properly calculated, the money wages of the U.S.S.R. accordingly should include the premium or payroll tax. The exclusion of this element from the category wages in Soviet statistics is an exception to the statement, made in the introduction to this chapter, that these money wages are the increment of costs incurred when an enterprise hires additional labor. But since the amount of the tax is proportionate to wages the exclusion or inclusion of it is a matter of indifference so far as relative wages are concerned.

There are qualifications, however. The identity between the tax and an insurance premium paid out of earnings would be complete if the benefits depended only on the amount contributed by the insured through the tax, and on actuarial principles. Actually, without any variation in the payroll tax among workers in the same industry, but with a variation as between industries, the benefits vary with the general characteristics of work done (e.g., underground workers and workers in specially dangerous and difficult occupations receive old-age pensions earlier than other workers). The benefits also vary with such factors as the number of dependents and membership in a trade union; and women are granted maternity benefits and disability pay-

---

[19] Aside from the lump-sum funeral and maternity benefits. A recent compilation of the Soviet regulations on social insurance is R. Kats i N. Sorokin, *Sotsial'noe Strakhovanie*, second edition (Moscow, 1936).

ments during pregnancy and childbirth.[20] These variations together produce a discrepancy between command over real income and money wages, which though unsystematic is analogous
to that caused by the progressive tax. Finally, the total insurance tax collections have been considerably higher than the current benefits paid. In 1934 the collections were 6.9 billion
rubles, and the benefits, 2.0 billion rubles. The difference was
spent on health care, housing construction, and education. It is
likely that the Soviet social insurance system has not yet struck
its gait so that part of the excess of receipts over outgo has an
actuarial basis. But in so far as the revenue is not actuarially
required to cover payments properly financed by it, the payroll
tax must be regarded simply as a proportionate income tax. The
equivalence of *relative* money wages and the *relative* command
over real income afforded by these money wages, however, is
unaffected by the excess.

3

Rationing. Commodity rationing, which had been a characteristic of the period preceding the inauguration of the New
Economic Policy, appeared again in the U.S.S.R. beginning in
the latter part of 1928. The rationed distribution of bread was
decreed by the city of Odessa in the second quarter of the year,
and Moscow and Leningrad soon followed.[21] In the ensuing
years, as heavy industry strode towards the goals of the five-
year plan, and as the struggle for agricultural collectivization
was intensified, the scope of the rationing system was extended.
By 1932 bread was rationed in virtually all the cities and work-

[20] In addition, in the case of old-age payments, the amount of the benefit depends on length of service. But this is to be expected, since the total contribution varies likewise. The disability benefits, in the first days of disability, also
depend on the length of time a worker has been employed in a given establishment (two years are required for the maximum rate to be paid), and on the
total length of service (three years are required for the maximum rate).

[21] A detailed account of the introduction of rationing is given in G. IA.
Neiman, *Vnutrenniaia Torgovlia SSSR* (Moscow, 1935), pp. 170 ff., and G.
Zberzhkovskii, "Proidennyi Etap," *Sovetskaia Torgovlia*, November–December
1934.

ers' settlements of the U.S.S.R. Other foods were added to the ration lists from 1929. In 1934, after the number of goods rationed had passed its peak, flour and grits, meat, herring, butter and vegetable oil, and sugar, in addition to bread, still were subject to the restricted distribution.[22] The rationing of these goods continued until January 1935, when bread, flour, and grits were derationed. In October of the same year the remaining goods followed.

The rationing system, so far as it involved the distribution of goods according to established norms, did not extend to industrial commodities. But a number of these goods were distributed at a dual set of prices, and, depending on the conditions of supply, purchases at the lower price were restricted. The outlets for the low-priced goods were the closed shops, which were organized from 1930 to serve the workers of a particular establishment or group of establishments. The distribution of industrial goods in this manner continued until January 1936, when a single open-market price was restored.

The Soviet consumers' goods market during the period of rationing, thus, was far from a free market. The first set of Soviet wage data which will be studied in the later statistical investigation relates to March 1928, and precedes the imposition of restrictions. But the second set relates to October 1934. In view of the distributive system employed at the time, it would be justifiable to question at the outset the possible usefulness of these statistics. Their claim to attention, of course, must rest on the inferences that can be gathered from them. To the extent that the data can shed light on the inequality of *money* wages and the principles according to which they were determined in 1934, they reflect also on the inequality and determinants of *real* wages in the period following the restoration of the open market. On this score alone the data deserve study. Some in-

---

[22] Potatoes also may have been among the commodities rationed. Flour is not included (at least not separately from bread) among the rationed products listed by Zberzhkovskii, *Sovetskaia Torgovlia*, November–December 1934, pp. 15, 16, but it is listed among the products which the state ordered derationed in January 1935.

formation is available, however, on the discrepancy, which appeared under the rationing system, between money wages and real income purchasable with money wages.

From the outset Soviet rationing was accompanied by a differentiation in the amounts of rationed goods allocated to different population groups. The basis for discrimination at first varied locally, though a widely used criterion was membership or non-membership in a consumers' coöperative society. Progress towards a uniform classification of the population into ration categories was made in 1930, and in the following year a classification of all ration recipients in cities and workers' settlements in the U.S.S.R. was adopted. With numerous alterations in detail this remained in effect through 1934.

The classification scheme used was twofold.[23] First the ration recipients were classified into three groups. In the first class, receiving the highest rations, or norms of supply, were the industrial wage earners. Salaried workers and their families, and the families of wage earners — in both cases except for children under fourteen — followed in the second class; and children under fourteen were placed in the third. Some salaried workers in industry, however, were placed in the first ration class, and their classification changed in the course of time. Other ration recipients than industrial workers and their families also were distributed in the three ration classes, though the norms of supply of certain workers in the first class were differentiated from those of industrial wage earners. The cross classification of ration recipients segregated the workers of different industries and, in certain cases, of different localities, plants, and plant departments into different ration categories. With many variations in each category there were four main groups of workers each receiving different norms. As of the fourth quar-

[23] For the detail of the classification see Postanovlenie Kollegii Narkomsnaba SSSR, January 13, 1931 (*Zakonodatel'stvo i Rasporiazheniia po Torgovle SSSR*, 1931, no. 5, pp. 22 ff.) ; Zbershkovskii, *Sovetskaia Torgovlia*, November–December 1934, pp. 17, 18; and the decrees ordering wage adjustments for the different ration categories when bread and grits were derationed (*B.F.Kh.Z.*, 1935, no. 1, pp. 36 ff.; no. 3, pp. 32 ff.; no. 8, pp. 32 ff.; and other numbers in the same year).

ter 1934, the highest group, or special list, included such workers as the industrial workers of Moscow, Leningrad, and Baku, and the coal miners, metallurgical and machinery workers of the Donbass.

The goods distributed according to established norms were not supplied without charge, nor were the rations the only source of supply. But the prices of the rations were far below the amounts charged elsewhere. The government itself sold limited quantities of the rationed foods in the open market in the latter part of the rationing period. The bread and flour sold in this manner in 1934 absorbed about one-fifth of the total flour distributed, and the open-market sale of grits was a similar proportion of the total. In Moscow and Leningrad in October 1934, when the gap between open-market prices and ration prices already had narrowed, the ratio of the state commercial price of rye bread to the ration price was 4:1, and of wheat bread 2.9:1.[24] For the non-grain foods the disparity between commercial prices and ration prices was greater, and in the farm markets, where the collective farmers were permitted to dispose of surpluses in excess of the amounts collected by state agencies, prices were higher than the state commercial prices.[25] Under these circumstances it is more than doubtful that the patrons of the open market comprised any but the least favored workers, and persons who were denied ration booklets (tradesmen, priests, the remaining persons living on unearned income, etc.).

From the characteristics of the rationing system it might be expected that among industrial wage earners, and in particular among the wage earners of any given industry, Soviet food rationing would have had an equalizing effect on the distribution of real income, as compared with the distribution of money income. A doubt would have to be registered, however, with respect to the effect of the differentiated ration norms for the workers in particular trades, departments, and plants.

[24] Z. Bolotin, "Edinaia Tsena i Ocherednye Zadachi Tovarooborota," *Planovoe Khoziaistvo*, 1935, no. 8, p. 97.　　[25] Neiman, *op. cit.*, p. 260.

If we may accept, as a measure of the equalizing effect of rationing, the adjustment in money incomes that would have to be made if the real incomes of the different workers were procured in an open market, it is possible to obtain a rough notion of its magnitude for the most important rationed good, bread, together with grits and flour. When these three commodities were derationed on January 1, 1935, an elaborate set of wage adjustments was undertaken, with the stated purpose of compensating the ration recipients for the establishment of single open-market prices on a level higher than the old ration prices, and at the same time to preserve the superiority as to supply of workers in the preferred ration categories.[26] How closely the wage increases realized these objectives is uncertain, but from the detailed adjustments ordered by the individual commissariats it does appear that the objectives were followed.[27]

The amount allocated by the government for the adjustment of wages in large-scale industry, on a monthly basis, averaged approximately 21 rubles per worker.[28] From the increment of wages actually realized after January 1, 1935, when the pay increase was effective, however, it seems likely that the adjustment carried out was somewhat less than the allocated amount. The realized increase was 19 rubles for wage earners of large-

---

[26] *Vsesoiuznaia Kommunisticheskaia Partiia (b) v Rezoliutsiakh ee S'ezdov, Konferentsii i Plenumov (1898–1935)*, fifth edition (Moscow, 1936), part ii, pp. 621, 622.

[27] In interpreting the wage adjustments a not unimportant reservation must be made for the fact that with an increased supply, the adjustments would have differed from those required for the same purpose in October 1934. A qualification is required also for the gains accruing, to those who had used the open market, from the establishment of the new single prices at a lower level than the old open-market prices. There is reason to believe that those gains were taken into account by the adjustments. But it is doubtful in any case that they were important for workers in large-scale industry.

[28] This figure is computed from the wage statistics given in the first and second editions — pp. 196 and 641 respectively — of the annual plan for 1935 (Gosplan. *Narodno-Khoziaistvennyi Plan na 1935 god*, Moscow, 1935). The planned wages of the first edition are revised in the second to allow for the wage adjustment accompanying derationing.

scale industry.[29] The latter figure is 12 per cent of the average monthly wage of 157 rubles in the fourth quarter 1934.

As between industries, and within each industry, the pay increases ordered by the different commissariats varied in accord with the cross classification of ration recipients. They also varied regionally, to accord with the locally differentiated market prices. Several examples of the adjustment ordered for workers in the Moscow Oblast — a region occupying an approximately middle position so far as the size of the adjustments is concerned — are inserted in Appendix A. The adjustments there exhibit no distinct positive variation with earnings as between industries.[30] Within the different industries the various special adjustments probably varied positively with wages. But it is fairly certain that the variation would not have overcome the equalizing effect for the whole industry.

These calculations for bread, flour, and grits do not exhaust the effect of Soviet market restrictions on the relation of real wages to money wages. But the remaining effect was not entirely an additive one. Contrary to the policy followed in the case of the rationed foods, the distribution of deficient industrial goods favored the more productive workers. The discriminatory distribution of these goods was initiated in 1931, after a declara-

---

[29] It is stated in Gosplan (*op. cit.*, second edition, p. 329) that wages for 1935 (presumably without the wage adjustment) were planned to remain on the level of the fourth quarter 1934. Assuming this to refer to wage rates, the increase of 12.8 per cent in the daily wage from the latter period to the first quarter 1935 would indicate that 19 rubles of the 173 rubles average monthly wage for the first quarter 1935 was due to the rationing adjustment. I have said that the adjustment probably did not exceed this amount because the 1935 wage plan was overfulfilled. But the important deviation from the plan appears to have occurred in the latter part of the year. See TSUNKHU, *Trud v SSSR* (Moscow, 1936), pp. 85 ff., 97.

[30] However, for one industry studied in the example, cotton, the realized wage increase from the fourth quarter 1934 to the first quarter 1935 was the highest among nineteen branches of large-scale industry: 16.5 per cent. In the woolen industry, which is included in the example also, the increase was 14.3 per cent, while in fourteen branches of large scale industry the increase was between 9 and 15 per cent (TSUNKHU, *Trud v SSSR*, Moscow, 1936). Daily wage rates are compared in these computations. See above, n. 29.

tion by the party Central Committee on the importance of using the supply of goods to increase the productivity of work and to assure the fulfillment of the plan. Instructions were issued to the trading outlets at that time to give preference as to supply to workers fulfilling and overfulfilling their productive tasks.[31] It was ordered specifically that such workers — shock workers — should have first claim on the most deficient industrial goods (overcoats, suits and shoes) and that in general they should not have to wait in line to make their purchases. The application of these instructions does not appear to have been energetic until after 1932,[32] when those closed shops which were administered by the consumers' coöperative organs and which served the larger industrial establishments were transformed into factory departments of workers' supply. The remaining coöperative closed shops at the same time were in large measure subjected to the control of the factory administration, though nominally remaining a part of the coöperative net. Thereafter special privileges as to supply were extended to workers in the more important occupations and departments, as well as to shock workers. Beyond the forms of discrimination provided for in the 1931 instructions, preference was shown these workers in the sale of the small independent collections of foods — including rationed foods — obtained from the collectives or from its own farms by the closed shop or supply department (the ration norms applied to the supplies received from the higher trading organizations).[33] In the restaurants organized in the larger factories the privileged workers also were supplied with better meals.

The rationing of non-grain foods should have introduced a discrepancy between money wages and real wages additional and similar to that caused by the rationing of bread, flour, and

---

[31] Instruktsiia VTSSPS NKSNABA SSSR i TSENTROSOIUZA, *B.F.Kh.Z.*, 1931, no. 11, pp. 17, 18.

[32] Cf. Neiman, *op. cit.*, p. 180.

[33] W. Nodel, *Supply and Trade in the U.S.S.R.* (London, 1934), pp. 89–90; Z. Bolotin, *Voprosy Snabzheniia* (Moscow, 1934), ch. ii and pp. 33, 36, 40.

grits. But the discriminatory distribution of other goods would have had a contrary effect. It would be foolhardy to attempt an estimate of the net result of these two forces, but it is of interest that the rationed sales of non-grain foods and the low-priced sale of industrial goods occupied a nearly equal position in the retail turnover. From an estimate, the former were 5 per cent of retail sales in 1934, and the latter, 6.5 per cent.[34] These figures considerably understate the importance of rationed and other low-priced sales to *industrial* workers, but it is likely that both types of sales varied similarly as between the more and less favored categories of consumers.[35, 36] It seems likely, then, that the net effect on the relation of real and money wages of the low-priced sales other than those of bread, grits, and flour, whatever its direction, would have been distinctly less than the effect of the latter. It is significant on this score that in contrast with the procedure followed in the case of grain foods no adjustment in the wages of workers in the various ration categories was made for the remaining commodities to compensate for the restoration of the open market.

Rent. Unlike the prices charged in a free market, the price of one commodity, living quarters, in the U.S.S.R. varies with the income of the purchaser, and also with the number of his dependents.[37] In Table 2 are indicated the monthly rental rates

[34] The chief source of information for the estimates is G. Zberzhkovskii, "Itogi Tovarooborota v I Kvartale 1935 g.," *Sovetskaia Torgovlia*, April 1935, p. 6. It is possible that certain of the single priced goods for which as a sum Zberzhkovskii gives turnover statistics, were restricted in some form, for not all were sold in the commercial shops. But Bolotin designates both the single priced and the higher of the two-priced sales "commercial trade."

[35] The gap between commercial and closed shop prices, however, was narrower, and the proportion of goods sold in the open market larger, for industrial goods than for the foods. Cf. Bolotin, *Planovoe Khoziaistvo*, 1935, no. 8, p. 97; Neiman, *op. cit.*, p. 241.

[36] See the turnover statistics in "Sovetskaia Torgovlia v Tsifrakh," *Sovetskaia Torgovlia*, May 1935, pp. 78, 79.

[37] In this respect the rental rates resemble the fees for education. The latter, however, were not significant for the bulk of wage earners.

for wage earners and salaried workers in Moscow in October 1934. The rates are for workers having three dependents. Separate schedules were effective for workers having up to five or more dependents, e.g., for a worker earning 80 rubles a month and having no dependents the monthly rental rate was 44

TABLE 2

PARTIAL SCHEDULE OF MONTHLY RENTAL RATES IN MOSCOW, OCTOBER 1934, FOR WAGE EARNERS AND SALARIED WORKERS WITH THREE DEPENDENTS AND EARNING THE AMOUNTS SPECIFIED

(*Earnings and Rent in Rubles*)

Monthly Earnings	Rent per Square Meter of Living Quarters
Less than 31	.055
31	.154
50	.198
80	.352
100	.396
145	.440
195	.605
295	.935
430	1.320
More than 430	1.320

Sources: N. Bronshtein, *Zhilishchnye Zakony* (Moscow, 1935), pp. 356 ff.; Zhilishchnoe Upravlenie Mossoveta, *Zhilishchnyi Spravochnik* (Moscow, 1936), ch. i, pp. 117 ff.

In computing living quarters floor space, kitchens, bathrooms, and corridors are not included, special rates being established for the remaining space to allow for these items if present. The earnings on the basis of which rent is computed are the highest of any member of the family.

kopeks a square meter, while a worker with five or more dependents was charged 24 kopeks. Also, the rates in Table 2 are basic rates. Standard deductions were established for living quarters in poor locations (distant from schools and shopping centers, etc.), or with no piped water, electricity, etc. Additions were made if the living quarters had special conveniences such as a bathroom or a centralized hot-water system, or if heat were supplied from a central source. Finally, the rates in Table 2 generally applied only to space of up to 13.5 square meters per occupant. But local authorities were permitted by the central government to allow a larger amount of space at the ordinary rates.

Though the rates in Table 2 are for Moscow workers, they

illustrate also the rate structure in other cities and workers' settlements. The local organs in general were permitted to establish, for a worker earning 145 rubles a month and having no dependents, a rental between 35 and 44 kopeks a square meter. But in relation to this rate the rates for other workers were determined according to a centrally established formula. The standardized system of rates applied to all residences in urban localities and workers' settlements with three exceptions: a relatively small number of apartment houses built and operated by coöperative building societies, the members of which shared, according to floor space and quality of lodgings but without reference to income, the costs of amortizing construction loans and operating costs; private homes, the owners of which had been given special privileges to encourage them to extend or reconstruct their residences; and houses in rural workers' settlements administered by industrial undertakings, where the rates did not take into account family size and earnings.

The rental rates for different levels of earnings effective in March 1928 differed only slightly from those in Table 2.[38] At that time, however, there was no variation in the rates according to number of dependents. Furthermore, in certain industries the pre-war custom of supplying workers lodgings without charge in quarters owned by the employing establishment (this is not to be confused with the short-lived and more general practice in Soviet cities during the period of War Communism) still prevailed. According to the last detailed statistics published, for September 1926, 72 per cent of the wage earners in the coal and oil extraction industries were receiving lodgings without charge from the establishment in which they were employed.[39] In cotton and woolen textile and wood products industries the proportions were between 20 and 27 per cent, and in the remaining industries, the wages of which we shall later study, the proportion was less than 17 per cent. The supply of

---

[38] See N. I. Bronshtein, *Oplata Zhilykh Pomeshchenii* (Moscow, 1928).

[39] N. Shesterkina, "Kvartirnoe Dovol'stvie i Uderzhanie iz Zarabotka . . . ," *Statistika Truda*, 1927, no. 7, pp. 12–13.

free lodgings by the employing establishment continued until August 1928, when the rental system which has been described was extended to these quarters.[40] To compensate the workers for the change, adjustments were made in wages to cover the rental charges.

Administratively the Soviet rental system was a much more complex means of discrimination than the progressive income tax. But its effect was similar, and among industrial workers its significance was about the same. For example, for the income levels marking off 25, 75, and 90 per cent of the industrial workers, that is 107, 220, and 321 rubles, respectively, the corresponding rental rates in Moscow would have been 44.0, 68.6, and 101.9 kopeks a square meter for a worker having three dependents. For a floor space of 5 square meters per person — this it is likely was approximate to the Moscow average in 1934 —[41] it would follow that the worker having an income of 107 rubles would have had to pay 8.80 rubles rent, or 4.92 rubles less than a worker with an income of 220 rubles, and 11.58 rubles less than a worker with an income of 321 rubles.[42] Workers having different incomes probably would not have occupied the same floor space, but the comparison yields a rough notion of the discrimination involved in the Soviet rental system.

4

Privileges to Order Bearers. The significance of inequalities in money wages in the U.S.S.R. is qualified perhaps no more than in capitalist countries by forms of discrimination which

[40] The decrees relating to this subject are given in N. Bronshtein, *Zhilishchnye Zakony*, pp. 387 ff.

[41] According to S. M. Kingsbury and M. Fairchild (*Factory, Family, and Women in the Soviet Union*, New York, 1935, p. 198), the average floor space per person in Moscow in 1932 was 4.3 square meters.

[42] These rentals are surprisingly low — relative to income — in comparison with rentals in capitalist countries. The explanation is partly that Soviet rental rates are low. But it is also true that the usual living space is quite small. Then, too, the rental rates are raised as much as 10 per cent when such conveniences as a gas range, a bathroom, and a central hot-water heater are available, and the rates are increased additionally when heat is supplied from a central source.

bear little or no relation to the size of a worker's income. A novel form of discrimination, however, has been fostered by the Soviet state itself. Though the discrepancy between money-wage differentials and differentials in real income which results probably is not systematic, mention ought to be made here of the special privileges accorded the minority of Soviet workers who hold orders of honor.

Soviet honorary orders and titles are awarded for outstanding service to the community.[43] Not only heroic exploits, such as that of the aviators who participated in the non-stop flight to the United States in 1937, but the distinguished performance of common labor is *honoris causa* in the Soviet Union. The "best group" among all the trade unionists, it was reported to the ninth trade union congress in 1933, was

the group of Comrade Yanovsky, comprising 34 mill cutters and drillers, of the Karl Marx Plant in Leningrad. This group has been awarded the Order of the Red Banner. . . . This group systematically overfulfilled its industrial and financial plan — 110 per cent in production and 119 per cent in productivity of labor. Bad work has been done away with altogether. This group has effected economies in metal to the value of 1336 rubles. Each member of the group has been awarded a bonus.[44]

The chief orders of all-union significance awarded to wage earners and salaried workers in the Soviet Union are, according to rank, the Order of Lenin, the Order of the Red Banner of Labor, and the Badge of Honor. The last of these orders was created in 1935. The honorary title "Hero of the Soviet Union" is conferred upon individuals who have distinguished themselves in the highest degree; recipients are awarded the Order of Lenin as well. There is also a title "Hero of Labor" which is conferred upon workers who have performed special service and

---

[43] The numerous regulations on honorary orders and titles in the Soviet Union have been compiled by B. M. Vinogradov in *Ordena i Pochetnye Zvaniia* (Moscow, 1937).

[44] Report of Shvernik to the Ninth All-Union Congress of Trade Unions, 1933 — S. and B. Webb, *Soviet Communism* (New York, 1936), II, 760.

(with certain exceptions) who have worked for hire thirty-five years or more.

The honorary orders doubtless are in themselves incentives to serve. But what gives them special interest here is that the appeals are not without a buttress of material gain. Recipients of the Order of Lenin, the Order of the Red Banner, and the Badge of Honor receive respectively an income of 25, 15, and 10 rubles a month besides their wages. Order bearers also ride tramways without charge; for them the number of years service required for receipt of social insurance benefits is reduced by a third; and their rent is reduced by 10 to 50 per cent. Heroes of the Soviet Union receive a bonus of 50 rubles a month instead of 25. The Hero of Labor receives a larger old-age pension. His income, as well as that of the order bearers, is partially exempt from taxes, and rental rates are computed on the basis of only 50 per cent of his pension.

To the extent that these special rewards and privileges are granted workers who produce record outputs, of course, they are in a sense a form of wages and might properly be valued and recorded in books as such. Since in practice they are not, however, they must be regarded as another cause of a disparity between money wages and the real rewards of labor, and as such they probably tend in some measure to increase the inequality of real income relatively to that of money wages. In this respect the special rewards to order bearers are in contrast to the various payments and charges described in the preceding sections.

5

The measure of inequality that is studied in the subsequent statistical investigation depends on *relative* rather than *absolute* differentials in money earnings. In order that the inequality in command over *real income* also may be gauged from this study, an effort will be made in Chapter X to summarize the effect of the different factors which cause a systematic discrepancy between relative money earnings and relative command over real income. The upshot, as must be evident, is that the inequality in real rewards is less than the inequality in money earnings, but it may be added here that the discrepancy is by no means as great as our conscientious catalogue of the vagaries of the Soviet distributive system might suggest. For the present, inequalities in money earnings may be studied with the assurance that they are a most important element in Soviet economic life.

The Soviet social security taxes, since they are proportional to wages, are excluded from this reckoning, and also the heavy turnover taxes which are levied at various points in the Soviet industrial process. The latter taxes, which are simply sales taxes, are a major source of revenue in the Soviet budget. In 1934 they yielded over 30 billion rubles, while direct taxes on income yielded not much more than 2 billions.[45]

But both the social security and the turnover taxes necessarily are reflected in the prices of the goods the Soviet worker must buy, and on this account they must be reckoned with the income tax, the progressive rental rates, and the rationing system as factors which make the established *money* wage differentials less attractive to the worker than they otherwise would be. Thus these items together exert a long-run pressure for greater *inequality* in money earnings, for a larger money wage differential than otherwise would be the case is needed to attract an adequate supply of labor into the more skilled, more responsible and more onerous occupations. The supply of education without charge to a growing number of workers, however, would have a contrary effect.

A further consequence of the hiatus between money wage differentials and differentials in command over real income in

---

[45] TSUNKHU, *Sotsialisticheskoe Stroitel'stvo SSSR* (Moscow, 1936), pp. 644 ff.

The Soviet worker's discretion over two sorts of expenditures in addition to those mentioned in the text, perhaps, is sufficiently limited to warrant note of them here. Reference is to trade union dues and state loan subscriptions. The trade union dues, however, are proportional to earnings — from August 31, 1933, they amounted to roughly 1 per cent of wages — and so also, I believe, are the loan subscriptions.

the Soviet Union is that the money costs recorded in the books of a Soviet enterprise differ from the real incomes attracting workers into the different occupations. Money costs, thus, deviate from social costs as defined by the workers' *own* evaluation of work done. In this light the Soviet accounting system is deficient. But there is hardly basis for assuming that the Soviet administrators have in fact ignored the workers' values and that they have undertaken to determine labor costs from a consideration of their own values. No patchwork of values that would make the Soviet accounting system flawless could be plausible. And without resort to such a rationalization the shortcomings of the system are at least understandable.[46]

---

[46] The factor which introduced more disorder in the Soviet accounting system than any other, rationing, is explainable only as an emergency measure. The shortages which appeared as the five-year plan unfolded doubtless were responsible for its adoption. The circumstances attendant on the abandonment of the open market are reviewed briefly in Appendix A.

CHAPTER IV

THE STATISTICAL PROCEDURE

THE WAGE STATISTICS which are used in the present study consist mainly of data on the number of wage earners in various industries whose earnings during a given period of time were within each of successive income classes. That is to say, the materials studied are frequency distributions of wage earners classified according to earnings. From this data it is possible to calculate directly the proportion of the earnings bill received by various proportions of the workers investigated. This has been done for comparable sectors of industry in the Soviet Union at different periods and in pre-war Russia. The resultant data on the distribution of the earnings bill are presented in Chapter X.

For purposes of studying the principles of Soviet wage determination, however, much can be gained by studying the inequality of earnings industry by industry. Such an investigation also is undertaken, but here a summary measure of inequality is used. The measure adopted is simply the ratio of the wage of the worker whose earnings are higher than those of 25 per cent and lower than those of 75 per cent of the workers to the wage of the worker whose position in the frequency distribution is the opposite.[1] In other words the ratio of the first and third quartiles of the frequency distribution of wage earners is con-

---

[1] More precisely one should speak of the wage, or point in the frequency distribution, which satisfies the condition specified in the text rather than of the wage of *the worker* who does so. The interpolation formula used to calculate the quartiles is $l + (h/f)c$. Here l is the lower limit of the class containing the quartile; h equals 25 (or 75) minus the percentage of workers having earnings less than l; f is the proportion of workers whose earnings are within the limits of the quartile class; and c is the class interval. This formula differs slightly in form from others which have been used, but because of the large number of items in the frequency distributions we study there is no significant difference in results.

sidered. This ratio, properly regarded, is a coefficient of the variation, or dispersion, of the frequency series, and as such it serves well enough the purpose of illuminating Soviet wage principles. But like many another such coefficient the quartile ratio is also an intuitively acceptable summary measure of inequality. Indeed, one relatively complex coefficient which has been used to measure the inequality of earnings may be expressed directly in terms of the quartile ratio.[2] The quartile ratio also commends itself to attention here on a practical ground. Its value can be determined despite the presence of large all-over and all-under earnings classes in several of the frequency distributions studied.

The position of the two quartiles for the frequency distribution of machinery and metal products wage earners in March 1928 is indicated graphically by the points denoted Q_1 and Q_3 in Chart 1. The chart is drawn so that the area under the rectangles between any two points is proportional to the number of workers whose earnings are between those values.

The value of the quartile ratio obviously is unaltered by a shift in the position of any but the twenty-fifth and seventy-fifth percentiles of the frequency distribution. Very disparate earnings distributions, thus, might be characterized by the same quartile ratio. This is not a possibility unique with the quartile ratio. It arises whenever a summary measure is used to characterize a frequency distribution. But it is none the less disturbing. A check on the relation of the quartile ratio and other percentile ratios for different earnings distributions is clearly warranted. In the comparison of wage variation in corresponding industries in pre-war Russia and in the Soviet Union which is undertaken in Chapter V, an effort is made to check graphically the over-all relation of the pairs of wage frequency distributions studied for each industry.

[2] Denoting the quartile ratio as Q, Professor Bowley's quartile coefficient of dispersion may be written as $(1 - Q) / (1 + Q)$. Pareto's measure of inequality also may be expressed in terms of the quartile ratio, for any distribution which obeys Pareto's law (cf. Bresciani-Turoni's interesting discussion of Pareto's and other measures of inequality, *Journal of the Royal Statistical Society*, vol. C, part iii, 1937, pp. 421 ff.).

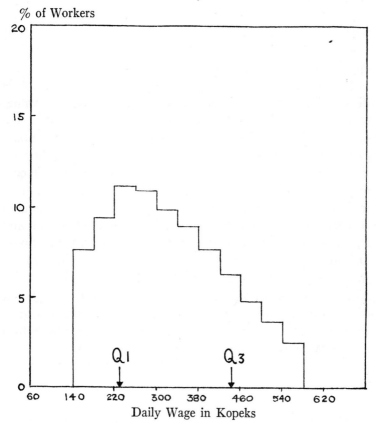

CHART 1

BLOCK DIAGRAM OF WAGE FREQUENCY DISTRIBUTION OF WORKERS IN
METAL PRODUCTS, MACHINERY AND EQUIPMENT INDUSTRY: U.S.S.R.
MARCH 1928 *

* Data in Appendix E. Frequency below 140 uncharted, 6.82%; above 580, 8.52%.

In Chapter VI a comparison is made of wage variation in corresponding industries in the Soviet Union and the United States, and in Chapter VII, of wage variation in corresponding industries in the Soviet Union at different times.

2

To compare wage variation in corresponding industries in the Soviet Union and in capitalist countries obviously is a promising course to take. Whether capitalist wage principles are indeed applicable to Soviet wages should be evidenced by the results.

The comparison promises the more because it appears little disturbed by a factor which itself might affect much the values of the quartile ratios. A cursory study suggests that at the periods which are investigated the techniques of production employed in the different countries compared do not differ substantially. If the techniques were identical, of course, and the conditions affecting the supply of labor in the different occupations were also the same, the quartile ratio ought to be the same in corresponding Soviet and capitalist industries. The same, that is, if Soviet wages are determined by capitalist principles. Doubtless these ideal conditions are not approximated in the wage comparisons undertaken. But the information on techniques that is readily available does sharpen the implications of the study. The particular pairs of periods investigated in the wage comparisons were selected for study partly from a consideration of this factor.

It must be acknowledged, however, that in this connection the results of a comparison of wage variation in several industries in the United States at distant periods undertaken in Chapter VIII are both surprising and reassuring. Despite the indubitable fact that techniques changed substantially in the interval between these periods, the quartile ratios are remarkably stable. These results necessarily deflate the importance of differences in technique as a disturbing factor in the comparison of wage variation. The study is confined, however, to various branches of the textile industry, and to the iron and steel and shoe industries. In the textile and metal industries the changes in technique which occurred probably were limited to improvements which left at least the main outlines of the technique intact.

3

The quartile ratio, it is clear, differs from a wage differential. As the latter term is used ordinarily, it refers to the relative wages of different kinds of workers. The value of the quartile ratio for a given industry depends not only on differentials in this sense, but also on the number of workers employed in the different occupations in that industry. On this score the ratio has been referred to as a measure of wage variation, rather than of the more familiar wage differentiation. To whatever extent the proportions of workers of different skills are stable in the comparisons of wage variation, however, differences in the quartile ratios must reflect directly differences in wage differentials. The casual study of techniques which is undertaken suggests that some such stability is realized at least in the comparison of pre-war Russian and Soviet wage variation. A parallelism in the movement of the quartile ratios and of wage differentials in this case and in a later comparison confined to the Soviet Union alone is evidenced more conclusively, however, by independent material on Soviet wage scales, which is presented in Chapters XIII and XIV.

4

Of the different sets of pre-war Russian and Soviet wage statistics studied, only that for 1928 could be chosen from among sets of data relating to neighboring years. Wage statistics suitable for the purposes of the present investigation are available for March in each of the years 1924 through 1930. The need to restrict the investigation to a manageable dimension was the primary reason for studying intensively only one of these sets of data. Concentration on the data for March 1928 in particular might not be difficult to support from a consideration of the level of Soviet technical and institutional development at this and other times. But the choice was determined largely by the relative statistical merits of the data for 1928 and for earlier years,[3] and by the fact that rationing was widespread in 1929 and 1930.

The present investigation is confined to industrial workers — in manufacturing and extractive industries — again primarily in order to lighten the task, though an additional consideration was the sparsity and scatteredness of materials available for other spheres.

The statistics in the next three chapters relate to the earnings of wage earners. This class of workers may be defined by distinguishing it from salaried workers. The latter category, as it is understood here, includes office workers, technical workers and engineers, administrative and supervisory workers and foremen. Other workers, including apprentices, are classified as wage earners. In Soviet statistics a more detailed classification of workers usually has been employed and the nearest Russian equivalents of "wage earner" (*rabochii*) and "salaried worker" (*sluzhashchii*) are at times used more narrowly.[4] But the grouping of workers used in the present investigation corresponds to that appearing in the earnings data for the capitalist economies studied.

---

[3] The coverage of the March 1928 data is greater than for the data relating to earlier periods, and the data for March 1928 are the first to include daily as well as monthly earnings statistics.

[4] The classifications of workers used in Soviet and pre-war Russian wage statistics are described in Appendix B.

CHAPTER V

WAGE VARIATION IN THE SOVIET UNION IN 1928 AND IN RUSSIA IN 1914

Russian Industry in 1914 and Soviet Industry in 1928. Whatever might be said of the tumultuous events which occupied the years following 1914 in Russia, it can scarcely be asserted that they were immediately favorable to the advance of industrial techniques. The shortages of fuel, materials, and transport which beset Russian industry soon after the outbreak of war [1] should have offered a strong incentive to technical change. But the opportunities to do more than rationalize the use of existing plant and equipment must have been severely limited. In the key metallurgical industry the output of pig iron declined from the outset of the war, and by 1917 the country was faced with a metals crisis which was spoken of as gravely as the food crisis. Of 231 blast furnaces in the Empire (excluding Poland) only 121 were active during that year.[2]

The hardy entrepreneurs who were able to launch new industrial ventures in the chaotic war period must have been few; in the ensuing years the revolutionary state which usurped their position was confronted with more pressing problems than the realization of technical improvements in the newly nationalized plants. When civil war was finally concluded in the latter part of 1920 the Soviet economy was prostrate. Coal output in 1921 was less than one-third of the pre-war amount; the production of pig iron, less than 3 per cent.[3] The enormous task

---

[1] The difficulties confronting Russian industry during the war are described at length by S. O. Zagorsky, *State Control of Industry in Russia during the War* (New Haven, 1928).

[2] TSU, *Trudy*, vol. VII, part 1, *Statisticheskii Sbornik za 1913–1917 gg.* (Moscow, 1921), pp. 76, 77.

[3] TSUNKHU, *Narodnoe Khoziaistvo SSSR, 1932* (Moscow, 1932), pp. 6, 7; TSUNKHU, *Sotsialisticheskoe Stroitel'stvo SSSR* (Moscow, 1936), pp. xxii, xxiii.

of rehabilitation confronting the Soviets occupied fully the period of the New Economic Policy. In Soviet literature the general level of economic activity of the pre-war period is not regarded as having been reattained until 1927.[4] The pre-war output of coal was first exceeded in that year, while the output of pig-iron was not surpassed until 1930.[5]

To the extent that the process of restoring Soviet industry after 1921 went beyond the repair and reintroduction into activity of old machines and equipment and involved their replacement by new ones, the change in some measure probably was associated with changes in production processes. In general, however, it would be surprising if the technical changes accomplished in the period of restoration, or in the seven years of war and revolution preceding it, were of a widespread or far-reaching character.

Accordingly, if we may turn to the point which concerns us here, a comparison of the inequality of earnings in the two years 1914 and 1928 would seem to be promising for the purposes of the present wage investigation. The most cursory study suggests, at least, that changes in techniques should not be an important factor affecting the general level of inequality.

But there is more specific information from which to judge the comparative status of Soviet and pre-war Russian industrial techniques. In the cotton-textile industry the revival after the civil war was accomplished largely with the same equipment as had been in use before 1914. Because of the long life of cotton-spinning machinery the fact that over three-fourths of the spindles in operation in 1925 had been installed prior to 1910 did not as yet present a serious problem, though the 15 per cent installed before 1890 were more pressing.[6] In the shoe industry the age of the machinery in use is uncertain, but its condition

---

[4] Cf. G. T. Grinko, *The Five Year Plan of the Soviet Union* (New York, 1930), pp. 31 ff.

[5] Cf. the references in n. 3 above.

[6] *Materialy Osobogo Soveshchaniia . . . pri Prezidiume VSNKH SSSR, Seriia I, Piatiletnie Gipotezy po Otrasliam Promyshlennosti, Kniga No. 27, Khlopchato-Bumazhnaia Promyshlennost'* (Moscow, 1926), pp. 33–34, 41.

as late as 1925 was such that the formulators of a tentative five-year plan in that year anticipated a new decline in output if the worn and antiquated equipment were not soon replaced.[7] In ferrous metallurgy, of the total capacity of blast furnaces in operation *in 1934*, over a third had been installed prior to 1918, and but 7 per cent were installed between 1918 and 1928.[8] Among the open-hearth furnaces, the corresponding ratios, as measured by hearth area, were 49 and 7 per cent. In all Soviet industry in 1928, of the total horsepower capacity of prime movers, the age of installation of which was known, over four-fifths had been installed prior to the war.[9]

Because of its importance for construction purposes, and because of the great potentialities of labor-saving machinery there, it might be expected that the glass industry would be among the first to be subjected to technical reconstruction by the Soviet administrators. Yet in 1928 the old hand technique of glass-blowing still prevailed. Attempts were made to introduce machinery in the existing factories in 1926. But, mainly because of the small size of the old glass furnaces, these first efforts proved unsuccessful. None of three factories which were mechanized continued in operation.[10] In the accounting year 1927–28 the machine output of window glass composed but 10 per cent of the output in large-scale establishments.[11] In the same year machine production of glass bottles, by weight, was 13 per cent of the total.

---

[7] *Materialy Osobogo Soveshchaniia . . . pri Prezidiume VSNKH SSSR, Seriia I, Kniga No. 22, Kozhevenno-Obuvnaia Promyshlennost'* (Moscow, 1926), p. 153.

[8] S. G. Strumilin, *Chernaia Metallurgiia v Rossii i v SSSR* (Moscow, 1935), p. 295.

[9] Gosplan, *Energeticheskoe Khoziaistvo SSSR* (Moscow, 1932), II, 190. Establishments having a power capacity totaling less than 25 horsepower are excluded from the statistics.

[10] Gosplan, *Piatiletnii Plan Narodno-Khoziaistvennogo Stroitel'stva SSSR*, vol. II, part 1 (Moscow, 1929), p. 197. In the *new* factories the first machine output was more expensive than the hand output.

[11] VSNKH, *Promyshlennost' SSSR v 1927–28 godu* (Moscow, 1930), p. 487.

2

The Statistics. The 1914 wage data which are used in this chapter are a product of an investigation which was conducted in the fall of 1916 by the Russian Ministry of Trade and Industry. The investigation related to both June 1914 and 1916, replies to a questionnaire submitted to the employers being taken from the factory accounts under the supervision and control of the organs of factory inspection. The chief functions of the latter under the Empire were overseeing the application of the factory laws and conciliating the parties to labor disputes. But they were charged also with the collection and checking of statistics on establishments subject to the inspection. The system of factory inspection had been organized in 1882, and statistics gathered by it were published annually after 1900. The *annual* reports, however, did not extend to the subject of the 1916 investigation. Only data on average wages were included there.

The preparation of the 1914–16 wage materials for publication was not concluded under the ministry which initiated it. After the imperial government had crumbled, the preparatory work was continued under the succeeding one. It was not until 1918, after the second revolution had taken place, that the results were published. But throughout this turbulent period and despite the procession of governments, supervision of the work remained in the hands of one of the members of the imperial factory inspection staff of the Moscow Province, I. M. Koz'minykh-Lanin. It was under his name that the study finally appeared.[12]

[12] This original publication, it may be noted, has not been obtained by the present writer. In its stead a detailed reproduction, as a part of a statistical collection of materials relating to the years 1913–1917, has been used. The collection was published by the Central Statistical Administration of the U.S.S.R. (then the R.S.F.S.R.) in 1921.

It is noted in the Soviet publication that the upper frequencies of the wage distributions are grouped into larger classes than was done in the original. This condensation is of little import to our investigation, but on the possibility that the original publication might contain also wage statistics classified in more detail

The wage statistics for March 1928 are the product of an investigation of wages initiated in March 1924 and conducted annually by the Central Bureau of Labor Statistics of the U.S.S.R. The bureau was subordinate to the Commissariat of Labor, the Central Council of Trade Unions, and the Central Statistical Administration and united the work of these three agencies relating to labor statistics. The Central Statistical Administration (TSU) had been organized in 1918 and was an administrative unit independent of the commissariats. Its head was an *ex officio* and after 1926 a full member of the Council of Commissars. Under its supervision were planned, conducted, and published the major Soviet statistical investigations. The annual wage investigations in March were designed to supplement the data on average wages which were received by the Central Bureau through periodic reports made, for shorter intervals, by the industrial plants. The statistics for March of each year were collected under the supervision of agents of the bureau.

As is to be expected in the use of statistics gathered by different organizations at widely separate points of time, there are a number of factors other than those in which we are interested which might affect the measures of wage variation compared:

(1) *Coverage.* The 1914 statistics do not relate to all wage earners subject to the Russian factory inspection, but mainly to those employed in large establishments. The extent of the investigation and the size of the establishments included may be judged by comparison with industry subject to factory inspection. Comprised in factory-inspection industry were all manufacturing establishments other than small handicraft shops.[13] Between these two spheres no sharp line existed either

---

for the various industries studied, and thus enable us to avoid the polyglot industry groups which appear in Table 4, an extensive effort to obtain the publication was made, without success.

[13] There were certain exceptions. Metallurgical plants engaged in the conversion of metals, together with any finishing departments attached to them, were

in law or in administrative practice. The general rule followed was that establishments using mechanical power or employing sixteen wage earners or more were included in industry subject to inspection. But, at the discretion of the administrative organs, larger handicraft shops might be excluded and smaller ones included on the basis of other considerations.[14] In all, the 1914 wage investigation covered 1.06 million wage earners, or 54 per cent of the number in factory-inspection industry. The number of establishments studied was but 7.9 per cent of the total. The number of workers to which our comparison of 1928 and 1914 wage variation relates is somewhat less than the total number covered by the 1914 wage investigation: 924.1 thousand. These wage earners are distributed among eight industries and industry groups and comprise 67 per cent of the total number of wage earners subject to factory inspection in *those* industries. The latter number, in turn comprises 71 per cent of the number of wage earners in all factory-inspection industry.

The coverage of the 1914 wage investigation in the different industries considered varies. The smallest, 37 per cent, is that in the saw mills, plywood group. The largest, 88 per cent, is that in the cotton-goods industry. The detailed statistics on coverage are inserted in Appendix D, Table 1.

To appraise the coverage of the 1928 study it is necessary to shift the standard of comparison to Soviet large-scale, or census, industry. The general criterion (there are a number of exceptions) distinguishing large from small-scale industry is the employment of sixteen or more wage earners with mechanical power or thirty or more wage earners without mechanical

---

subject to the mining inspection. State establishments also were excluded from the factory inspection as well as mining inspection, but this exclusion was mainly important in the latter field. On the other hand, the Baku oil fields were included in the factory inspection. In these respects the scope of the 1914–16 wage investigation was the same as that of factory-inspection industry.

[14] The writer has been informed by Col. M. A. Platoff, a former factory inspector, that the administrative discretion extended to the inspectors themselves, though their rulings were subject to appeal.

power.[15] For the eight industries and industry groups to which the 1914–28 wage comparison relates, 641.9 thousand wage earners were included in the March 1928 wage investigation. This number was 35 per cent of the number subject to the census in these industries. The largest coverage, 65 per cent, was that in the rubber products, etc., industry group; the smallest, 20 per cent, that in the saw mills, plywood group.[16]

While the coverage of the 1928 investigation was more restricted than that of 1914, the former study, too, related mainly to the larger establishments. This apparently was from a consideration of the ease of obtaining mass statistics by such means rather than from an effort on the part of the Soviet authorities to assure comparability with the 1914 data. For manufacturing industry roughly comparable in scope to that included in the entire 1914 wage investigation the average number of wage earners per establishment was nearly the same in 1928 (990) as in the earlier year (960).

(2) *The region studied.* Of the territory lost by the U.S.S.R. in the war and post-war adjustments and hence not included in the 1928 wage investigation, a large part was excluded from the reports of the factory inspection after 1913 due to the war activities. Though it is not certain, it may safely be assumed that this area was excluded as well from the 1914 wage statistics, which it will be recalled were gathered in 1916. Reference is to the Warsaw factory region, which comprised the Polish provinces and the provinces of Kovno, Grodno, and Vilna. Finland, which also was separated from the rest of the Empire by the war, was not included in any case in the factory inspection, nor in the 1914–16 wage study.

Besides these regions there are certain others which were lost to the U.S.S.R. but which were included in the 1914–16 factory-

---

[15] The characteristics of large-scale industry, as well as of factory-inspection industry, are described in greater detail in Appendix B. The scope of large-scale industry extends beyond manufacturing establishments to mining establishments. These, aside from establishments engaged in oil extraction, were excluded from the industry subject to factory inspection in 1914.

[16] Cf. Appendix D, Table 1.

inspection reports. Accordingly these probably were included in the special investigation of wages in 1916. These are the provinces of Courland, Livonia, Esthonia, Bessarabia; a part of the provinces of Minsk, Vitebsk, and Volnynia. The number of wage earners subject to factory inspection in 1914 in the area lost was roughly 165 thousand, or about 8 per cent of the total.[17] The losses were fairly evenly distributed among the industries included in the present wage comparison.

It should be noted finally that the factory inspection was extended for the first time to Asiatic Russia in 1915. Whether any wage earners in this region are included in the 1914 wage statistics used here is doubtful. But in any case the area of *European* Russia swept sufficiently beyond the Urals to include the important industrial centers on the eastern slope. In the vast expanse of Asiatic Russia the number of wage earners in large-scale industry as late as 1929 amounted to not more than 5 per cent of the total.

(3) *The definition of wages; the wage earners included.* Besides the differences in region and coverage there are two other differences between the 1914 and 1928 wage data which should be remarked. In both years the studies relate to actual earnings rather than to basic rates, and in both years daily earnings are considered. But in 1928 overtime pay as well as any money payments made to cover the workers' rent were excluded from the sum into which the number of days worked by the wage earner was divided. In 1914 these payments were included, though in calculating the number of days worked no extra allowance was made for overtime hours. The sum excluded in 1928 varied in the different industries, but in general was close to 5 per cent of the average daily wage as computed.

Finally, the 1928 investigation related only to those workers who were on the lists of a given establishment during the whole month of March. Those who were newly employed or who left the establishment during the month were excluded.

---

[17] In addition, certain Transcaucasian regions were lost to Turkey. The number of wage earners in these was not significant in the factory-inspection statistics.

Significance of the Statistical Factors. The various statistical factors that have been described necessarily affect the values of the quartile ratios, but, needless to say, this fact in itself is not a matter of great concern. To the extent that the effects are largely erratic, the wage comparison that is undertaken still may illuminate the economic forces at work. What matters, rather, is whether the statistical factors might give rise to differences in the overall level of the quartile ratios in the two years studied.

Though the 1914 coverage is in general greater than that of 1928, the difference in coverage varies widely among the different industries. This, together with the similarity in the size of the establishments studied, is adequate reason to conclude that the effects of the differences in coverage are primarily of an idiosyncratic rather than uniform character. There is certain additional evidence, however, which has interest in itself. In Appendix D, Table 2, are inserted, by industries, the average daily wages for March 1928 as determined from the 1928 wage investigation and from current reports on wages. The current reports relate to all establishments employing 250 or more workers. In these establishments were employed approximately 85 per cent of the total number of wage earners in large-scale industry. As appears from the table, the two sets of averages approximate each other closely. For only one industry is the difference greater than 5 per cent. At the same time, the relation of the averages varies among the different industries. For two of them the current statistics average is greater than that of the 1928 investigation; for the rest, to a varying extent, it is less. Not only do these results support the view that the effects of the differences in coverage were primarily erratic, but also it appears from them that the wage data studied here are likely to be representative of a much larger sphere than they comprise.

Besides the data on daily wages collected in the March 1928 investigation, information was collected on monthly earnings for those workers who were on the payroll lists the entire month. Overtime payments and other payments which were excluded from daily wages were included in the monthly earnings. Accordingly, the effect of this factor on the quartile ratios may be gauged — though in association with the effect of variation in the number of days worked per month — from the difference in the ratios for the monthly and daily earnings distributions. For the cotton-goods industry, the quartile ratio is slightly greater (.7 per cent) for the monthly than for the daily earnings distribution. For the woolen and worsted goods industry, it is slightly less (.6 per cent).

Aside from the fact that the definition of daily wages differs in the 1914 and 1928 investigations, it is to be remarked that it is *daily* rather than hourly wages which are studied. Since it is to be expected that the length of the working day was more uniform in the Soviet Union than in capitalist Russia, there is an additional statistical factor affecting the quartile ratios to be reckoned with. As to its import, it is possible to quote an example far afield, for wage earners studied in the United States in 1910. The investigation, which will be referred to again, relates to the hourly and full-time weekly earnings[18] of workers in the iron and steel industry. While there is little reason to expect the variation of working time, or the correlation of the length of time worked with hourly wages, to be approximate in the United States and in pre-war Russia, the result is nevertheless of interest. The quartile ratio for the weekly earnings distribution is 1.3 per cent less than for that of hourly earnings.

The limitation of the March 1928 investigation to wage earners who were on the employment rolls the entire month has the result that any position occupied by more than one worker during the month is excluded. In the June 1914 study such a position would be included, and with a representation equal to the number of workers occupying it. Since the labor turnover in the U.S.S.R. is large (it is true, much larger in the later years

---

[18] Full-time weekly earnings are calculated as the average hourly earnings times the number of hours customarily worked per week by each wage earner in the position filled by him.

of the first five-year plan than in 1928),[19] and since it might be
expected that the turnover among low-paid wage earners would
be greater than among the highly paid, the difference between
the two investigations would seem significant. From the comparison already referred to, of the average daily wages derived
from current reports with the average daily wages derived from
the March 1928 investigation, however, it appears that the
difference could not have been consistently important. For three
textile industries the largest difference between the averages is
2.3 per cent. Only the effect of counting the excluded positions
once, however, is allowed for here.[20] The direction of the effect
of the difference in scope of the 1914 and 1928 wage investigation should have been upward with respect to the 1928 quartile
ratios. The effect also should have been more nearly general
than that of the other factors with which we have to deal.

The illustrations cited are neither exhaustive nor conclusive.
Larger effects than those observed for industries other than the
ones considered are by no means precluded. In the case of the
variation in working time, indeed, for an industry which em-
ploys a large number of women and children, and where accordingly a positive correlation of hours worked and hourly earnings
might be expected, a greater effect is plausible. In the comparison, made in section 4, of the change in wage variation
among adult males alone, this factor is excluded. But granting
the possibility of a larger effect of the statistical differences than
is shown by the examples, it still appears likely, for most of the
differences, that such effects would be primarily of an erratic

*

[19] The total accessions in the plants of all large-scale industry in 1928 were
100.8 per cent of the average monthly working force for the year. Departures
were 92.8 per cent. The turnover was mainly important in the mining industries, however. These are not included in the 1914–28 wage comparison. In
the cotton industry the annual accession and separation rates were respectively
37.2 and 31.2 per cent; in the metal-working and machinery industry, 76.8 and
62.4 per cent. On a monthly basis of course the rates would be proportionately
less.

[20] The average daily wage in the current reports is computed as the total
in the position filled by him.

character. In general, it is believed, not more than a minor share of the difference observed in the *general level* of the quartile ratios can be attributed to the statistical factors.

The Industries and Industry Groups. The industry classes which are used in the present comparison of wage variation are as detailed as the wage statistics permit. Nevertheless, certain of the classes are exceedingly heterogeneous in content, and in one case the "industry" studied is little more than a hodgepodge. To include such an industry at all in the investigation is certainly a questionable procedure. But in general the composition of the industry classes probably did not change very substantially in Russia between 1914 and 1928. It is also reassuring to observe that to the extent that the quartile ratios are affected by changes in the composition of the industry classes, the effect should be erratic rather than uniform.

Between the industries and industry groups compared in 1914 and 1928 there are a number of disparities which, because of the differences in classifications used in the two investigations, it was not possible to avoid. One of these disparities deserves mention here. Others are indicated in the notes to Table 3 (below). Plants engaged in converting ferrous and non-ferrous metals (iron ore into pig iron, pig iron into steel, etc.), together with any finishing departments attached to them, were excluded from the 1914 investigation. Independent rolling mills and other finishing plants were included. The latter divisions employed 22.6 per cent of wage earners in the whole metal products, machinery, and equipment group in that year. In the 1928 wage investigation the ferrous and non-ferrous metallurgy industries were studied as a whole. On the presumption that the average level and the variation of wages in the converting departments approximates more the level and variation of wages in the finishing departments than in the entire metal-products, machinery, and equipment group, the metallurgy industries have been included in the metal products, etc., group in 1928 with the weight of the finishing departments alone rather than with the entire weight of the metallurgy industries.

3

Wage Variation. In Table 3 are the results of the comparison between Soviet wage variation in 1928 and Russian wage variation in 1914. Quartile ratios are presented for eight industries and industry groups. It is to be observed first that for seven

TABLE 3

QUARTILE RATIOS OF WAGE FREQUENCY DISTRIBUTIONS OF WORKERS STUDIED IN
SPECIFIED INDUSTRIES: RUSSIA 1914; U.S.S.R. 1928

		QUARTILE RATIO (Q_1/Q_3 IN %)	
	Industry	Ministry of Trade Study, Daily Wages, Russia, June 1914	Central Bureau of Labor Stat. Study, Daily Wages, U.S.S.R., March 1928
1.	Cotton goods	57.8	63.5
2.	Linen goods, hemp products ...	51.6	61.1
3.	Saw mills, plywood, furniture, and other wood products	48.0	56.5
4.	Woolen and worsted goods	44.5	55.5
5.	Metal products, machinery and equipment	43.0	51.7
6.	Paper, printing	40.0	51.0
7.	Leather, shoe	38.5	53.7
8.	Rubber products, oil extraction and refining, chemical products, matches	54.2	52.7

Besides the description of the statistical investigations contained in the text of the present chapter (section 2), the reader is referred to Appendix C for information on the sources of the data and on certain estimates used.

Each of the textile industries in the table includes the dyeing and finishing of the corresponding textiles. It is uncertain to what extent they include also the various initial processes of preparing raw materials for spinning (wool scouring, etc.). Wood pulp, with minor qualifications, is included in the paper and printing industry; also included is the printing and binding of books. The more important "other wood products" are lathed and shaped articles (bobbins, shoe lasts, etc.); cooperage and boxes, corks and stoppers. Among the components of the metal-products, etc., group are agricultural, electrical, and transport machinery and equipment.

There are a number of minor allied industries which in 1914 were *classified* in the various industry groups and which may have been included in the 1914 wage investigation but which were not included in the 1928 study. I say "may have been included" because, as has been indicated, the 1914 investigation related mainly to the larger establishments in the different industry classes, and for this reason I believe the comparability with 1928 is greater than it otherwise would be. The more important discrepancies are listed below. In each case, except for the paper, printing group, where the magnitude is unknown, the total number of wage earners who might be covered in one of the two years studied and not in the other, it is fairly certain is less than 10 per cent of all wage earners in large scale industry in the relevant industry group in 1928:

Linen goods, hemp products: In 1914 jute products are included. In 1928 hemp products were given the weight of both hemp and jute (the hemp and jute products are bagging, rope, and twine).

Paper, printing: Among the allied products in the 1914 industry class are wallpaper, blank-books, cardboard boxes, bags, and envelopes. The last three, at least, are excluded in 1928.

Rubber products, etc.: The chief rubber product is rubber footwear, but in 1928 rubber tires and tubes are included.

The chemical products include basic chemical products, and paints and varnishes. In the 1928 study soap and other fat products are included also, but not in 1914.

Leather, shoe: The 1914 industry class includes soap and other fat products.

of the eight industries and industry groups the ratios are distinctly greater in 1928 than in 1914. In view of the magnitude and consistency of the change, *the conclusion is inescapable that the variation, or inequality, of wages among industrial workers was less in the Soviet Union in 1928 than in Russia in 1914.* While the possibility that statistical factors were partly responsible for this general change has been noted, it is believed that a large share of the movement must be explained otherwise.

The data in Table 3 reveal also a very striking and significant relation. *For six of the eight industries and industry groups studied the order, or rank, of the quartile ratios is identical in 1914 and in 1928.* For a seventh industry the deviation in 1928 from its rank in 1914 is only in relation to its two close neighbors in the latter year. The invariance in the results is not exhausted by a consideration of the rank of the ratios. If all the ratios were widely separated in one year their order might be maintained in the other despite a considerable change in their relative values. It is of great interest, then, to observe in Table 3 that any two quartile ratios which are approximately equal in one year are likewise equal in the other. If one member of the pair is distinctly less in one year it is also in the other. Considering the tumultuous events intervening, the tenacity of this relation is impressive.

It is not to be passed over that the stability in the relative position of the quartile ratios is only approximate, and that exceptional changes did occur. The two industry groups segregated by a double space at the foot of Table 3 are both industries for which the difference in quartile ratios as between 1914 and 1928 deviates from the average difference by more than 5 per cent: leather, shoe; and rubber products, etc. The writer is in no position to explain these two unusual movements, but for the second industry group — rubber products, etc. — which exhibits the most exceptional change in the quartile ratios, it is highly plausible that the motleyness of the group, as compared with all others, is the relevant factor.

The curves plotted in Chart 2 represent graphically the fre-

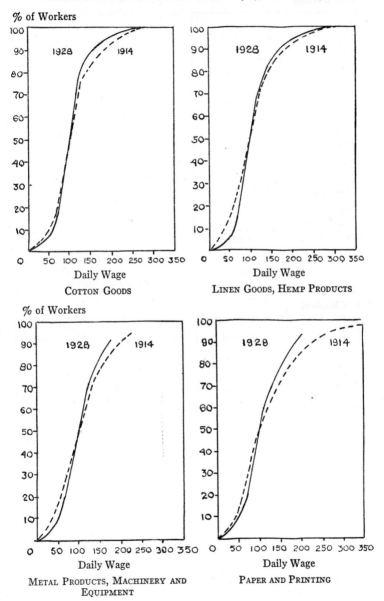

CHART 2

CUMULATIVE FREQUENCY CURVES OF INDUSTRIAL WORKERS CLASSIFIED
ACCORDING TO DAILY WAGES: RUSSIA 1914; U.S.S.R. 1928 *

% of Workers

COTTON GOODS

LINEN GOODS, HEMP PRODUCTS

% of Workers

METAL PRODUCTS, MACHINERY AND
EQUIPMENT

PAPER AND PRINTING

* Data in Appendix E. Median of each distribution = 100.

CHART 2 (*continued*)

Cumulative Frequency Curves of Industrial Workers Classified according to Daily Wages: Russia 1914; U.S.S.R. 1928 *

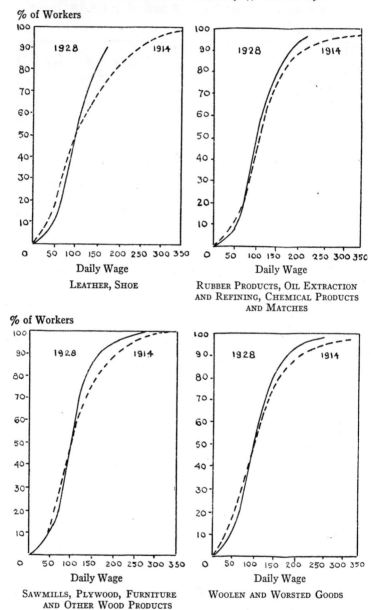

% of Workers

Daily Wage

Leather, Shoe

Daily Wage

Rubber Products, Oil Extraction and Refining, Chemical Products and Matches

% of Workers

Daily Wage

Sawmills, Plywood, Furniture and Other Wood Products

Daily Wage

Woolen and Worsted Goods

* Data in Appendix E. Median of each distribution = 100.

quency distributions from which the quartile ratios in Table 3 are computed. Each curve in the chart shows, reading vertically, the cumulative proportion of wage earners receiving less than any given wage indicated on the horizontal scale. The wage read on the horizontal scale is a percentage: prior to plotting, the class limits in each distribution were expressed as a per cent of the average wage for that distribution, the average selected being the median. The approach to a vertical line of the S-shaped cumulative curves which appear in the chart would indicate the approach of all percentiles to each other, and an increased equality of wages. It is apparent that the curves which represent the 1928 frequency distributions in Chart 2, with one exception, are consistently more erect than those for corresponding industries in 1914. There is a greater concentration of workers in the moderate wage classes in 1928, a greater dispersion in 1914. Each pair of curves thus bears out the conclusion reached from the study of the quartile ratios alone, that there was a greater variation or inequality of earnings in 1914 than in 1928.

4

The Relative Wages of Male and Female Workers. It might be suggested immediately as an explanation of the shift in the values of the quartile ratios between 1914 and 1928 which is revealed in Table 3 that it was mainly due to a leveling-up of the earnings of women relative to those of men. This hypothesis in turn probably would be based on the often expressed belief that in a capitalist economy women are paid less than proportionately to their productivity, because of (say) their weaker bargaining position. In a socialist economy, it is usually assumed, such exploitation would cease.

Whatever might be said of the correctness of this argument as to the earnings of women, there is an inherent implausibility in it so far as it is used to explain a *general* change in wage variation. Nevertheless it is profitable to examine the relevant facts.

In Table 4 are data on the relative daily wages of male and female wage earners in June 1914 and March 1928, for the same industries and wage earners as were studied in Table 3. A rise in the wages of women relative to those of men is ex-

TABLE 4

RELATIVE DAILY WAGES OF ADULT MALE AND FEMALE WAGE EARNERS, AND RATIO
OF THE NUMBER OF ADULT MALES AND FEMALES TO TOTAL NUMBER OF
WAGE EARNERS IN SPECIFIED INDUSTRIES: RUSSIA, JUNE 1914;
U.S.S.R., MARCH 1928

Industry	Wage of Adult Female in Per Cent of Wage of Adult Male		Number of Adult Males and of Females as Per Cent of Total			
	June 1914	March 1928	June 1914		March 1928	
			M.	F.	M.	F.
1. Cotton goods	72.1	73.9	39.2	51.0	35.8	57.5
2. Linen goods, hemp products	65.3	70.9	34.9	45.9	32.2	56.6
3. Saw mills, plywood, furniture, and other wood products	44.3	65.9	74.4	12.3	74.7	19.8
4. Woolen and worsted goods	67.8	76.6	50.1	37.3	47.8	45.9
5. Metal products, machinery and equipment ...	41.1	64.4	86.4	4.4	85.8	7.2
6. Paper, printing	46.5	70.0	62.0	22.1	72.7	19.4
7. Leather, shoe	58.2	76.5	65.0	21.0	73.3	23.1
8. Rubber products, oil extraction and refining, chemical products, matches	64.5	84.2	69.7	23.0	74.9	21.2

Cf., for information on the materials used in composing Table 4, the notes appended to Table 3, and in Appendix C.
It is uncertain whether or not "adult" in 1914 includes workers seventeen years of age. In 1928 "adult" refers to workers eighteen years of age and over, except that apprentices, some of whom exceeded this age, are excluded.

hibited clearly. The increase varies, however, from 1.8 per cent in the case of workers in the cotton-goods industry to 23.3 per cent in the case of paper and printing wage earners. This leveling to no more than a minor extent was due to changes in the length of the working day. From an investigation in 1913 of the hours of work of wage earners in industry subject to factory or mining inspection, the customary day [21] of adult females in the cotton-goods industry was slightly shorter (2.5 per cent) than that of males. It was slightly longer (1.5 per cent) in the paper and printing industry, and in all industry was 3.4 per cent shorter.[22] In 1928, for the two industries just referred to, the difference in the customary working day of adult males and females was less than one per cent. In all industry the hours of adult male wage earners were 1.9 per cent less than those of females.[23]

While there was an increase in the earnings of women relative to those of men in the Soviet Union, the differences in the increase as between industries and the great diversity in the proportion of women employed, which is exhibited also in Table 4, leave little basis for ascribing the overall change in the values of the quartile ratios to this factor. The data in Table 4 suggest instead what in any case is very plausible, that the changes in the relative wages of male and female workers and in the proportions of these workers employed were a cause of the erratic changes in the quartile ratios for the different industries. That this was in fact the case is strikingly established by the data in Table 5.

Among the industries listed in Table 4 there are five in which the proportion of adult males employed was approximately the same in 1928 as in 1914. The increase in adult females was at the expense of the number of minors employed. The largest change in the proportion of adult males among the five industries is that in the cotton-goods industry where it is 3.4 per cent. It is plausible, in view of the constancy of the proportion of adult males employed, that the type of work performed by them

[21] Overtime and shortened hours on Saturdays and holiday eves are not taken into account.

[22] Ministerstvo Torgovli i Promyshlennosti, *Dannye o Prodolzhitel' nosti . . . Rabochego Vremeni . . . za 1913 god.* (St. Petersburg, 1914). The averages for all industry are taken from the Soviet source in the footnote following.

[23] TSU, *Rabochii Den' v Fabrichno-Zavodskoi Promyshlennosti v 1928 g.* (Moscow, 1929). Only workers in the day shift are studied. Overtime is excluded.

in the two periods also was similar. On the presumption that this was so, the quartile ratios in 1914 and 1928 have been computed for adult male wage earners alone in these industries. The comparison accordingly excludes the effects of changes in relative wages of male and female workers. It eliminates at the same time the effect of changes in the proportion of minors employed. The latter changes, as may be seen by adding the separate columns of Table 4, were not unimportant.

The results of the comparison are presented in Table 5. A

TABLE 5

QUARTILE RATIOS OF WAGE FREQUENCY DISTRIBUTIONS OF ADULT MALE WORKERS
STUDIED IN SPECIFIED INDUSTRIES: RUSSIA, JUNE 1914;
U.S.S.R., MARCH 1928

	QUARTILE RATIO (Q_1/Q_3 IN %)	
Industry	Ministry of Trade Study, Daily Wages, Russia, June 1914	Central Bureau of Labor Stat. Study, Daily Wages, U.S.S.R., March 1928
1. Cotton goods	54.7	62.2
2. Saw mills, plywood, furniture, and other wood products	54.8	61.8
3. Linen goods, hemp products	55.8	58.2
4. Woolen and worsted goods	50.4	57.9
5. Metal products, machinery and equipment	48.0	56.4

Cf. the notes attached to Tables 3 and 4.

general movement in the quartile ratios, applying as well to industries employing large proportions of female workers as to other industries, still is exhibited clearly. But the uniformity of the movement — and at the same time the constancy in the relative values of the quartile ratios — is remarkable. *For four of the five industries the increment of the ratios is between 7.0 and 8.3 per cent.*

5

Wage Principles. The striking similarity in the relative values of the quartile ratios in different industries in Russia in 1914 and in the Soviet Union in 1928 can hardly be attributed either to statistical error or to coincidence. The only plausible explanation is the one suggested already in Chapter II, that the principles of wages applied in the Soviet Union were capitalist principles and that Soviet wages like the wages of pre-war Russia varied systematically in accord with the productivity of different workers.[24] In the stability of the relative values of the quartile ratios no peculiarity of socialist wages is discernible.

This cannot be said, however, for the general level of the quartile ratios. The overall reduction in the inequality of earnings which is revealed in Table 3 might well have been supported by an overall change in the conditions affecting the supply of labor in the different occupations. A smaller incentive might have been adequate in all industries to maintain the supply of skilled labor. But no less plausible on the face of it is it that administrators of equalitarian proclivities reduced Soviet wage differentials regardless of whether the conditions affecting the labor supply were favorable or no. To the extent that the supply of labor was affected in consequence there would have been an overall departure from capitalist wage principles in the Soviet Union. To this interesting possibility we shall return.

---

[24] In view of the heterogeneous character of the "industries" that are studied, the invariance in the relative position of the quartile ratios suggests that the principles of commodity evaluation as well as the wage principles applied in the Soviet Union were capitalist principles, and that the relative values of the different commodities in a given industry as well as the relative wages of different workers were proximate in the U.S.S.R. and in pre-war Russia. Since the different commodities embraced by each industry are allied, the proximity of their relative values in the Soviet Union and in pre-war Russia is indeed plausible. It is likely, however, that the type of labor employed in the production of the different commodities in each industry were similar, sufficiently so to assure that wages in the various broad occupation groups, through movements in the supply of labor, would be proximate even if the relative commodity values were quite different.

CHAPTER VI

WAGE VARIATION IN THE SOVIET UNION IN 1928 AND IN THE UNITED STATES IN 1904

Soviet Industry in 1928 and American Industry in 1904. A comparison of wage variation in the United States in 1904 with that in the Soviet Union in 1928 doubtless will strike the reader as a strenuous statistical maneuver. Certainly it was undertaken with some trepidation.

In the light of the information on Soviet and pre-war Russian techniques that has just been presented, however, the comparison would not seem unpromising for our purposes. If Soviet industry in 1928 had progressed little beyond the technical level of Russian industry in 1914, as the scattered information suggests, a comparable stage in the technical development of such an advanced capitalist country as the United States evidently must have appeared, if at all, well before 1914.

Needless to say, the available statistics on American wages do not permit one to be choosy in this matter. Except for scattered statistics for various industries, the data for 1904 are the only available pre-war statistics on earnings in the United States which are satisfactory for the purposes of the present investigation.[1] But a cursory glance at the technical development of several industries suggests that the year 1904 is not an unfavorable one to study and that an even earlier year might have been preferable.

(1) *The glass industry.* The year 1904 preceded by one the introduction of automatic machinery in the most important division of the American glass industry, the manufacture of glass containers. The change did not represent a complete

---

[1] The earnings statistics in the Special Report of the Census Office for 1900 might have been suitable for the present investigation, but their slender coverage precludes their being given serious consideration.

break with the technique in use prior to that time. In the manufacture of wide-mouth ware [2] various semi-automatic devices had already been applied successfully in the preceding decade. But the number of containers produced by this division of the industry was only one-fifth of the total. Only 10 per cent of the skilled workers and apprentices engaged in the production of glass containers in 1905 were operators of semi-automatic machines.[3] The remainder of the workers continued to be employed in the traditional process of hand blowing. The characteristic of the most highly developed of the semi-automatic machines was that the hand blower was replaced by a device which, with the attendance of skilled workmen, combined glass blowing and pressing. The automatic machine which was introduced in 1905, the Owens Automatic, dispensed entirely with the need for skilled operators and made output independent of the speed of the attendant. This machine was used not only for the production of wide-mouth ware, but in other divisions of the industry. In the manufacture of narrow-mouth ware, improved semi-automatic devices, first employed about 1908, continued to be used for some time thereafter.

The mechanization of the flat glass industry in the United States followed that of glass-container production. A mechanical window-glass blower, the cylinder machine, was not introduced until 1903. This continued to be used until after 1917, when commercial production of window glass in sheets was initiated. The latter process eliminates two skilled operations, splitting and flattening, which still were required in the use of the cylinder device.

The technique of the Soviet glass industry in 1928 has been sketched in an earlier chapter.[4] But juxtaposition of it with the American technical development brings out all the more sharply the Russian backwardness. More than thirty years after the

[2] Milk jars, fruit jars, and packers' goods.

[3] G. E. Barnett, *Chapters on Machinery and Labor* (Cambridge, 1926), pp. 67–70, 85.

[4] Chapter V, p. 59.

commercial application of labor-saving machines in the United States the bulk of the Soviet output was produced by hand blowing. Only one-eighth of the output of glass bottles in 1927/ 28 was machine output. The proportion of the output of window glass produced with the use of machinery was one-tenth. As far as it has been possible to determine, neither the semi-automatic nor the cylinder machine was applied in the U.S.S.R. In the production of glass bottles, automatic machines, either of the feed and flow or of the Owens type, followed directly the hand technique, while in the production of window glass the Fourcault sheet machine was introduced in the same manner. But despite these differences, the Soviet glass industry in 1928, like the American glass industry of 1904, was still predominantly a hand industry.

(2) *Ferrous metallurgy.* Soviet ferrous metallurgical technique in 1928 differed markedly in the two important and widely separate regions in which the industry was centered. The historic branch of the industry was the Urals, whence Europe long since had drawn a large part of its metals. The methods employed there still bore the imprint of the early development. One writer has described the region as continuing up to the war at the technical level of the eighteenth century.[5] Charcoal remained the basic fuel through the 'twenties, and in association with this the furnaces were tiny. With the same number of blast furnaces the Ural region in 1928 produced but one-third as much pig iron as its great rival, the southern district.[6] The latter, centered in the Ukraine, was primarily a coke region. In this respect it resembled much more closely the American iron and steel industry than did the Ural branch of Soviet metallurgy.

The relative development of metallurgy in the different Soviet regions and in the United States may be gauged from the avail-

---

[5] N. Mikhailov, *Soviet Geography* (London, 1937), p. 79.

[6] TSUNKHU, *Sotsialisticheskoe Stroitel'stvo SSSR* (Moscow, 1936), pp. 136–138. Cf. also the description by V. E. Den, *Kurs Ekonomicheskoi Geografii*, third edition (Moscow, 1928), pp. 443–445.

able statistics relating to productivity. The average output of pig iron per blast-furnace wage earner in the United States in 1904 was 473 tons, an increase of more than 200 tons over the 1889 output, and of 100 tons over the 1899 figure. For the whole U.S.S.R., the average output per wage earner in the accounting year 1927–28 was 135 tons, and in the Ukraine, 192 tons.[7] These figures, however, must be subject to important qualification. Aside from possible differences in quality of output, the working time of the Soviet and American wage earners differed widely in the two periods studied. The pre-war working week in the American blast-furnace industry was nearly 80 hours, two-shift continuous operation being generally applied.[8] For a week of equivalent length the average working time for workers in all branches of Soviet metallurgy in 1928 was slightly more than half this amount, 41 hours.[9] If this overall figure is taken as representative,[10] the productivity of the Soviet blast-furnace worker in 1928, when adjusted for differences in working time, approximates the 1889 productivity for the United States. The Ukrainian figure for 1928, however, falls between those for 1899 and 1904.

(3) *Power capacity.* Data on primary power capacity per wage earner can be interpreted as an index of technical development only with great reserve.[11] But the positive association of

---

[7] Output statistics are from TSUNKHU, *Sotsialisticheskoe Stroitel'stvo SSSR* (Moscow, 1936), p. 137. The statistics used on wage earners employed are estimates derived from various sources. An error of 10 per cent in the productivity figure on the latter account is not unlikely.

[8] Senate Document No. 301, 62nd Congress, Second Session, *Summary of the Wages and Hours of Labor* (Washington, 1912), p. 37. Only customary working time is considered.

[9] See TSUNKHU, *Trud v SSSR* (Moscow, 1932), p. 74; and S. G. Strumilin, *Chernaia Metallurgiia v Rossii i v SSSR* (Moscow, 1935), p. 310.

[10] In the Soviet blast furnace division, in contrast with the American practice, it is likely that the hours per week were less than the overall figure because of the Soviet custom of shortening the hours in dangerous and heavy trades.

[11] This use of power capacity data is discussed in detail in W. F. Thorp, "Horsepower Statistics for Manufactures," *Journal of the American Statistical Association*, December 1929; and in H. Jerome, *Mechanization in Industry* (New York, 1934), chapter vi.

this ratio with other indicators of technical development, which is revealed by studies of mechanization in American industry, lends much interest to a comparison of power capacity in the United States in 1904 and in the Soviet Union in 1928.

Taking together all the industries included in the present wage comparison except brewing (see Table 6), the primary power capacity per wage earner in census establishments in the United States in 1904 was 4.3 HP.[12] In large-scale establishments in the corresponding sector of Soviet industry in 1928 the ratio was but 1.3 HP.[13] In the industries considered, only a small proportion of the workers were employed in very small establishments, so that the discrepancy between the Soviet and American ratios is affected very little by the fact that the criteria of a census establishment and of a large-scale establishment are not the same.[14]

Primary power capacity here is the sum of the capacity of prime movers (steam engines and turbines, gas engines, water wheels and water turbines, power drills, etc.) and electric motors run by power received from an outside generating plant.[15] Because the electric motors used in industry are ordinarily not in use simultaneously there is a possibility, in any particular case, that the second element in this sum would be inflated sub-

---

[12] Data on primary capacity and on the number of wage earners in census industry were obtained from United States Bureau of Census, *Special Reports of the Census Office, Manufacturing*, 1905, part i (Washington, 1907).

[13] Data on primary capacity were obtained from TSUNKHU, *Narodnoe Khoziaistvo SSSR, 1932* (Moscow, 1932), pp. 30 ff., and data on the number of wage earners in large scale establishments, from V. Sats, "Chislennost' i Sostav Rabochikh i Sluzhashchikh v Promyshlennosti SSSR na 1-e IAnvaria 1929 g.," *Statistika Truda*, 1929, no. 5–6, pp. 1 ff. Soviet statistics in kilowatt units are converted into HP at the rate of 1 HP = .746 KW.

[14] Subject to a number of exceptions, American census establishments comprised all plants having annual sales of $500 or more.

[15] In the U.S.S.R. the capacity of electric motors run by mixed power is also included. Mr. Leverne Beales of the United States Census Bureau has informed the writer that to the extent that there was a mixed power capacity in the United States it is likely that this was classified either with the capacity driven by outside ("rented") power or with that driven by inside power according to which of these sources of power predominated.

stantially by idle capacity.[16] A check of the Soviet and American power data, however, reveals that it is the Soviet power ratio which is likely to be the more inflated on this account.

Surprisingly the denominator of the power ratios, much more than the numerator, is a questionable element in the comparison that has been made. To the extent that workers are employed in more than one shift, the proper figure to relate to power capacity is not the total number of wage earners, but the number in one shift, and if the shifts differ in size, the number in the largest shift. What makes this consideration important here, of course, is that shift work was far more widespread and intensive in Soviet industry in 1928 than in American industry in 1904. With the shortening of the working day in the Soviet Union, second and even third shifts were employed, not only in industries where technical factors required shift work, but in industry in general.

Fortunately there are statistics available which permit adjustment of the Soviet power ratio for the number of wage earners employed in other than the largest shift. For the same sector of industry as was studied previously, the primary power capacity per wage earner in the largest shift in the U.S.S.R. in 1928 was 2.5 HP.[17] It is apparent that even the adjusted Soviet figure for 1928 is 1.8 HP less than the unadjusted one for the United States in 1904. Since shift work was important in the American metallurgy and paper industries and possibly the glass industry in 1904 — all these are included in the sector of industry studied here — the adjustment for the number of wage earners in other than the largest shift in the United States probably would be a significant one.[18]

---

[16] Thus when electric motors are supplied by outside instead of inside power, primary power capacity data are arbitrarily inflated. For all American manufactures, Thorp (*op. cit.*), p. 384, has estimated that the capacity of electric motors exceeds by as much as 50 per cent the capacity of prime movers which motivate them.

[17] Data on shift work are from TSU, *Rabochii Den' v Fabrichno-Zavodskoi Promyshlennosti v 1928 g.* (Moscow, 1928), pp. 42–43.

[18] The importance of differences in shift work as a factor affecting the signif-

2

The Statistics. The statistics on wages in the United States in 1904 which are used in the present chapter were collected as a part of the census of 1905, the inquiry on wages being included in the regular census schedule. The Soviet data for March 1928 are the product of the same investigation as the data used in Chapter V for comparison with Russian wages in 1914. As with the statistics studied in the earlier chapter, the two sets of data which are considered in the present one differ in a number of respects other than those which we are interested in measuring.

(1) *Coverage; the size of establishments studied.* Large-scale industry, that is, all establishments employing 16 or more wage earners with mechanical power, or 30 or more wage earners without mechanical power, is again taken as a standard of comparison for the coverage of the Soviet wage investigation. Relative to large-scale industry, the coverage of the Soviet study, among the thirteen industries which are considered in the wage comparison, varied from 28 per cent for the glass industry to 87 per cent for the rubber products industry.[19]

The United States Census investigation was projected to include all of census industry. With minor qualifications, this comprised all establishments having annual sales of more than $500. But because of the large number of defective returns, the actual coverage was much less.[20] In the glass industry, which as in the Soviet study had the smallest coverage, 42 per cent cf wage earners in census industry were included in the investigation. In the rubber products industry the proportion was 70 per cent. In all thirteen industries together the American

---

icance of power capacity ratios has been ignored consistently by students of American power capacity data.

[19] The coverage of the Soviet and the American wage investigation is indicated for all industries in Appendix D, Table 3.

[20] No explanation of the defective returns is given. But it is likely that the fact that the 1905 wage investigation was a first attempt of its sort to canvass census industry as a whole is relevant.

investigation included 53 per cent of the census wage earners in those industries. The number of workers studied was 745 thousand. In the Soviet wage investigation the number of workers studied in all thirteen industries was 413 thousand, or 37 per cent of the total number of workers in all large-scale establishments in these industries.

As in Chapter V, the Soviet wage statistics used here relate primarily to the larger establishments. Because of the large number of defective returns in the American investigation it might be expected that larger establishments would have been given a disproportionately large weight here also. Actually this did not turn out to be the case. The average size of the investigated establishments approximates the average for all census establishments. The consequence of the difference in the scope of the Soviet and American investigations was that the difference in the size of establishments studied, which in any case would have been large, was greatly magnified. A moderate example is the cotton-textile industry. Here the average number of wage earners per establishment in the Soviet study was 14 times the average number (384) in the American one.[21]

It is plausible that the effect on wage variation of the disparity in the size of establishments studied in the Soviet Union and in the United States, together with the effect of differences in coverage, would be primarily idiosyncratic. Any uniformities observed in the quartile ratios could be attributed to other factors. Beyond this, there are grounds for the view that, within broad limits, the effect of the first difference was small as well. For a few branches of industry in the American census wage investigation, wage frequency distributions are classified according to establishment size. For one of these branches, print-

---

[21] As far as it has been possible to ascertain, there was no important difference in the definition of establishment in the Soviet and American wage investigation. It would have represented no discrepancy in definition, however, if kindred products produced by separate establishments in American industry had been produced by departments of a large unit in Soviet industry, and this unit called an establishment in the Soviet wage investigation. The Soviet proclivity to giantism might well have been expressed in such conglomerative establishments.

ing and publishing, book and job, the quartile ratios of the
frequency distributions has been calculated for establishments
of different size. The results indicate a marked stability in
wage variation with respect to this variable. In the highest two
establishment classes containing a small number of wage earners the quartile ratio fluctuates widely. But if these two classes
are grouped the ratio varies from a lower limit of 33.2 per cent,
for establishments employing more than 300 workers, to 37.6
per cent for establishments employing from 10 to 50 workers.
The first large change occurs for the class of establishments
employing fewer than 10 workers, for which the quartile ratio
is 43.5 per cent.[22]

While this information is reassuring, several minor industries
have been omitted from the wage comparison because of the
disparity in the size of the establishments included in the Soviet
and American investigations. Since in these industries the
American establishments are on the average proximate in size
to the *smallest* establishments in the printing and publishing,
book and job industry, the computation just presented for
that industry is more indicative of the importance of the disparity between these and the Soviet establishments than of the
converse. An example is the printing industry as a whole. Here
the average number of workers per establishment in the American investigation is 8, and in the Soviet investigation, 270.
In cases such as this the results of a comparison of wage variation are a foregone conclusion. While the character of the

[22] The quartile ratios for wage earners in the different sizes of establishments
are as follows:

No. of Wage Earners	Proportion of Wage Earners (%)	Quartile Ratio (%)
Over 500	4.0	27.3 ⎫ 33.2
300–500	3.5	42.1 ⎭
150–300	10.1	33.7
50–150	16.9	35.3
10– 50	24.9	37.6
0– 10	40.6	43.5
All	100.0	

establishments studied would be a ready explanation of the exceptional relations that could be expected to result, it was deemed wiser to exclude such industries from the comparison at the outset.[23]

The thirteen industries which are included in the wage comparison employed 46 per cent of the 2.3 million wage earners in Soviet large-scale (non-extractive) industry in 1928.

(2) *Definition of wages; the wage earners studied.* Both the American and Soviet wage data are data on actual earnings rather than on basic wage rates. The period of time to which the American earnings relate, however, is one week, while the Soviet statistics used are for monthly earnings. Also, the Soviet data relate only to wage earners who were on the payroll lists the entire month of March.

Among workers included in the Soviet study, the variation in working time is not of large import. The examples used in Chapter V apply as well here. For two Soviet textile industries, the quartile ratio of the distribution of wage earners by monthly earnings in March 1928 was in one case .7 per cent greater, and in the other case, .6 per cent less than for the corresponding distribution by daily earnings.

The restriction of the Soviet data to workers who were on the payroll lists the entire month, as before, has the result that positions occupied by more than one worker during the month

---

[23] In all, four industries employing 6 per cent of the wage earners in Soviet large-scale (non-extractive) industry were omitted on this account. The industries omitted, besides printing, and the average size of establishments in the Soviet and American investigations were: baking (153;4); milling (128;4); and clothing (1035;31). The last was a borderline industry, but, because of doubts as to its comparability in the United States and the U.S.S.R. in any case, it was omitted.

For two other industries, rubber products and electrical machinery, the *relative* size of Soviet and American establishments was comparable to that of the excluded industries (for all other studied, the ratio was less than the cotton-textile ratio of 14:1). Since the American establishments in these industries were large absolutely, their exclusion was not indicated as clearly as was that of the industries listed in the preceding paragraph. Accordingly they were retained. But it is interesting that for one of these two industries the result of the wage comparison is exceptional.

are not represented. In the American data, positions occupied more than once during the week studied are included with a weight equal to the number of workers occupying the position. This statistical difference was encountered in the wage comparison of Chapter V.[24] But in the present comparison, its significance is enhanced because the American wage statistics are earnings for a week, rather than daily or hourly earnings. All workers who were employed only part of the week would tend to be pushed downward in the weekly earnings distribution. The results of a wage comparison for American industries alone, to be made in Chapter VIII, indicate that this statistical factor operates fairly uniformly to reduce the quartile ratios. Though other factors obtrude, it appears there that on the average the reduction may have been as much as 4 per cent.

In the Soviet wage investigation in 1928, statistics on both daily and monthly earnings were collected. The reader will recall that the former were used in the comparison with Russian daily wages in 1914. Which, if either, of these sets of data would be preferable in the present comparison is open to question, there being grounds for either choice.[25] The computations which were presented earlier suggest at once that the difference in the results would be slight in any case. Under these circumstances our choice has been guided by a practical consideration. Since for a later comparison with Soviet monthly wages in 1934 the use of monthly wages in 1928 is clearly indicated, and since the industries studied now will be studied then, the use of the same data now reduces considerably the statistical labor.

(3) *Geographical dispersion.* More than in the earlier in-

---

[24] The week selected for study in the American investigation was one for which, in each establishment studied, employment was at a maximum for the year. It is difficult to say whether this would have enhanced or reduced the influence of the turnover factor.

[25] So far as the monthly earnings include rents and tramway fares paid to the workers they are preferable to daily earnings. But the position is the reverse insofar as it is uncertain whether, whatever further variation in working time was involved in the use of monthly earnings, this would be similar in effect to that involved in the use of weekly earnings in the United States.

vestigation of Russian and Soviet wages the present investigation should be affected by the fact that the workers in each industry are not concentrated in one locality but are scattered in different regions. From a cursory examination of a number of industries for which regional data are presented in the American investigation this factor does not appear in general to have the importance which a first thought might give it. Without a more painstaking study it is safe to presume in any case that the geographic dispersion, as with the differences in establishment size, would explain the exception rather than the rule in the wage comparison.

In one industry, cotton textiles, however, the regional data for the United States reveals an unusually large wage differential between the two important producing regions, the North and the South. Whether this differential was entirely "geographic" is open to question. But it is clear in this case that wage variation should be calculated separately for the two regions. In Table 6, which summarizes the results of the wage comparison, this has been done. But because of the large number of children employed in the southern mills (nearly 25 per cent of the total number of wage earners) the figure for the northern region alone has been inserted there, for comparison with the Soviet cotton ratio.

A similar course has been followed in the case of one Soviet industry, ferrous metallurgy. Here the motivating consideration was primarily the striking difference in techniques in the two important and widely separate producing regions, though, too, there was a large regional differential. In Table 6 the quartile ratio for Ukrainian metallurgy alone is inserted. That for the Urals is noted. Ferrous metallurgy is the only industry for which regional data are available in the Soviet investigation.

(4) *The industries studied.* The industries which are studied in the present wage comparison, fortunately, are narrower in scope than those studied in Chapter V. Because of the fact that two different countries are compared, however, it is doubtful

whether on balance the composition of the output of the various industries is more similar at the two points of time studied than it was in the earlier comparison. Where possible, in industries having a very heterogeneous product, and for which it seemed that the composition of the working force would be affected particularly on that account (the electrical machinery, apparatus industry is an example), a check of the composition of the output has been made. The object was to assure that the outputs did not differ so widely in the United States and U.S.S.R. as to make a wage comparison out of the question.[26]

3

Wage Variation. In Table 6 are presented the quartile ratios of the wage frequency distributions of Soviet workers in 1928 and American workers in 1904. For convenience those industries for which the quartile ratio in the two countries differs by 5 per cent or more from the average difference for all industries are segregated from the others.

It is apparent that the general level of the quartile ratios in the two countries is remarkably proximate. In general the wage variation in the U.S.S.R. is less than that in the United States, that is, the quartile ratios are greater. *But, among the first eight of the industries in Table 6, the maximum difference in the quartile ratios in the two countries is 5.4 per cent, and the average difference is 3.2 per cent. For all industries together the average difference, taking absolute differences, is 5.4 per cent.* On balance this difference would be reduced if allowance were made for the statistical factors which were described in section 2,[27] and in a number of industries the American quartile ratios might slightly exceed the Soviet ones. It may be concluded that in general the inequality of earnings among Soviet industrial

[26] The relative value of the different products of the electric machinery apparatus industry in the U.S.S.R. and the United States was surprisingly similar. On the other hand, in the agricultural machinery industry the difference was so wide as clearly to indicate the exclusion of this industry.

[27] The effect of the earnings period used in the two wage investigations, and of the workers included in the investigations, is referred to particularly.

TABLE 6

QUARTILE RATIOS OF WAGE FREQUENCY DISTRIBUTIONS OF WORKERS IN SPECIFIED
INDUSTRIES: U.S.S.R. 1928; UNITED STATES 1904.

Industry	QUARTILE RATIO (Q_1/Q_3 IN %)	
	Central Bureau of Labor Study, Monthly Wages, U.S.S.R., 1928	Census Office Study, Weekly Wages, U.S., 1904
1. Cotton goods	64.2	62.6
2. Matches	63.6	59.5
3. Woolen goods	63.5	60.4
4. Linen goods	63.4	61.6
5. Ferrous metallurgy	58.7	60.3
6. Worsted goods	58.2	52.8
7. Electrical machinery, apparatus	53.4	49.6
8. Shoes	52.1	48.1
9. Rubber products	67.5	59.0
10. Glassware	43.0	31.1
11. Brewing	58.3	64.5
12. Paper	54.2	61.8
13. Leather	53.8	64.6

The reader is referred to Appendix C for information on the sources of the statistics and on certain estimates used.

The Soviet ferrous metallurgy figure refers to the metallurgy of the Ukraine. For the Urals the wage ratio is 54.4 per cent. The cotton goods quartile ratio for the United States is for North Atlantic States. The ratio for the South Atlantic States is 53.3 per cent.

The wage ratios for Soviet ferrous metallurgy, and glassware, are calculated from daily earnings rather than monthly earnings distributions.

With respect to the contents of the different industries the following should be remarked:

(1) The textile industries in the American wage study do not include wage earners in independent dyeing and finishing establishments. In the Soviet study, dyeing and finishing establishmens are included with the various textile industries.

(2) To make the Soviet woolen goods industry more comparable with that in the United States, I have excluded from it a sub-class, "coarse woolen goods." This class of goods is made from wool which I believe would be designated carpet wool in the United States. A large amount of peasant and military cloth was made from it.

(3) Ferrous metallurgy, for the United States, comprises the two census classes, "iron and steel: blast turnaces," and "iron and steel: steel works and rolling mills."

(4) Electrical machinery, apparatus includes dynamos and motors, cable and wire, batteries, telephone and telegraph apparatus, and other minor products.

(5) The rubber products are rubber footwear, belting and hose, and various rubber and elastic goods.

(6) Glassware includes bottles and jars, and various forms of pressed and blown ware.

(7) Paper in the United States includes independent wood pulp establishments. It is unlikely that they are included in the Soviet wage statistics for the paper industry. But the number of wage earners employed in separate wood pulp establishments in the U.S.S.R. was less than 4 per cent of the total number in this branch and the paper industry proper.

(8) In the American wage statistics a number of minor divisions of different industries are classified as separate industries. Cotton small wares, for example, is presented as a separate industry from cotton goods. To what extent these minor branches were included with the main branches of the different industries in the Soviet wage study is uncertain. But since, in the United States, the number of wage earners in these minor branches is quite small, I have not troubled to calculate what the wage ratios would be if they were included.

workers in 1928 was closely proximate to that among American industrial workers in 1904.

A number of the Soviet quartile ratios in Table 6 are bunched at the upper end of the scale, and differ by only a fraction of one per cent. Under this circumstance a comparison of the rank of the ratios in the Soviet Union and the United States is not of special interest. But if we turn directly to the more significant characteristic, relative value, the comparison is interesting indeed. Similarity in the relative values of the quartile ratios is taken, as before, to mean that if the ratios for two industries are approximate in one country they are so in the other, and if the ratio for one industry is distinctly less than that for another in one country it is distinctly less also in the other. *In Table 6 for seven of the thirteen industries (numbers 1 through 8, excluding 5), the relative position of the ratios in this sense is nearly identical in the two countries. For nine of the thirteen industries (the above, plus numbers 5 and 10) the relative values are strikingly similar.*

In view of the roughness with which the present wage comparison satisfies the ordinary requirements of homogeneity in other respects than those measured, it is not surprising that there are a number of comparatively large deviations from the general relation of the quartile ratios in the U.S.S.R. and United States exhibited in Table 6. Among the thirteen industries in Table 6 there are three for which the quartile ratios differ from the average difference by 5 per cent or more and for which the general relation of the quartile ratios is reversed. The ratio for the Soviet Union is less than that for the United States. For two of these industries, brewing and leather, it has been possible to obtain little information which would shed light on the exceptional results. It may be pertinent to the unusual result for the leather industry that a large proportion of Soviet upper leather production is a heavy vegetable-tanned type used primarily for the production of work shoes in the United States.[28] At least a third of the hides tanned in the U.S.S.R. in 1926–27, for the production of uppers, consisted of this type of leather.

---

[28] This is the so-called Mostov'e leather.

On the third industry for which the American quartile ratio exceeds the Soviet one by a relatively large amount, the paper industry, there is more definite information. Despite persistent efforts to develop its own newsprint branch of the paper industry, the Soviet Union satisfied most of its needs for this commodity abroad. In March 1928 but 6 per cent of the total paper output was composed of newsprint.[29] In the United States newsprint was one of the important branches of the paper industry, 36 per cent of the paper output in 1904 being composed of this product. While in general such a difference in composition of output might not be of particular import, it happens in the present case that there are significant differences in the methods of producing the different products which would be reflected in the overall measure of wage variation. At both the initial and the final stages of production, such branches of the paper industry as writing and book paper employ unskilled labor for operations which are of little or no importance in the newsprint branch. The sorting of rags and wastepaper, and the cutting, inspecting and sorting, and finishing of the final product (newsprint is ordinarily produced in rolls; book and writing paper in sheets) are operations of this character. The effect of the larger weight of these occupations in the Soviet paper industry, it is clear, would be to increase the Soviet wage variation, or reduce the quartile ratio relative to the American ratio.

In the American census wage investigation of 1900, which was referred to earlier,[30] wage data are given separately for the few establishments investigated. For one establishment, producing an output which appears comparable to that of the Soviet paper industry (the designation is "book, writing, and other paper") the quartile ratio of the wage frequency distribution is 50.7 per cent. The quartile ratio for a second establishment

---

[29] VSNKH, Tsentral'nyi Otdel Statistiki, *Ezhemesiachnyi Statisticheskii Biulleten'*, Mart-Aprel 1928, p. 57. The statistics refer to industry administered by the Supreme Economic Council, which in this case employed about four-fifths of the wage earners in census industry.

[30] Cf. p. 78, n. 1.

producing book and news paper is 80.1 per cent. The effect of the difference in product is exaggerated in this case by certain peculiarities of the second establishment.[31] But it is interesting that if the result for the first establishment could be taken as representative of a sector of the American paper industry comparable to the Soviet paper industry, this industry could be transferred from the exceptional group to those exhibiting the "rule" in Table 6. The quartile ratio is 3.5 per cent *less* than the Soviet ratio.

For two industries in Table 6, rubber products and glassware, the difference in the American and Soviet quartile ratios is comparatively large. But it is in the same direction as that generally exhibited in the table. In the rubber products industry the relative disparity in the size of the Soviet and American establishments was the largest among those which we study, the average number of workers employed in the Soviet establishments being 41 times the average number in American establishments.[32] In all Soviet large-scale industry there were but four giant rubber establishments. Of these, three were included in the wage investigation. While the effect on wage variation of differences in establishment size in general might be discounted, it is plausible that the exceptional discrepancy in the rubber industry was responsible for the unusual result in Table 6.

The hand technique of production in the glass industry is one with which, in capitalist countries, large wage differentials have been peculiarly associated. From the detailed examination of techniques in this industry, it appears that the hand technique was predominant in both the Soviet Union and the United States at the time of our wage comparison. Accordingly, the wage variation observed for the glass industry in a socialist country has a special interest. For the branch of the industry

[31] This establishment used no rags even for the book paper and purchased its own sulphite.

[32] This ratio is comparable to that for such industries as printing, which the reader will recall were excluded from our comparison. My reason for not excluding this industry as well is indicated on p. 87, n. 23.

for which it was possible to compare wage variation, glassware (this includes bottles and jars, and pressed and blown ware, but does not include window and plate glass), it is clear from Table 6 that the quartile ratios in both countries are markedly below the ratios for all other industries, and *pari passu* the wage variation is much greater. But the difference between the Soviet and American ratios is comparatively large, the ratios being respectively 43.0 and 31.1 per cent. Of this difference perhaps 1, and not more than 2, per cent can be attributed to the fact that it was necessary to use daily wages instead of monthly wages in computing the Soviet quartile ratio. But there remains an idiosyncratic difference of some 5 or 6 per cent to be explained.

The proportions of the two groups of products in the glassware industry, bottles and jars, and pressed and blown ware, in value terms, are surprisingly proximate in the United States and in the Soviet Union in the years which we consider. In both cases the former composes slightly more than three-fifths of the total. There is one further factor, however, which may be relevant to the large discrepancy between the Soviet and American quartile ratios. This is the union organization in the American glass industry. In 1910 the unionized members of the glass industry comprised 34 per cent of the total number of wage earners in this branch of production. This figure was among the highest in American industry.[33] More significant than the extent of organization, however, is the fact that the glass unions were notoriously strong. The glass bottle blowers, for example, over a period of years had built up an elaborate system of collective bargaining with the association of bottle manufacturers. Further, the unions were primarily organizations of skilled workers.[34] The organizations, accordingly, were in a specially favorable position to extract monopolistic advantages for skilled workers, and at the same time to resist the encroachment of

[33] Cf. Leo Wolman, *The Growth of American Trade Unions, 1880–1923* (New York, 1924), pp. 146 ff.

[34] According to G. E. Barnett (*op. cit.*, p. 106) the Glass Bottle Blowers' Union included only skilled workers as late as 1914. In that year packers and other unskilled workers were taken into membership.

the machine on these advantages. It is clear that at least the latter policy was accomplished for a period by the bottle blowers.[35]

Whether or not the strong union organization in the American glass industry accounted for the relatively large variation of wages observed there, it is worth noting that the total gain of skilled over unskilled workers that could be attributed to the union measured but 5 or 6 per cent in terms of the quartile ratio. For other American trade unions than that of the glass workers, it is clear, the showing in Table 6 is less "favorable." But here because of the generally small extent of unionization their effect may be less adequately expressed in the quartile ratio. In any case, however, in view of the importance that has been attached to the subject of the monopolistic gains of craft unions in wage literature, these results can claim a special interest.

4

Wage Principles. The remarkable proximity of the general level of the quartile ratios in the Soviet Union in 1928 and in the United States in 1904 was hardly to be anticipated. Certainly the framework of capitalist wage principles is broad enough to embrace at the same time inequalities in earnings which differ substantially in two different countries at opposite portions of the globe and at periods of time separated by a quarter of a century. But the fact that the level of the quartile ratios is proximate in the U.S.S.R. in 1928 and in the United States in 1904 is not to be dismissed as a coincidence. The results must be regarded as further support for the conclusion that Soviet wages varied in accord with capitalist principles. When to the proximity of the general level of the quartile ratios is added the similarity in their relative position, the evidence is certainly impressive.

[35] Cf. Barnett's analysis (*op. cit.*, p. 82) of the effect of the semi-automatic on standard rates and on the working day.

CHAPTER VII

SOVIET WAGE VARIATION, 1928 AND 1934

IF SOVIET WAGE POLICY ever were to take a course peculiar to a socialist society, the year 1928 might be expected to mark the turn. In a brief interval immediately preceding that year the New Economic Policy, which was embarked on in 1921, was rapidly liquidated, and the bulk of private trade brought into the hands of the state. The fourth quarter 1928 marked the inauguration of the first five-year plan, this to be succeeded in ensuing years by a second and third. The five-year plans were not the first Soviet attempt at planning. But with them planning crystallized into a relatively effective administrative technique. The first five-year plan was preceded by only one set of annual control figures which, like it, were confirmed by the government as directives for the whole state sector of the economy. In the years immediately following 1928, planning was to become the more effective as the Soviet peasantry followed private trade into a socialist mold. By 1932 over three-quarters of the sown area was administered by collectives, or by state and other coöperative organizations.

In the light of these developments a comparison of Soviet wage variation in 1928 and in 1934 has more than the ordinary interest of "additional observations." Did the great strides towards communism finally augur the tardy equalization of Soviet wages? Was the payment of wages according to productivity merely a transient among Soviet institutions, to disappear with the more complete development of a socialist administrative technique, and with the establishment of socialist forms of organization in other spheres? Or was it a relatively stable element of the economy?

The momentous events which give special interest to a comparison of wage variation in the Soviet Union in 1928 and in

1934, however, were associated with a drastic overhauling of Soviet industry. In Soviet economic literature the first five-year plan marks the end of the period of industrial "restoration," the beginning of the period of "reconstruction." In part the industrial development that took place in the later period was merely expansive. The working force of large-scale industry in 1934 was more than double the 3.1 millions employed in 1928. This expansion in itself is noteworthy. But technically, too, the years after 1928 were ones of marked change. Descriptions of the period by Soviet writers as one of "profound technical revolution," or as one in which the U.S.S.R. moved from a backward country "into the front rank of technically and economically highly developed countries," perhaps overdo the matter. But in six years after 1928 primary power capacity per wage earner in large-scale industry increased 40 per cent.[1] This increment compares favorably with that achieved in American manufacturing industry in a period when the recorded annual rate of growth was at its peak. In the ten years 1899 to 1909 primary power capacity in American census manufacturing establishments increased 34 per cent.[2]

In view of the technological development that took place, then, the comparison of wage variation in 1928 and 1934, though interesting to undertake, is hardly favorable for the study of wage principles. Changes in techniques as well as in institutions are reflected in the changes in wage structure.

---

[1] From data in TSUNKHU, *Sotsialisticheskoe Stroitel'stvo v SSSR* (Moscow, 1936), p. 3; and TSUNKHU, *Trud v SSSR* (Moscow, 1936), p. 91.

[2] Harry Jerome, *Mechanization in Industry* (New York, 1934), p. 217.

In view of the relative backwardness of Soviet industry in 1928 it might be suggested that 1934 would have been an even better year than 1928 to use in the comparison of Soviet wage variation with that in the United States in 1904. But the tempestuous character of Soviet industrial development after 1928 and the likelihood of technical short-cuts — such as occurred in the glass industry — are considerations favorable to the use of the 1928 data. It is to be recalled also that the period 1929–34 was a period of rationing in the Soviet Union. Since the quartile ratios for various Soviet industries in 1934 are presented in the present chapter, however, the results of the different alternatives are readily compared.

2

The Statistics. The statistics used in the present wage comparison are more homogeneous than any used thus far. The 1928 data are the same as those used for the Soviet-American wage comparison in Chapter VII. The 1934 statistics were collected by the Central Administration of National-Economic Accounting (TSUNKHU), the successor to the Central Statistical Administration. While the 1934 investigation was not simply a continuation of the 1928 one (the last of this series was that of March 1930) the data are similar in most important respects. In 1934 as well as in 1928 the study relates mainly to wage earners in large establishments. In both cases monthly earnings are investigated, and workers not on the payroll lists the entire month are excluded. Of the total number of wage earners employed in large-scale establishments, in industries which are included in the present wage comparison, the 1928 study covered 32.4 per cent, and that of 1934, 28.5 per cent. Among the different industries, however, the coverage varies widely. In 1928 the largest proportion of wage earners studied was in the rubber products industry, where it was 87 per cent, and the smallest proportion was for furniture, 11 per cent. The corresponding figures for 1934 are 58 and 8 per cent, for tobacco and liquor, respectively.[3]

The 1934 wage investigation, like that of 1928, covered virtually all of Soviet large-scale industry, including extractive industry. On this account, and because of the similarity in classification, it is possible to extend the present wage comparison considerably beyond the limits of the earlier ones. In all, twenty-six industries are included. These industries, in 1934, employed 4.2 million wage earners, or 70 per cent of the number employed in all large-scale industry.

The 1934 wage data relate to October, and the 1928 statistics, as before, to March. As far as may be gathered from monthly data on the number of workers employed in the different indus-

[3] Coverage in different industries is indicated in Table 4, Appendix D.

tries, the comparison is not disturbed by seasonal factors on this account.

3

Wage Variation. The results of the comparison of Soviet wage variation in 1928 and 1934 are in Table 7. Industries for which the quartile ratios in the two years deviate from the average difference by 5 per cent or more are again segregated at the foot of the table.

The change in wage variation from 1928 to 1934 exhibited in the table is surprisingly small. *The average difference in the quartile ratios for all industries (disregarding sign) is 3.5 per cent.* For seventeen of the twenty-six industries the change is less than this. These small changes are counterbalanced in the average by large movements in a few industries.

But the direction of the change in the quartile ratios from 1928 to 1934 is consistently downward. This is so in seventeen of the twenty-six industries, and in only three of the remaining nine industries is the change in the opposite direction large. *Thus, instead of a further equalization of earnings, the period 1928–34 in the Soviet Union witnessed an increase in inequality.*

Though it was not to be anticipated for the period 1928–34, the relative position of the quartile ratios in Table 7 also is somewhat stable. The fact that the ratios cluster in groups obscures this relation. But in industries in which the ratios are proximate in one year they tend to be so in the other, and likewise if the ratios are less in one group of industries than in another. This result is exhibited graphically and, in view of the large number of industries, more clearly in Chart 3. Here the quartile ratios for each industry are plotted, the 1934 ratio against the vertical axis and the 1928 ratio against the horizontal axis. Though the points by no means fall on a straight line as would be the case if their relative position remained unchanged, there is a tendency (it is more clear if for the moment the three extreme items designated by a circle are disregarded) towards a linear scatter.

TABLE 7

QUARTILE RATIOS OF WAGE FREQUENCY DISTRIBUTIONS OF WAGE EARNERS IN
SPECIFIED INDUSTRIES IN THE SOVIET UNION, 1928 AND 1934.

Industry	QUARTILE RATIO (Q_1/Q_3 IN %)	
	Central Bureau of Labor Stat. Study, Monthly Wages, March 1928	TSUNKHU Study, Monthly Wages, October 1934
1. Rubber products	68.9	67.7
2. Tobacco	66.5	64.0
3. Cotton goods	64.2	61.6
4. Matches	63.6	62.5
5. Linen goods	63.4	62.6
6. Liquor	62.8	64.6
7. Confectionery	61.9	60.9
8. China, porcelainware	57.9	55.9
9. Saw mills, plywood	57.3	51.1
10. Electric power	55.6	49.4
11. Basic chemical products	55.1	52.2
12. Woolen and worsted goods	54.9	57.4
13. Paper	54.2	53.5
14. Leather	53.8	55.1
15. Non-ferrous metallurgy	53.8	54.6
16. Metal products, machinery and equipment	53.6	50.5
17. Ferrous metallurgy	53.5	50.9
18. Shoe	52.1	52.6
19. Printing	50.9	51.3
20. Coal	50.1	46.1
21. Oil extraction, refining	62.5	54.0
22. Milling	55.0	44.2
23. Furniture	53.4	43.5
24. Clothing	56.1	63.2
25. Baking	54.1	59.9
26. Glass	41.9	47.5

The sources, and certain other information, are inserted in the notes to this table in Appendix C. On the industries compared the following should be remarked:

Tobacco: It is uncertain whether makhorka is included in 1934. In the table this product is included in 1928, but without it the quartile ratio is 73.0 per cent.

China, porcelainware: It is uncertain whether sanitary porcelainware and insulators and other electric and technical ware are included. The former composed but a small part of the total output in both 1928 and 1934 (2.3 and 6.1 per cent respectively), but the latter was 16.0 per cent of the total output in 1928 and 36.0 per cent in 1934.

Basic chemical products: Of the basic chemical products, the products of chlorine and soda are included in 1934 only.

Leather: The caption for the industry in the 1934 study is "leather-fur," but from other evidence it does not appear that fur workers received important representation. The industry also includes in 1934 a number of leather products (pocketbook, gloves, and others) which, it does not appear, were included in 1928.

Metal products, machinery and equipment: The line between this industry and the metallurgy industries is not clear cut. The metal products included appear to be primarily ferrous metal products, the working up of non-ferrous metals being included primarily in the non-ferrous metallurgy industry. This is more clear for 1934, though, than for 1928.

The three industries which are designated by a circle in Chart 3 are glass, clothing, and baking. These three industries are among six for which the change in the quartile ratios from 1928 to 1934 differs by 5 per cent or more from the average change. But they are distinguished from the other three by the fact that the movement is the reverse of the general trend. The quartile ratio for the glass industry increases 5.6 per cent; that for baking, 5.8 per cent; and that for clothing, 7.1 per cent. In the case of the first of these industries the reason for the contrary movement in wage variation is not far to seek. The period of the first five-year plans witnessed the introduction of machinery which displaced the important and highly skilled hand crafts in the industry. This explanation, it seems likely, is appropriate also for the change in wage variation in the baking industry. If American experience can serve, the mechanization of bread factories, which took place in the U.S.S.R. during the period of the five-year plans, must have taken a toll of the skilled bench hands, or hand bakers. The Soviet clothing industry, like glass and baking, was primarily a hand industry in the 'twenties. Though hand processes continued to be important in ensuing years, in the words of a Soviet economist, it was "transformed into a large scale mechanized industry with a number of factories which are the largest in the world." [4] Whether here also the impact of mechanization was on the highly skilled trades is uncertain, but in the light of the developments in the other industries, it is not implausible.

4

Wage Principles. It will be interesting to inquire in a later chapter why the trend towards the equalization of earnings in the Soviet Union was reversed after 1928. But, whatever the explanation, it would certainly be difficult to discern in the new course a peculiarly "socialist" wage policy. If the equalization achieved prior to 1928 was a deviation from capitalist principles

[4] *Report of the State Planning Commission, Summary of the Fulfillment of the First Five Year Plan* (Moscow, 1933), p. 142.

of remuneration, the socialist administrators surely lost no time in expiating their waywardness.

More positive evidence of the persistence of capitalist wage principles is the rough stability in the relative position of the quartile ratios. The idiosyncratic movements exhibited in the glass and baking industries must be regarded here as exceptions that prove the rule.

CHART 3

SCATTER DIAGRAM OF QUARTILE RATIOS, WAGE FREQUENCY DISTRI-
BUTIONS OF SOVIET INDUSTRIAL WORKERS: 1928 AND 1934 *

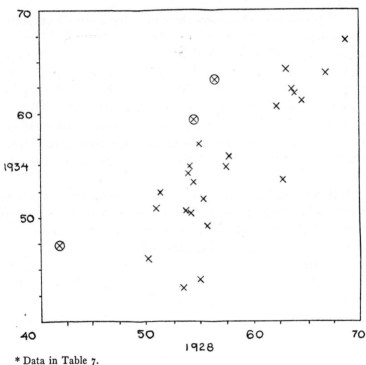

* Data in Table 7.

CHAPTER VIII

NOTE ON WAGE VARIATION
IN THE UNITED STATES, VARIOUS YEARS

In Table 8 are presented the quartile ratios of wage frequency distributions for several industries in the United States at various periods of time. The computations are limited to industries in Table 6 [1] for which data were available for a later year than 1904.

Like previous comparisons, those in Table 8 suffer from statistical differences in the data used. The most important factor to be reckoned with is the difference in the period for which wages were calculated. The 1904 data, which were used in the comparison of American and Soviet wage variation, relate to the earnings of workers for one week in the year studied. All other data, except one of the 1911 ferrous metallurgy distributions, relate to hourly earnings. This difference should have reduced the 1904 quartile ratios relatively to the ratios for the later years.

If the comparison is restricted to the quartile ratios calculated from the hourly earnings distributions a remarkable stability in wage variation is exhibited. The comparison can be made readily for three of the four industries in Table 8. *For these industries, cotton, ferrous metallurgy, and wool and worsted, the quartile ratio changes less than 1 per cent from 1910 (or 1911) to 1930.* The 1904 quartile ratios for the last two industries are some 5 per cent less than the corresponding 1910 (or 1911) ratio.[2] In the cotton goods industry as a whole there is an 8 per cent difference. But in the Northern States alone the difference is but 3 per cent. It is plausible that the relatively low

---

[1] Cf. p. 91.

[2] For ferrous metallurgy the difference between the 1904 quartile ratio and the 1911 ratio computed for the full time weekly earnings distribution is 5 per cent. For the 1911 hourly earnings distribution the difference is 6 per cent.

TABLE 8

QUARTILE RATIOS OF WAGE FREQUENCY DISTRIBUTION OF WAGE EARNERS
IN SPECIFIED INDUSTRIES: UNITED STATES, VARIOUS YEARS

Industry and Time of Study	Quartile Ratio $(Q_1/Q_3$ in %)	Type of Wage Data
1. *Cotton goods*		
1904	52.7	Earnings for one week
1911	60.6	Hourly earnings, one week
1930	60.2	Hourly earnings, one pay period
2. *Cotton goods*		
(Northern states)		
1904	62.6	Earnings for one week
1911	65.5	Hourly earnings, one week
3. *Ferrous metallurgy*		
1904	60.3	Earnings for one week
1910	65.3	Full-time weekly earnings, one month
1910	66.6	Hourly earnings, one month
1931	66.1	Hourly earnings, sixteen days
4. *Woolen and worsted*		
goods		
1904	55.7	Earnings for one week
1911	62.4	Hourly earnings, one pay period
1930	62.6	Hourly earnings, one pay period
5. *Shoes*		
1904	48.1	Earnings for one week
1930	52.7	Hourly earnings, one pay period

The sources used in this table are noted in Appendix C.

For the textile industries in 1911 it is uncertain whether the wage data for time workers are hourly earnings or hourly wage rates. For piece workers the data are hourly earnings. For the ferrous metallurgy industry in 1910 full-time weekly earnings for each worker are calculated as the hourly wage rate times the number of hours in a customary full-time working week for that worker.

In all cases the hourly earnings were calculated for a selected payroll period in the years indicated.

From the wage data for the cotton goods and woolen and worsted goods industries in 1911, I have excluded a small group of overseers. If these workers are included the quartile ratios are reduced by less than 1 per cent.

Ferrous metallurgy comprises blast furnaces, and steel works and rolling mills. The 1910 data do not include fabricating and assembling departments even when these are operated in conjunction with steel works. Steel foundries are also excluded in the table, but if included, the quartile ratio of the hourly earnings distribution is 65.8. The *textile industries* in every case do not include independent dyeing and finishing mills. The 1911 cotton goods also excludes all finishing, and the 1930 cotton goods excludes the dyeing as well as the finishing departments of cotton mills. The 1930 woolen and worsted goods data relate only to mills the principal products of which were dress goods, or coat and suit cloth. The data for the *shoe industry* in 1930 relates only to factories the principal products of which were welt, McKay, or turned shoes.

In obtaining a quartile ratio for the frequency distribution of cotton-goods wage earners in both the northern and southern states together in 1911, the frequency distribution for wage earners in the southern states was given a weight twice that of the frequency distribution of wage earners in the northern states. This weighting is in rough accord with the relative number of cotton-goods wage earners in these two regions in the Census of 1909.

ratios for 1904 are accounted for primarily by the statistical differences referred to in the preceding paragraph, rather than by economic changes.[3]

These striking results beg explanation. But whether they are sports or not the writer is at loss to say. The American metallurgy and textile industries were both "mature" even before the turn of the century, and it is questionable whether there were any changes in technique thereafter which would have substantially altered the composition of the working force. Even in the shoe industry, according to Harry Jerome, "machinery went through its initial stages of development in the 'eighties and 'nineties, and changes since then have been for the most part refinements of the basic devices."[4] Certainly it is unlikely that wage variation in an industry such as glass was also stable in the period in question. But whether technical changes in the industries investigated in Table 8 were all merely "improvements" or "refinements," the stability of the quartile ratios deflates the significance of changing techniques as a factor affecting wage variation. At the same time the stability of wage variation in at least the metallurgy, textile, and shoe industries of the Soviet Union over the period 1928–34 is the more understandable.

Statistical factors additional to that already cited obstruct a direct comparison between wage variation in the U.S.S.R. in 1934 and in the United States in 1905.[5] But if an indirect route is taken via the previous comparison for 1928 and 1904, the results indicate clearly that the inequality in wages in the U.S.S.R. is closely proximate to that now prevailing in the United States.

[3] The smaller change in the quartile ratio from 1904 to 1911 for the cotton goods industry, when the northern states alone are considered, also indicates that the large change for the entire United States was accounted for by regional variations in working time.

[4] *Mechanization in Industry* (New York, 1934), p. 115.

[5] Geographical factors obstruct the comparison in the cotton goods and metallurgy industries. In the woolen and worsted goods industry, it is not possible to exclude from the Soviet 1934 data a large but relatively low-paid division of the industry producing coarse woolen goods. This division was not studied at all in the United States in 1930.

CHAPTER IX

SALARIES IN THE U.S.S.R., 1928 AND 1934

THE OBJECTS of communal malevolence do not fit easily in the confines of a precise statistical category, but it is probably correct to say that large groups of the "salaried workers" of the present study, with varying intensity and for a period extending at least through 1930, were regarded with distrust in the Soviet Union. It was to be expected that the more secure and prosperous workers should greet the October Revolution with less than proletarian enthusiasm. But the Russian employee class was by no means passive in its displeasure. In the latter part of 1917 and in 1918, strikes among the employees of government institutions were widespread. Their purpose, it seems clear, was to hasten the expected downfall of the revolutionary government.[1] Strikes of white-collar workers, and supervisory and technical personnel in industrial and commercial establishments, and open conflicts of employees with the wage earners in these establishments also occurred.[2]

Counter-revolutionary activity on the part of important sections of the Russian employee class at a critical period was not soon to be forgotten by the Soviet revolutionaries. As late as 1930 E. T. Grinko, the vice-chairman of the State Planning Commission, could still refer to the "active opposition and sabotage of the old technicians" as "pages from the history of the October Revolution . . . fresh in everybody's memory."[3]

But the recollection had doubtless been sharpened in the

---

[1] A detailed account of the strikes is presented in D. Antoskin, *Professional'noe Dvizhenie Sluzhashchikh, 1917–1924 gg.* (Moscow, 1927), pp. 99 ff. This is a Soviet source. Mr. N. A. Rodionoff, a participant in the strikes and now of Washington, D. C., has affirmed to me their political character.

[2] *Ibid.*

[3] G. T. Grinko, *The Five Year Plan of the Soviet Union* (New York, 1930), p. 235.

interim by the much-publicized case of the Shakhty engineers. Whatever the merits of the government's charges of sabotage and conspiracy with foreign agents [4] which were levied against this group of engineers and technical workers of the Shakhty mine fields, the trial at least temporarily increased the distrust with which the Soviet specialist was regarded, and in consequence, his insecurity. The proceedings, it is reported by a Soviet source, created a "panic emotion" among the specialists. Their fears subsided somewhat, the report continues, when the government declared that not all technical personnel but only a "criminal clique" were implicated.[5]

Apparently no such discernment was displayed by the Soviet authorities when another group of engineers was brought to trial in December 1930. The charges were sabotage, conspiracy with foreign agents to overthrow the government, and the organization of a secret political party. According to an American observer,

this much discussed prosecution of Prof. Ramzin and his colleagues inaugurated a veritable reign of terror against the intelligentsia. Nobody regarded himself beyond suspicion. . . . Thousands were sent on administrative exile to distant parts of the country. Evidence was not necessary. The title of engineer served as sufficient condemnation. The jails were filled . . . and chiefs of the Supreme Economic Council commenced to complain that by its wholesale arrests of engineers the G.P.U. or O.G.P.U. . . . was interfering with industrial progress. . . . The year 1930 was the blackest year in the history of the intelligentsia.[6]

The trial of British and Russian engineers in January 1933, the Metro-Vickers case, doubtless increased again the insecurity of Soviet technical personnel, but no such drastic events ensued as followed the Ramzin trial.

[4] A brief account of the case is given in *Bol'shaia Sovetskaia Entsiklopediia*, vol. LXII (Moscow, 1933), pp. 14 ff.

[5] *Profsoiuzy S.S.S.R. 1926–1928, Otchet VTSSPS k VIII S'ezdu Professional' nykh Soiuzov* (Moscow, 1928), p. 519.

[6] Louis Fischer, *Machines and Men in Russia* (New York, 1932), pp. 222–223. Quoted with the permission of the author.

2

Disabilities of the Salaried Worker. Suspicion, and the accompanying threat of imprisonment and exile, are not ordinarily comprised in the economist's concept of real income. But they surely have been important negative elements in the welfare of the Soviet employee, and must have qualified the significance for him of any pecuniary advantage derived from his position. It is not surprising, too, that being suspect and insecure should not exhaust the woes of Soviet salaried personnel, and that they should be subject also to more material disabilities. These disabilities are not readily assayed in pecuniary terms, but they must not be passed by in a study of the inequality of Soviet earnings.

Though Lenin spoke often of the necessity of weaning the pre-revolutionary specialists to the proletarian cause,[7] it was inevitable, after the outbreak of opposition to the revolutionary government among these workers, that efforts should be made by the Soviet authorities to train cadres from the proletarian sector of the population. Discrimination to this end among the candidates for admission to the institutions of higher education became an accepted principle of Soviet education. In the frank words of E. T. Grinko, dated as of 1930,

> The free admission of bourgeois elements is limited deliberately and on principle. With equal deliberateness and firmness, every preference in the admission of students is given to representatives of the proletariat and the peasantry. It is not merely the law, it is the binding principle of the dictatorship of the proletariat.[8]

For Mr. Grinko, the evidence of sabotage produced at the Shakhty trial only affirmed the wisdom of this course.[9]

As the policy of class selection was applied in practice, the children of persons living on unearned income and of other individuals who were denied election rights were excluded entirely

[7] Cf. Grinko, *op. cit.*, pp. 235 ff.
[8] *Ibid.*, p. 259. Quoted with the permission of International Publishers.
[9] *Ibid.*, p. 239.

from the universities and technicums. The children of salaried workers were not as a group in this unenviable position, but in comparison with the proletarian elements they suffered a disability which was expressed in various ways. The statement of party policy in 1926 required that a major share of the new places in the universities be reserved for the graduates of the adult schools for workers and peasants who had been engaged in physical labor.[10] Seventy-five per cent of those admitted into the technicums, or secondary vocational schools, were to be members of the proletarian (*rabochii*) [11] and peasant classes.[12] The party's concern with the social composition of the student body was not relaxed in the ensuing years. In the period 1927–29 the party called regularly for increases in the proletarian and peasant sectors of the student body at the institutions of higher education. The matriculation requirements in the universities, higher technical institutes, and technicums were to be eased for wage earners, peasants and their children, and other measures were to be instituted to aid and encourage matriculation from these classes.[13] While the institution of exams for all candidates for admission to the universities in 1926 apparently had an "adverse" effect on the social composition of the

[10] According to N. Hans and S. Hessen (*Educational Policy in Soviet Russia*, London, 1930, pp. 154–156) 35 per cent of the admissions in the universities in 1926 (this probably means the school year 1925–26) were reserved specifically for graduates of Workers' Faculties. At the same time 10 per cent were reserved for the children of the working intelligentsia. The party's directive of June 1926 directed that the allocation for these categories be maintained. Cf. Tsirkuliar TSK VKP(b), June 14, 1926, in A. IA. Podzemskii, compiler, I. D. Davydov i I. G. Klabunovskii, editors, *Direktivy VKP(b) po Voprosam Prosveshcheniia*, third edition (Moscow, 1931), p. 157.

[11] "Proletariat" is a decidedly free translation of the Russian word *rabochii*, but it probably conveys the intended Russian meaning more correctly than does the literal translation "laboring man." An acceptable equivalent, too, is "wage earner," and this translation is used here and elsewhere in the present investigation, except when exact statistical categories are considered. In the latter context "wage earner" is usually used as a somewhat more comprehensive category than *rabochii*.

[12] Podzemskii, *op. cit.*, p. 157.

[13] Cf. the circular and resolutions of the central committee of the party, Podzemskii, *op. cit.*, pp. 158–162.

student body, the party noted successes in this sphere in 1928.[14] Furthermore, the goal established for the technicums in 1926 was declared realized in 1927,[15] and in the latter part of 1929 the party noted that the proletarian sector in the higher technical institutes had increased. A further increase to 70 per cent was called for.[16]

There is scattered evidence also, and it is not surprising, that the discrimination as to admissions to the institutions of higher education in this period was supplemented by discrimination in the awarding of stipends, and, in the elementary schools, in the charging of fees.[17]

Whether it was because of a distrust of the specialist and other members of the employee class, or simply because of their inferior position on the Soviet scale of social values, or for other causes, the disabilities suffered by the Soviet salaried worker and his children were not confined to the discrimination against them in the sphere of education. In those industries where the Soviet old-age pension system was first established in 1929 and 1930, the right to pensions was granted only to wage earners, to workers who had been promoted from this rank not more than five years prior to their application for a pension, and to a limited number of salaried workers who were engaged directly in production.[18] Under the rationing system, as it had crystallized by 1931, wage earners were in a preferred ration category, together with those engineers and technical workers who were

[14] Tsirkuliar TSK VKP(b), April 13, 1927; and Postanovlenie TSK VKP(b), February 22, 1928, Pódzemskii, *op. cit.*, pp. 158–161.

[15] Tsirkuliar TSK VKP(b), April 13, 1927, Podzemskii, *op. cit.*, p. 158.

[16] Postanovlenie TSK VKP(b), November 16, 1929 in S. Livshits, *Kadry Spetsialistov* (Moscow, 1931), p. 17.

[17] Hans and Hessen, *op. cit.*, pp. 33, 95, 156, 157; Postanovlenie TSK VKP(b), July 26, 1929, Podzemskii, *op. cit.*, p. 161.

[18] Postanovlenie TSIK i SNK SSSR, May 15, 1929, *Izvestiia NKT SSSR*, 1929, no. 25–26, p. 403; Pravila Utverzhdennye SSSS pri NKT SSSR, May 23, 1929, *Izvestiia NKT SSSR*, 1929 no. 25–26, pp. 405 ff.; Postanovlenie SSSS pri NKT SSSR, October 31, 1929, *Izvestiia NKT SSSR*, 1929, no. 48–49, pp. 778–779; also R. Kats i N. Sorokin, *Sotsial'noe Strakhovanie*, second edition (Moscow, 1936), pp. 153–154.

engaged directly in production, and, during their first year of work at the new task, wage earners who had been promoted. Other salaried workers were in a lower category.[19] From the laws passed later to improve the general position of salaried workers, it is clear, the discrimination against the employee class at this time extended also to other spheres.[20]

It is not surprising that under the pressure of the five-year plan an exception should have been made under the rationing system for engineers and technical workers engaged directly in production. The equating of the rations of these workers to those of wage earners was decreed in May 1930, and the explicitly stated purpose was to attract more such workers into industry. At the same time it was ordered that these specialists should be given rights equal to those of wage earners under the social insurance system, and with respect to the supply of housing.[21]

The decree of 1930 must have been of substantial value to the special class it favored. But the rights it conferred and others as well were extended to a much broader group of workers in the following year.

On June 23, 1931, Stalin delivered before a meeting of factory managers an address which was to have vast import for the Soviet worker. Among the subjects discussed was the position of the specialist in the Soviet Union. The speech followed shortly upon the excesses accompanying the Ramzin trial.

Stalin observed first that the hostile elements among the old technical intelligentsia had now been quelled, and that, with the Soviet successes on the agricultural front and the failure of the ever hoped-for intervention to materialize, the attitude of the old technicians towards the Soviet power had changed decidedly for the better.[22] Accordingly, Stalin called in a few

[19] Postanovlenie Kollegii Narkomsnaba SSSR, January 13, 1931, *Zakonodatel' stvo i Rasporiazheniia po Torgovle SSSR*, 1935, no. 5, pp. 22 ff.

[20] See below.

[21] Postanovlenie TSIK i SNK SSSR, May 13, 1930, *B.F.Kh.Z.*, 1930, no. 16, pp. 42–43.

[22] I. Stalin, *Voprosy Leninizma*, tenth edition (Moscow, 1934), p. 460.

words for a sharp change in policy towards these persons. Instead of being "smashed," the engineers and technicians of the
old school were to be shown "attention and care," in order to
"attract them to work." A great expansion in the technical
cadres arising from the proletariat also was called for. Non-
membership in the party was to be no bar to promotion.[23]

Stalin's speech has been called by one writer the "Magna
Charta" of the Soviet intellectual. The designation is probably
extravagant, but on August 1 the Central Executive Committee
and the Council of Commissars [24] promulgated jointly a decree
which altered radically the material position of Soviet engineers
and technical workers.[25] It was directed that the children of
engineers and technical workers (all such workers, and not
merely those engaged directly in production) be admitted to
educational institutions on the same basis as the children of
industrial wage earners, and that, where there were norms of
admission, the children of engineers and technical workers
be included in the norms of admission established for the children of wage earners. Insurance benefits for those temporarily
incapacitated for work were to be paid to engineers and technical workers on the same basis as to industrial wage earners.
The privileges in the supply of consumers' goods of engineers
and technical workers and their families were equated to those
of industrial wage earners. Places in rest homes and sanatoria,
and housing space in general, were to be received on a basis of
equality with industrial wage earners, and the engineers and
technical workers were given certain rights to extra housing
space. Finally, the income tax for technical personnel having a
monthly income of more than 500 rubles was fixed at a constant

[23] *Ibid.*, pp. 457–461.
[24] Under the pre-1936 constitution the members of the Council of Commissars
were appointed by a bicameral assembly, the Central Executive Committee
(TSIK). The latter in turn was elected by the All-Union Congress of Soviets,
and, in between meetings of the congress, was entrusted with the powers of the
latter.
[25] Postanovlenie TSIK i SNK SSSR, August 1, 1931, *S.Z.R. SSSR*, 1931,
Part I, no. 48, section 322, pp. 585–586.

rate, 3.5 per cent, in place of the previously applied scale of progressive rates.

One year later, in August 1932, the Soviet authorities were able to claim that these measures had been largely accomplished, and that already in consequence many sections of engineers and technical workers showed a "model socialist attitude towards their work." [26] Shortcomings in the execution of the new policy in the supply of consumers' goods and housing space were noted, however, and measures were directed to remedy them. The organization of dining rooms for the exclusive service of engineers and technical workers was called for. Closed retail shops, apparently, already had been organized for these workers. The supply of goods to the engineers and technical workers in the dining rooms and in the shops, it was reiterated, was to be equal to that of wage earners. There is reason to believe that in the ensuing period this directive was more than realized.[27]

The new privileges of engineers and technical workers were extended in 1932 to specialists and technicians in the field of distribution and to chief and senior bookkeepers and their assistants in enterprises and institutions in the socialized sector.[28] The terms engineer and technician, it should be noted also, are interpreted broadly in Soviet *statistical* usage to include even the director of a factory, supervisors of production departments, and foremen. Though it is uncertain, the *legal* usage may well have been as comprehensive.

For the rest, however, there is evidence that the Soviet authorities soon relaxed their vigil over the social composition of the student body.[29] The rationing system was liquidated in

---

[26] Tsirkuliar NKT SSSR, NKSnaba SSSR, Tsentrosoiuza, Vsekoopita i VMBIT VTSSPS, August 1, 1932, *B.F.Kh.Z.*, 1932, no. 53–54, pp. 67 ff.

[27] W. Nodel (*Supply and Trade in the U.S.S.R.*, London, 1934, pp. 65, 89–90) states that the specialist received *preferred* treatment under the rationing system.

[28] Postanovlenie TSIK i SNK SSSR, January 17, 1932, *S.Z.R. SSSR*, 1932, part I, no. 4, section 21, p. 26, and Postanovlenie SNK SSSR, September 29, 1932, *S.Z.R. SSSR*, 1932, part I, no. 72, section 440, pp. 719 ff.

[29] In a decree of 1932 fixing the stipends of students in universities and tech-

1935 and 1936, and at least by 1934 the progressive income taxes on incomes above 500 rubles a month had been replaced by a straight 3.5 per cent tax for all salaried workers.[30] In August 1936 the practice of distributing passes to sanatoria and rest homes to workers in accord with their class status was abandoned.[31] But as late as 1936, the inferior treatment of salaried workers other than engineers and technical workers still was a characteristic of the social insurance system.[32]

3

Wage Differentials and Wage Variation. Against a background of shifting non-pecuniary rights and privileges, the significance of differences in the earnings of salaried workers and wage earners in the U.S.S.R. necessarily is reduced. But interest in the pecuniary differentials is hardly extinguished. Their investigation is a worthy part of our agenda.

Unfortunately the Russian factory inspection wage data — both the data compiled annually and that collected for June 1914 and June 1916 — relate only to the earnings of wage earn-

---

nicums scholarship is declared the only criterion which is to determine the recipient of the stipend and its extent (Postanovlenie TSIK i SNK SSSR, July 7, 1932, *Biulleten' NKProsa RSFSR*, 1932, no. 41, section 525, pp. 2–3).

With respect to admissions, a long list of preferred categories still was incorporated in the rules on admission promulgated for the school year 1932/33 for the universities under the Commissariat of Education of the R.S.F.S.R. Graduates of the adult workers' schools were to be given precedence over all other candidates, and preference was to be shown wage earners and their children, and the children of specialists, among others (Pravila Priema . . . na 1932/1933 Uchebnyi God, *Biulleten' NKProsa RSFSR*, 1932, no. 32, section 407, pp. 11 ff.). But in 1935 a step was taken to liberalize admissions. The long-standing rule against admitting to the universities and technicums students dependent on persons living on unearned income and on other individuals deprived of election rights was abolished (Postanovlenie TSIK i SNK SSSR, December 29, 1935, *S.Z.R. SSSR*, 1936, part I, no. 1, section 2, p. 2).

[30] See Table 1, p. 33.

[31] Postanovlenie Presiduuma VTSSPS, June 28, 1936, *Biulleten' VTSSPS*, 1936, no. 11, quoted in IA. Kiselev, *Spravochnik po Trudovomu Zakonodatel' stvu*, second edition (Moscow, 1939), p. 82.

[32] Cf. R. Kats i N. Sorokin, *Sotsialisticheskoe Strakhovanie*, second edition (Moscow, 1936), particularly pp. 110 ff.

ers. But the Soviet studies of March 1928 and October 1934 embrace salaried workers as well as wage earners. Accordingly, it is possible to extend the present investigation to the inequality of earnings among wage earners and salaried workers together at these dates.

It is well to recall here that the term "salaried worker" is used in a broad sense in this investigation. Not only are clerical workers, economic, accounting, and technical personnel of all sorts included, but also all supervisory personnel from the director of the factory down to and including foremen. In a word, all workers in industrial establishments other than "wage earners" are comprised in the category "salaried workers." [33]

In Table 9 are shown the ratios of the average earnings of salaried workers to the average earnings of wage earners for each of twenty-six industries in March 1928 and in October 1934. The ratio varies widely in both periods. The lowest ratio in March 1928 is that for the baking industry, 113.4 per cent, and the highest, that for linen goods, 206.5 per cent. The extremes in October 1934 were 149.6 and 235.4 per cent, for the milling and coal industries. A marked increase in differentials is general, however. For all but four of the industries the ratio is larger in October 1934 than in March 1928. For all twenty-six industries together the differential was 172.0 per cent in March 1928 and 192.0 per cent in October 1934.

The quartile ratios of the earnings frequency distributions of wage earners and salaried workers together also have been computed for each of the twenty-six industries. The results are shown in Table 10. As was the case for the earnings distributions of wage earners alone, there is a clear overall increase in the inequality of earnings. In only four industries of the twenty-six is the ratio of the first to the third quartile of the earnings distribution greater in March 1928 than in October 1934. As might be expected, the increase in inequality is more marked for the all-worker earnings distributions than for the wage-

---

[33] See Appendix B for a list of the Soviet statistical categories corresponding to the categories "wage earner" and "salaried worker" used here.

TABLE 9

RATIO OF AVERAGE EARNINGS OF SALARIED WORKERS AND WAGE EARNERS
IN SPECIFIED INDUSTRIES IN THE SOVIET UNION, 1928 AND 1934

Industry	AVERAGE EARNING OF SALARIED WORKERS IN PER CENT OF AVERAGE EARNING OF WAGE EARNERS	
	Central Bureau of Labor Stat. Study, Monthly Earnings, March 1928	TSUNKHU Study, Monthly Earnings, October, 1934
1. Baking	113.4	167.3
2. Clothing	128.2	179.8
3. Electric power	131.2	211.5
4. Shoe	131.4	178.4
5. Leather	138.9	183.2
6. Furniture	139.0	197.4
7. Metal products; machinery and equipment	144.7	176.0
8. Non-ferrous metallurgy	150.2	206.6
9. Rubber products	151.1	199.9
10. Tobacco	157.6	184.4
11. Printing	158.1	184.8
12. Ferrous metallurgy	168.1	218.5
13. China, porcelainware	168.2	178.3
14. Liquor	168.9	203.7
15. Basic chemical products	169.6	211.0
16. Confectionery	170.0	186.1
17. Milling	170.3	149.6
18. Saw mills, plywood	171.2	160.6
19. Glass	171.3	189.6
20. Woolen and worsted goods	172.3	206.7
21. Cotton goods	176.7	189.7
22. Match	180.5	191.7
23. Paper	184.9	212.9
24. Oil extraction; refining	193.4	183.8
25. Coal	196.1	235.4
26. Linen goods	206.5	202.1
All industries	172.0	192.0

See the notes to Table 7, p. 101.

TABLE 10

QUARTILE RATIOS OF EARNINGS FREQUENCY DISTRIBUTIONS OF WORKERS
IN SPECIFIED INDUSTRIES IN THE SOVIET UNION, 1928 AND 1934

| Industry | Quartile Ratios (Q_1/Q_3 in %) | |
	Central Bureau of Labor Stat. Study, Monthly Earnings, March 1928	TSUNKHU Study, Monthly Earnings, October, 1934
1. Rubber products	67.5	64.1
2. Tobacco	66.6	59.9
3. Cotton goods	63.5	60.7
4. Linen goods	62.1	60.9
5. Match	61.9	59.4
6. Liquor	61.4	54.3
7. Confectionery	60.9	54.9
8. China, porcelainware	57.0	53.0
9. Oil extraction; refining	56.8	49.4
10. Saw mills, plywood	56.3	49.6
11. Baking	55.0	56.6
12. Woolen and worsted goods	54.0	55.7
13. Leather	53.9	52.2
14. Basic chemical products	53.8	49.2
15. Non-ferrous metallurgy	53.6	51.1
16. Ferrous metallurgy	53.1	49.0
17. Paper	53.1	50.5
18. Milling	53.0	45.5
19. Metal products, machinery and equipment	53.0	48.0
20. Shoe	52.4	49.9
21. Printing	49.9	48.0
22. Coal	49.1	43.5
23. Electric power	54.9	46.3
24. Furniture	53.9	42.6
25. Clothing	55.6	60.5
26. Glass	40.9	45.7

See the notes to Table 7, p. 101.

earner earnings distribution alone. The average decrease in the quartile ratios is 3.5 per cent for the former distributions, and 1.6 per cent for the latter.

4

Wage Principles. The increase in the earnings differentials of salaried workers after 1928, like the increase in wage variation among wage earners, hardly describes a distinctly socialist turn in Soviet wage policy. The explanation of the upward movement in the inequality of earnings in this period, clearly, must be sought elsewhere.

Though the lack of a comparison with pre-revolutionary differentials is to be regretted, the extent of the average earnings differential of salaried workers that has persisted in the Soviet Union is in itself noteworthy. In view of the removal of the barriers to the attainment of higher education by the masses and the positive encouragement of proletarian efforts in this direction in the U.S.S.R., the weight traditionally assigned these barriers in the explanation of *capitalist* wage differentials requires reëxamination. Reference is to the explanation of the differences in the earnings of salaried workers and ordinary workers by the theory of non-competing groups.

CHAPTER X

THE DISTRIBUTION OF THE WAGE BILL AMONG INDUSTRIAL WORKERS: RUSSIA 1914; U.S.S.R. 1928 AND 1934

Earnings Distributions. The quartile ratios which have been computed in this study to illumine Soviet wage principles serve at the same time as useful summary measures of the inequality of earnings. The ratios have been computed, however, only for individual industries. It is also of great interest to determine the extent and changes in the inequality of earnings for Russian industrial workers as a group. For this purpose it is no longer desirable to limit ourselves to a summary measure.

The form of presentation used in Chart 4 is particularly appropriate for the detailed study of the distribution of the earnings bill. A point plotted there measures horizontally the cumulative per cent of workers whose earnings are studied, and vertically, the per cent of the total wage bill received by these workers. The cumulation, horizontally, is from lower-paid to higher-paid workers. An equal distribution of the wage bill would be represented by a diagonal of the chart (lower left to upper right). The further the curve representing a given wage distribution departs from the diagonal, the greater is the inequality in earnings.[1]

The curves in Chart 4 relate to wage earners in all the industries which were studied in the comparison of Soviet 1928 and Russian 1914 wage variation in Chapter V. These industries in 1914 employed 1.388 million wage earners in plants subject to factory inspection, or 71 per cent of the wage earners in all industry subject to factory inspection.[2] In 1928 the same

---

[1] A curve plotted on the chart is known as a Lorenz curve.

[2] The coverage of the 1914, and 1928, wage investigations, in relation to the

industries employed 1.695 million wage earners, or 73 per cent of the total number in large-scale (non-extractive) industry. Accordingly, the curves relate to a major sector of the Russian working force.

CHART 4

DISTRIBUTION OF THE DAILY WAGE BILL AMONG INDUSTRIAL
WAGE EARNERS: RUSSIA, JUNE 1914; U.S.S.R., MARCH 1928 *

% of Wage and Salary Bill

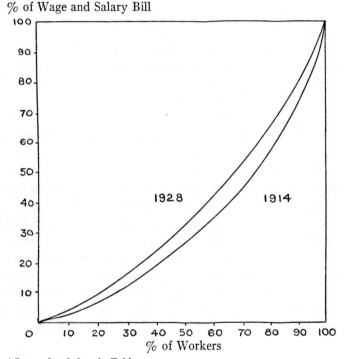

% of Workers

* Interpolated data in Table 11.

The wage data used to construct Chart 4 are the same as the data used in the earlier wage comparison. The curves in the chart show the distribution of the *daily* wage bill among the workers studied, one for June 1914 and the other for March

total number of wage earners in the industries studied, is indicated in Appendix D, Table 1.

1928. Thus, in contrast with income distributions which are often presented, the curves are affected little by variation in working time in each period.[3] In Chart 4 both curves depart from linearity, but the Russian curve is distinctly to the right of the Soviet one. Data corresponding to points on the two curves are presented in Table 11. There it is indicated, to take one pair of items, that the upper 20 per cent of the wage earners received 44.0 per cent of the wage bill in 1914, and 36.1 per cent of the wage bill in 1928. A decided inequality of distribution, thus, still prevailed among Soviet wage earners in 1928, but the inequality was less than that in Russia in 1914. As was true of the comparison of wage variation, some part of the change in inequality (probably a minor part) is due to the statistical factors mentioned in Chapter V.[4]

In Chart 5 the comparison of the distribution of the wage bill is extended to the years 1928 and 1934. In this comparison the sector of industry studied is larger than in the 1914–28 one. All the industries included in the study of Soviet wage variation in 1928 and in 1934, in Chapter VII, are included here. In 1928 these industries employed 2.265 million wage earners, or 85 per cent of the wage earners in large-scale industry (including extractive industry).[5] The corresponding figures in 1934 are 4.208 million wage earners, and 70 per cent.

The wage data in Chart 5, like the data used in the comparison of wage variation in Chapter VII, are data on monthly earnings. The curves exhibit the distribution of the wage bill for one month in each year. In 1928, March is studied, and in 1934, October. Both curves again depart clearly from linearity,

---

[3] The curves in Chart 4 may be regarded either as showing the average distribution of the daily wage bill in June 1914 and in March 1928, or alternatively as showing the distribution of the earnings bill for a whole month as it would have been if all wage earners were employed the same number of days during the month.

[4] Cf. pp. 61 ff.

[5] The coverage of the 1928 and 1934 wage investigations, in relation to the total number of wage earners in the industries studied, is indicated in Appendix D, Table 4.

TABLE 11

DISTRIBUTION OF THE WAGE BILL AND WAGE AND SALARY BILL AMONG INDUSTRIAL WORKERS: RUSSIA 1914; U.S.S.R. 1928 AND 1934

Cumulative Per Cent of Workers	CUMULATIVE PER CENT OF WAGE BILL					
	Daily Wage Bill		Wage Bill for Month, U.S.S.R.		Wage and Salary Bill for Month, U.S.S.R.	
	Russia June 1914	U.S.S.R. March 1928	March 1928	Oct. 1934	March 1928	Oct. 1934
10	3.0	3.9	3.6	3.4	3.5	3.0
20	7.4	9.1	9.0	8.7	8.8	7.8
30	12.6	15.5	15.2	15.0	15.0	13.7
40	18.3	23.0	22.9	22.3	22.0	20.6
50	25.8	31.7	31.4	30.5	30.5	28.4
60	34.0	41.2	40.8	39.9	39.9	37.3
70	43.8	52.0	51.7	50.5	50.6	47.5
80	56.0	63.9	64.4	62.7	63.0	59.7
90	72.6	79.1	79.0	77.7	78.2	75.7
100	100.0	100.0	100.0	100.0	100.0	100.0

The wage data used are the same as the data used in Tables 3 and 7. The source of the 1928 salary data is the same as that of the 1928 wage data. The source of the 1934 salary data is TSUNKHU, *Zarabotnaya Plata Inzhenerno-Technicheskikh Rabotnikov, Sluzhashchikh i Uchenikov v Sentiabre-Oktiabre 1934 g.* (Moscow 1936).

The sector of industry to which the *daily* wage bill data relate is comprised of the industries listed in Table 4. The *monthly* wage and salary data relate to the industries listed in Table 7.

In computing the data in Table 11 it was necessary first to combine the earnings *frequency* distributions for individual industries into a single earnings frequency distribution for each period studied. The weights used in combining the individual frequency distributions are in Appendix D, Tables 5 and 6. The aggregate frequency distributions are in Appendix D, Tables 7–10. The distribution of the earnings bill in each period studied was computed from the aggregate earnings frequency distributions, the results were then plotted in enlarged replicas of Charts 4, 5, and 6, and the data in Table 11 were obtained by interpolating from the curves plotted in these charts.

The computation of earnings distributions from the combined frequency distributions, and certain errors originating in this computation, are discussed in Appendix C. The slight discrepancies between the 1928 earnings distributions in Table 11 and those which appeared in an earlier publication ("Distribution of the Earnings Bill among Industrial Workers in the Soviet Union," *Journal of Political Economy*, April 1942) are due to a change in the interpolation procedure.

but the 1934 curve is somewhat to the right of that for 1928. The change in inequality is less than might have been expected from a study of the quartile ratios in Table 7, and suggests that the increase in inequality among the wage earners in individual industries was partly offset by relative movements in

CHART 5

Distribution of the Wage Bill among Industrial Wage Earners: U.S.S.R., March 1928 and October 1934 *

% of the Wage Bill

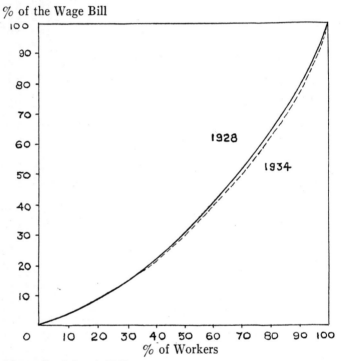

% of Workers

* Interpolated data in Table 11.

the average earnings in different industries. In any case, it appears, the direction of change in Soviet inequality was reversed in the period following 1928. Quoting again from Table 11, the upper 20 per cent of the wage earners received 35.6 per cent of the wage bill in March 1928, and 37.3 per cent of the wage bill in October 1934.

The 1928–34 comparison of the distribution of the wage bill is affected little by differences in the statistics used. But the data in Table 11 all were computed from frequency series, and on a number of counts errors of interpolation and extrapolation were unavoidable.[6] The errors to which limits can be assigned are uniformly small, but in the comparison of the wage bill distribution in March 1928 and in October 1934 the change in inequality that is exhibited might have been accounted for by statistical error. The changes in wage variation which are exhibited in Tables 7 and 12, however, are convincing evidence to the contrary.

From Table 11 it is apparent that the monthly and daily wage bill distributions for March 1928 are nearly the same.[7] Because of this an otherwise strenuous step is permissible. This is to compare the 1914 and 1934 distributions. In June 1914 the upper 20 per cent of the wage earners received 44.0 per cent of the daily wage bill, while in October 1934 they received 37.3 per cent of the wage bill for the month. *Thus in 1934 inequality of reward still was less than that which prevailed in 1914.*

In both the 1928 and 1934 investigations of wages, data on the earnings of salaried workers in industry were gathered as well. In view of the discussion that has arisen concerning the earnings of the latter workers in the U.S.S.R., it is of much interest to study the inequality of distribution among salaried workers and wage earners together.

In Chart 6 are curves showing the distribution of the wage and salary bill for March 1928 and October 1934. The industries represented are the same as those included in the distributions in Chart 5. Chart 6, like Chart 5, indicates that the inequality of distribution of the wage and salary bill increased from 1928 to 1934. But the change is distinctly greater than

---

[6] See the note to Table 11 in Appendix C.

[7] The reader should recall that the 1928 wage data (as well as the data for 1934) were collected only for workers who were on the payroll lists the entire month studied.

that for the distribution of the wage bill alone. The upper 20 per cent of the workers in 1928 received 37.0 per cent of the wage and salary bill, and in 1934, 40.3 per cent. Furthermore,

CHART 6

<small>DISTRIBUTION OF THE WAGE AND SALARY BILL AMONG INDUS-
TRIAL WORKERS: U.S.S.R., MARCH 1928 AND OCTOBER 1934 *</small>

% of Wage and Salary Bill

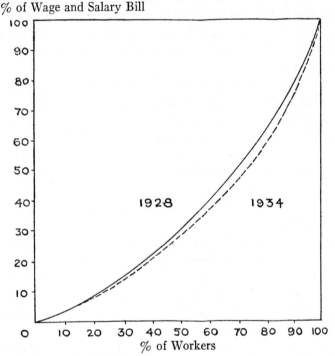

% of Workers

* Interpolated data in Table 11.

the inequality in distribution is greater for wage earners and salaried workers together than it is for wage earners alone. In 1934 the upper 20 per cent of the wage earners received 37.3 per cent of the wage bill (Table 11).

2

Wage Variation. It is interesting to compare, for the same sector of industry, the inferences as to inequality obtained from the quartile ratio with those obtained from the study of the overall distribution of the earnings bill.

In Table 12 are presented the values of the first and third quartiles and of their ratio for the same frequency distributions as those from which the earnings distributions in Table 11 were computed. The quartile ratio of the frequency distribution of wage earners according to daily wages in March 1928 is 9.7 per cent greater than that of the corresponding distribution in June 1914. The ratio for the frequency distribution of wage earners according to monthly earnings exhibits no significant change from March 1928 to October 1934, while that for the frequency distribution of wage earners and salaried workers together decreases 1.9 per cent in the same period.

The variation of the quartile ratio for the aggregate frequency distributions from 1928 to 1934, thus, is less than might have been expected from a study of the quartile ratios of the frequency distributions for individual industries. Again the contrast suggests that the change in the inequality of earnings among workers within the different industries was offset in some measure by changes in the inequality of earnings as between industries.

Except for the fact that the data in Table 11 exhibit a slight increase in the inequality of distribution among wage earners from March 1928 to October 1934, while the corresponding quartile ratios in Table 12 show no significant change, the change in the inequality exhibited by the quartile ratios is consistent with that exhibited by the overall data on the distribution of the earnings bill.

In Table 12 are shown also the values of the two extreme deciles of the earnings distributions, and their ratio. The percentage change in the decile ratio is strikingly similar to that in the quartile ratio. The decile ratio of the distribution of wage earners according to their earnings for the month, however, decreases slightly from March 1928 to October 1934.

Even if the highest and lowest-paid 10 per cent of industrial

TABLE 12

FIRST AND THIRD QUARTILES AND THEIR RATIO, AND FIRST AND NINTH DECILES AND THEIR RATIO FOR EARNINGS FREQUENCY DISTRIBUTIONS OF INDUSTRIAL WORKERS: RUSSIA, JUNE 1914; U.S.S.R., MARCH 1928, OCTOBER 1934

	Wage Earners Distributed According to Daily Wages		Wage Earners Distributed According to Wages for Month		Wage Earners and Salaried Workers Distributed According to Earnings for Month	
	Russia June 1914	U.S.S.R. March 1928	U.S.S.R. March 1928	U.S.S.R. October 1934	U.S.S.R. March 1928	U.S.S.R. October 1934
First quartile (in rubles)	.620	1.818	47.57	101.47	49.11	106.65
Third quartile (in rubles)	1.447	3.463	92.59	197.19	97.16	219.57
Quartile ratio (Q_1/Q_3 in per cent)	42.8	52.5	51.4	51.5	50.5	48.6
First decile (in rubles)	.420	1.355	34.22	73.07	35.11	77.32
Ninth decile (in rubles)	2.333	4.735	125.15	273.14	133.79	320.54
Decile ratio (D_1/D_9 in per cent)	18.0	28.6	27.3	26.8	26.2	24.1

The quartiles and deciles in this table are calculated from the frequency distributions in Appendix D, Tables 7–10. The first decile of the June 1914 distribution was extrapolated.

workers are left out of account, it is apparent that Soviet earnings vary over a wide range. The ninth decile of the distribution of wage earners and salaried workers according to earnings for October 1934 is 4.15 times the first.

The extremes of earnings among Soviet industrial workers cannot be determined from the earnings frequency distributions which have been studied because of the presence in them of all-over and all-under earnings class (See Appendix D, Tables 7–10). It is clear from the distributions, however, that in October 1934 some workers earned more than 1420 rubles while others earned less than 50 rubles (Appendix D, Table 10). Thus the earnings of the highest-paid Soviet worker were *more* than 28.3 times the earnings of the lowest-paid worker at that time.

3

Money Wage Variation and Real Wage Variation. The data in Tables 11 and 12 make it clear that a considerable inequality of earnings still prevailed among Soviet industrial workers in 1928, and that in the period after 1928 the inequality increased. But the question recurs: To what extent did the inequality in money earnings connote a corresponding inequality in command over real income? Information on the different factors causing a discrepancy between relative money earnings and relative command over real income in the Soviet Union already has been presented in Chapter III. But it remains to summarize here the effect of these factors on the inequality of earnings. Only three factors, rationing, income taxes, and the rental rates, will be considered. Each of these favored fairly consistently the workers at one money income level relative to those at another.

(1) *Rationing.* It has been indicated that the rationing system operated, in 1934, to equalize the distribution of real income relative to the distribution of money income. To the extent that this equalization is measured by the January 1935 wage adjustment for the derationing of bread, grits, and flour,[8]

[8] But see Chapter III, section 3.

some notion of the effect can be obtained by relating the adjustment to the measures of inequality that have been computed.

The workers in the cotton textile industry may be considered for purposes of illustration. The cotton textile workers were concentrated in the Moscow and Ivanov Oblasts, which districts were both in the same Soviet price region. The regional variation of the derationing adjustment, accordingly, does not obtrude in the calculation.

In October 1934 the quartile ratio of the wage frequency distribution for the cotton textile industry was 61.6 per cent. The first and third quartiles were respectively 97.4 and 158.1 rubles. The wage adjustments for derationing were 17.5 rubles and 21 rubles a month.[9] The latter adjustment was for wage earners in the "most important establishments." A hypothesis which should yield a likely lower limit for the effect of derationing is that all the higher-paid workers in the industry were in the "most important establishments," and the lower-paid workers in the less important ones. The result in this case is that the quartile ratio is increased to 64.0 per cent. A plausible upper limit is obtained if it is assumed that all workers received an equal and average adjustment of (say) 19 rubles. The quartile ratio, then, is increased to 65.6 per cent.

In two respects the effect of the derationing adjustment for the cotton textile workers is not likely to be typical. But these unusual aspects tend to cancel. First the relative wage adjustment, on the average, was relatively high in this industry.[10] This would result in a larger equalization than the typical one. But at the same time the inequality of wages in the cotton goods industry already was relatively low, and the quartile ratio large. The equalizing effect of the derationing adjustment on this account would be lessened.

Since the 1928 quartile ratio in the cotton goods industry was 64.2 per cent, the derationing adjustment overcomes, or

[9] Cf. Appendix A, n. 1.

[10] The realized increment of wages was 16.5 per cent in the cotton industry. In most other industries it was between 9 and 15 per cent.

more than overcomes, the increase in money wage variation which occurred from 1928 to 1934.

The impact of the derationing adjustment on the inequality of earnings among workers in all industries together may be gauged from the following data on the relative average monthly earnings of salaried workers and wage earners in the years 1928, 1934, and 1935: [11]

Year	Earnings of Salaried Workers in Per Cent of Earnings of Wage Earners
1928	180.9
1934	209.2
1935	191.0

Since the change in the relative earnings of wage earners and salaried workers must have been an important factor in the change in distribution from March 1928 to October 1934,[12] the effect of the rationing adjustment on the relative earnings of these workers is of particular interest. From the data presented it would appear that the rationing adjustment reduced the overall inequality of earnings, but not to the 1928 level.

The use of the wage adjustment for the derationing of bread, grits, and flour as a measure of the equalization in real income caused by the rationing system is admittedly a highly questionable procedure. At best the results can only be an approximation to the truth. But the data that have been presented have an interest of their own. For they enable us to gauge the inequality of earnings in the period immediately after rationing was abandoned. In 1935, apparently, money earnings were less unequal than in 1934, but perhaps somewhat more unequal than in 1928.

[11] TSUNKHU, *Trud v SSSR* (Moscow, 1936), p. 96. The earnings data relate to workers in all large-scale industry in the U.S.S.R. They were computed by dividing the average monthly earnings bill by the average number of workers employed during the year, the latter figure being presumably an average of the number of workers employed at a specified date in each month.

[12] The reader will recall that the change in the inequality of distribution among wage earners and salaried workers together was distinctly greater than the change in the inequality of distribution among wage earners alone.

In the latter part of 1935, however, a new factor tending to *increase* the inequality of earnings appeared: the Stakhonovite movement. To this we shall recur.

(2) *Income taxes.* The equalizing effect of the progressive Soviet income taxes on the distribution of real income may be gauged from the following computations. Two hypothetical workers, one at the first quartile and the other at the third quartile of the frequency distribution of wage earners and salaried workers according to earnings, are considered in the illustration. Each worker is assumed to have three dependents. The earnings of these workers before and after taxes were as follows: [13]

	MARCH 1928		OCTOBER 1934	
	Before Taxes	After Taxes	Before Taxes	After Taxes
First quartile	49.11	49.11	106.65	104.94 [14]
Third quartile	97.16	96.69 [14]	219.57	211.68
Quartile ratio				
(Q_1/Q_3 in per cent) ..	50.5	50.8	48.6	49.6

For workers at the first and ninth deciles of the earnings distribution, earnings before and after taxes would have been:

	MARCH 1928		OCTOBER 1934	
	Before Taxes	After Taxes	Before Taxes	After Taxes
First decile	35.11	35.11	77.32	77.32
Ninth decile	133.79	132.96	320.54	305.41
Decile ratio				
(D_1/D_9 in per cent)	26.2	26.4	24.1	25.3

Partly because of the change in the tax rates, and partly because the higher earnings in 1934 were confronted with the more progressive sections of the tax scale, the equalizing effect of the taxes was greater in 1934 than in 1928.

(3) *The rental rates.* Soviet rental rates, it will be recalled,

[13] The taxes referred to here are the Cultural and Housing Construction Tax and the Income Tax, so-called.

[14] If the hypothetical workers considered had been in the first of the four regions into which the Soviet Union was divided for tax purposes, taxes on incomes of less than 100 rubles in 1928 and 115 rubles in 1934 would have been zero.

vary with income, and in 1934 though not in 1928 they varied
with the number of dependents of the lessee. Also, the basic
rental rates vary regionally. This last fact plus the fact that
workers earning different incomes would occupy living space of
different quality and in different amounts makes it difficult to
judge the effect of the Soviet rental system in equalizing the
command over real income afforded by different money incomes.
But it is of interest to compare the rents charged our hypothetical workers at the extreme quartiles and deciles of the March
1928 and October 1934 earnings distributions under the assumption that these workers occupied the same living space,
and of a quality subject to the standard rental rates. For purposes of illustration it may be supposed that the basic rental
rate applicable to the quarters occupied by these workers was
40 kopeks per square meter. This figure is midway between
the limits of basic rental rates established by the central government.[15] For a living space of 20 square meters per family
— this probably approximated the national average for a family of four in 1932 [16] — our hypothetical workers would have
been charged the following rents in rubles per month: [17]

	MARCH 1928		OCTOBER 1934	
	Earnings	Rent	Earnings	Rent
First quartile	49.11	3.60	106.65	8.00
Third quartile	97.16	6.40	219.57	12.92
First decile	35.11	2.80	77.32	7.40
Ninth decile	133.79	8.00	320.54	19.58

Thus in March 1928 the worker at the third quartile would have
been charged 2.80 rubles more per month for the same quarters
than the worker at the first quartile, and the worker at the

[15] The figure, however, is lower than the basic rate of Moscow — 44 kopeks
a square meter — from which the schedule of rates in Table 2, p. 44, is constructed. The range of basic rates established by the central government was
35 to 44, but in special cases, for cities of less than 35,000 inhabitants, basic
rates as low as 30 kopeks a square meter might be established.

[16] See S. M. Kingsbury and M. Fairchild, *Factory, Family and Woman in the
Soviet Union* (New York, 1935), p. 198.

[17] To a reader familiar with workers' budgets in the United States these rents,

ninth decile would have been charged 5.20 rubles more per month than the worker at the first decile. The differentials in rent for the same pairs of workers in October 1934 would have been 4.92 rubles and 12.88 rubles, respectively. If earnings, *after taxes*, are adjusted for these differentials in rent, the March 1928 quartile ratio is increased to 52.3 per cent and the October 1934 quartile ratio to 50.8 per cent. The decile ratio for March 1928 is increased to 27.5 per cent, and that for October 1934 to 26.4 per cent.

4

Recent Changes in Wage Differentials. The wage policies which the observed changes in the inequality of Soviet earnings reflect are discussed in detail in the chapters following. It ought to be remarked here, however, that Soviet policy has operated recently to increase wage differentials beyond the levels at which the rationing adjustment of January 1935 left them.

(1) Recent wage-scale revisions in several industries for which information is at hand all incorporate increased differentials in basic wage rates. In the scales for wage earners, other than apprentices and service personnel, in the linen and hemp industries,[18] which the Commissariat of Light Industry decreed to be effective as of September 1, 1935, the ratio of the highest to the lowest basic wage rates was 3.5:1.[19] In the scale previously applying to the same category of workers in the linen industry, the ratio of extreme basic rates was 2.7:1 and in the hemp industry, 2.77:1. By a directive of the Commissariat of Heavy Industry of March 9, 1936, the scale applying to wage earners other than apprentices and service personnel in the electric precision tool industry, which incorporated a range

---

in relation to income, will appear surprisingly low. The rents quoted, however, are those charged for a standard type of housing which excludes a number of facilities, such as a gas range, bath room, etc.

   [18] Soviet wage scales are described in Chapter XII.

   [19] Postanovleniia NKLP, September 10, 1935, *B.F.Kh.Z.*, 1935, no. 36, pp. 34, 35.

of basic rates of 2.8:1, was likewise ordered replaced by one incorporating a range of 3.5:1.[20]

(2) One effect of the widely discussed Stakhonovite movement undoubtedly has been to increase the inequality of earnings. The movement was inspired by the output records achieved in August and September, 1935 by the Donbas coal miner, Alexei Stakhonov. Following Stakhonov's successes, an intensive campaign to increase the productivity of labor was inaugurated in the U.S.S.R. Great emphasis was given in the campaign to the improvement of work methods. But the campaign was associated also with a movement to extend the use of the progressive piece system.[21] The latter aspect of the Stakhonovite movement probably was the more important, as far as wage differentials are concerned.

The effect of recent revisions of wage scales and of the Stakonovite movement no doubt has been to raise the inequality of earnings in the U.S.S.R. appreciably above the level of March 1928.[22] Whether the inequality of earnings prevailing in October 1934 has been exceeded, however, is uncertain.

[20] Rasporiazhenie NKTP, March 9, 1936, *B.F.Kh.Z.*, 1936, no. 11, p. 28.

[21] The development of the use of piece work in the U.S.S.R. is discussed in Chapter XII, section 2.

[22] A comparison of the extremes of basic rates in recently promulgated wage scales with those prevailing in 1928 supports this conclusion. In view of the fact that the "supplements" to basic rates referred to in Chapter XII, section 2, still were substantial in 1928, and that the wage scales prevailing then relate to larger industrial sectors than those promulgated recently, however, the comparison is not as incisive as it might be.

In the one wage scale which prevailed in March 1928 for wage earners other than apprentices and service personnel in *all* metal-working industries, the range of basic rates was 2.8:1 (*Profsoiuzy S.S.S.R. 1926–28, Otchet VTSSPS k VIII S'ezdu Professional'nykh Soiuzov*, Moscow, 1928, p. 326). The range of basic wage rates effective in the electric precision tool industry at this time must have been distinctly less than that established by this directive.

The range of basic rates in the one scale applying to all textile wage earners other than apprentices and service personnel in March 1928 was 3.5:1 (*ibid.*). It seems clear, however, that in at least the linen industry the actual ratio of extreme basic wage rates at this time was less than that allowed by the all-textile industry scale. The highest average basic rate of wage earners in any basic occupation in the linen industry — that for sub-foremen — was 2.90 times the lowest basic rate in the textile scale (Tsentral'noe Biuro Statistiki Truda, *Differensiatsiia Zarabotnoi Platy v Fabrichno-Zavodskoi Promyshlennosti Soiuza SSR za 1927 i 1928 gg.*, Moscow, 1929, p. 180).

The range of the scale applying to wage earners other than apprentices and service personnel in the construction industry in March 1928 was 2.5:1 (*Profsoiuzy SSSR, 1926–28*, p. 326). In a decree issued by the Council of Labor and Defense on April 5, 1936, two scales were established for these workers. One, for ordinary construction workers, incorporated a range of 3.0:1; the other, for machine operators and metal workers, incorporated a range of 3.9:1 (Postanovlenie STO, April 5, 1936, *B.F.Kh.Z.*, 1936, no. 15, p. 34).

CHAPTER XI

WAGE ADMINISTRATION [1]

THE TENDENCY of wage differentials to proximate differences in productivity in a capitalistic economy expresses the interaction of two sorts of market forces. Business men, on the one hand, seek to economize their labor costs by adjusting in an appropriate manner the number of workers of different skills they employ. Workers, on the other, strive to enhance their material position by shifting from less to more remunerative employment. Since workers may be induced by a sufficient wage differential to change their occupation as well as their place of employment, and since new additions to the labor force are influenced also in their choice of occupation by the size of prevalent wage differentials, wage differentials tend to correspond not only to differences in productivity, but also to the marginal workers' evaluations of the relative material advantages of different employments.

These are long-run tendencies, and in a modern capitalistic economy, needless to say, the forces that they express are often attenuated. The labor market, perhaps, is among the least efficient of capitalist markets in providing information on prices and conditions of sale, and labor itself is notoriously immobile. Large employers of labor and organizations of employees are able to determine wages with little regard to market forces. Increasingly the ballot box encroaches on the market

---

[1] In seeking out legal materials on Soviet wage administration, I have found the following compendiums especially helpful: E. N. Danilova, *Deistvuiushchee Zakonodatel'stvo o Trude*, vols. I and II, second edition (Moscow, 1927); V. V. Shmidt, *Osnovy Trudovogo Zakonodatel'stva* (Moscow, 1929); IA. L. Kiselev i S. E. Malkin, *Sbornik Vazhneishikh Postanovlenii po Trudu*, second edition (Moscow, 1931), third edition (Moscow, 1931), fourth edition (Moscow, 1932), fifth edition (Moscow, 1935), sixth edition (Moscow, 1936), tenth edition (Moscow, 1938).

place itself as the testing ground for capitalist prices. All this is to say that competition in the capitalist labor market is neither pure nor perfect. If, withal, wage differentials exhibit some relation to differences in productivity, this must be attributed largely to the fact that employers still have much discretion to determine the composition of their working force.

But, however the capitalist labor market functions, a glance at it suggests at once the desirability of supplementing our statistical inquiry into the principles of Soviet wages by a study of Soviet wage administration. Is there any counterpart in the Soviet Union of the capitalist labor market? Is Soviet wage administration itself evidence that capitalist wage principles prevail? These are questions to which we may now turn profitably.

2

Utilization of Labor. In view of the far-reaching mechanization of industry which has been accomplished in the U.S.S.R. under the five-year plan, it needs no demonstration here that economy of labor is very much a motive of Soviet administrators. Significantly, however, it is *money* costs that the administrators seek to economize. The use of funds derived from economies in money costs to reward the workers responsible for their realization has become an established administrative practice in the Soviet Union. In August 1931, the Central Executive Committee and the Council of Commissars of the U.S.S.R. decreed that 50 per cent of the reduction in costs realized in a state enterprise by the first year's application of a new invention, technical improvement or rationalization be set aside as a fund for the payment of premiums to workers responsible for such cost reductions, and for the measures to further rationalize production.[2] This directive did not deviate in principle from an earlier one on the same subject issued in February 1927, and it was still in effect in 1937. The rewards

[2] Postanovlenie TSIK i SNK SSSR, August 13, 1931, *S.Z.R. SSSR*, 1931, part I, no. 52, pp. 615 ff.

of those responsible for the economies depend directly on the magnitude of the economy achieved.[3] The 1931 decree provided also for the establishment of a fund in each enterprise, amounting to one-half of 1 per cent of its total annual wage bill, for the payment of premiums to individuals or groups of employees for distinguished attainments in fulfilling or overfulfilling the plan, and in other spheres. This fund was to be derived from economies realized from socialist competition and shock work.

The 1931 decree presumably supplemented rather than replaced a directive of the Council of Labor and Defense[4] of June 1928 providing that from 25 to 50 per cent of the reduction in costs below initial estimates realized by a state industrial enterprise should be placed at the disposal of the director of the enterprise for use in further rationalization of the productive process and for the betterment of the employment and living conditions of the workers.[5] By a decree of April 1936,

[3] Instruktsiia Komiteta . . . pri STO, October 7, 1931, in Kiselev i Malkin, *op. cit.*, tenth edition, pp. 27 ff. So are rewarded, among others, persons whose innovation is sufficiently novel to warrant their being awarded, on application, a certificate of authorship. If the innovator desires a patent, so-called, as distinct from a certificate of authorship, for his invention, royalties must be arranged by agreement between the patentee and the administrative organ which wishes to make use of the patent. The inventor in this case must pay certain fees and taxes which he otherwise would be relieved of.

[4] The Council of Labor and Defense (STO) is a joint committee under the Council of Commissars, and its membership is drawn largely from the ranks of the latter organ. For a description of the organization and functions of the council, see S. and B. Webb, *Soviet Communism* (New York, 1936), I, 104 ff.

[5] Postanovlenie STO, June 14, 1928, *S.Z.R. SSSR*, 1928, part I, no. 42, section 384, pp. 794 ff. Economies arising from causes outside the control of the individual enterprise, for example from a reduction in the price of raw materials, were not to be included in reckoning the fund to be placed at the disposal of the director of the establishment. The actual amount of the fund, within the specified limits, was to be determined by the trust administering the establishment, with the participation of the director of the establishment. In a decree of December 2, 1931, however, the Council of Labor and Defense apparently fixed the fund uniquely at 50 per cent of the realized economies. By this decree, the payment of individual premiums from the fund was permitted.

The fund that has been described should be distinguished from a *normal* appropriation from the net profit of a trust (later, a combine or a trust) for

however, a single fund was established in each state enterprise engaged in production for the betterment of the employment and living conditions of the workers and for the payment of premiums to workers for distinguished attainments.[6] (The fund to reward inventors and the authors of rationalization proposals was not affected by the decree.) It was directed that not less than 50 per cent of the fund be expended for workers' housing, and that the remainder be expended for other improvements in living and working conditions, for the payment of premiums to workers who especially distinguished themselves, for additions to capital, and for rationalization measures. Four per cent of the profits realized by the enterprise from operation under the plan, and 50 per cent of the profits realized from measures not embraced in the plan, were to constitute the new fund. Gains arising from causes outside the control of the individual enterprise, such as gains from the reduction in the price of raw materials, were not to be included in reckoning the unplanned profits from which the fund was derived.

Under the decree of August 1931, 6 per cent of the means placed in the fund of an individual enterprise to reward workers for distinguished attainments with respect to the plan was to be transferred to an administrative organ superior to the enterprise (a combine, or if the trusts in an industry were not subordinate to a combine, a trust) for the payment of premiums, on the same basis, to the directors and directors' assistants in the firms administered by the higher organ.[7] This provision of the 1931 decree, it appears, supplanted a similar

---

housing construction and other similar purposes which was made as early as 1924. The decree of August 1931, organizing funds for the payment of premiums, however, directs, without specifying the source of the funds in question, that 10 per cent of the means intended for housing construction and like measures in the individual establishment should be placed at the disposal of the all-union or republican commissariats administering it for the payment of premiums, in the form of additional housing construction, to entire plants for attainments in fulfilling and overfulfilling the plan.

[6] Postanovlenie TSIK i SNK SSSR, April 1936, S.Z.R. SSSR, 1936, part I, no. 20, section 169, pp. 294–295.

[7] A fund to encourage inventions and technical improvements also was formed in the higher organ, and in the state department superior to it. In the latter

bonus scheme which had been established in March 1927, and it was in turn replaced by a short-lived arrangement initiated in June 1935. Whether the consolidated fund established by the decree of April 1936 is now used for the payment of premiums to the director of an enterprise as well as to members of his staff is not clear.

While the economies from which premium funds are derived in the Soviet Union usually are understood to be reductions in costs below planned costs, the reduction in money cost of production is at the same time one of the recurring directives in the annual plan itself. More recently, however, this directive has been detailed for individual categories of costs, and for some time physical coefficients of production also have been projected in the plan.[8] In respect to wages, five distinct funds are established for as many categories of workers[9] in the monthly and quarterly plans confirmed for each enterprise by the administrative organ superior to it, and in the yearly and quarterly plans confirmed for these organs by the commissariat administering the industry concerned. The promulgation of such detailed directives by the Soviet authorities may contribute to the fulfillment of the plan. But their strict observance — and such was intended — would tend to obstruct or at least to delay in certain instances realization of the unplanned economies, which the Soviet administrators have taken such pains to encourage. It is of some significance, then, that an establishment which overfulfills its production program is permitted to increase its wage expenditures provided the planned wage cost per unit of output is not exceeded in consequence.[10]

---

organ a fund was established, too, for the payment of premiums to entire establishments in the form of extra housing construction.

[8] See Gosplan, *Narodno-Khoziaistvennyi Plan na 1935 God*, second edition (Moscow, 1935), pp. 347 ff.

[9] These categories correspond to the classes of workers distinguished in the October 1934 wage statistics which have been used in the present study. (See Appendix B.)

[10] See Postanovlenie SNK SSSR, February 21, 1933, *S.Z.R. SSSR*, 1933, part I, no. 13, section 75, pp. 149 ff.

In total, the annual and quarterly wage fund for each commissariat is confirmed by the central government.

Whether the incentives to economize money costs which are provided in the Soviet Union are more or less effective than those existing in a capitalist economy is an interesting and oft-raised issue, but one which is not to be settled here. To the extent that money costs are economized, however, the upshot in a socialist economy is the same as in a capitalist one. The use of a resource is determined from a consideration of its yield on the one hand, and its price on the other. What concerns us here is that different kinds of labor tend to be allocated to tasks which yield a value product corresponding to their money wage. The employment of high-paid labor tends to be restricted to the more productive employments, while low-paid labor is used more freely. The "demand" for different kinds of labor is thus determined.[11] Whether not merely a rough correspondence but a proportionality of money wages to productivity would tend to be established depends, however, on whether money wages in turn are adjusted to assure that the "demand" for and "supply" of the different kinds of labor are proximate. Conceivably, even though a regime of money-cost economy were established, the socialist authorities might seek to realize an optimum allocation of labor without recourse to the mechanism of the market. The procedure used to allocate labor in the economy as a whole then would be much the same as that employed within a single business unit in a capitalist economy. In following such a course, however, the socialist administrators would sacrifice unnecessarily a valuable administrative technique.

Significantly, the director of the individual enterprise in the Soviet Union has been charged by the Central Committee of the Communist Party with direct responsibility for the fulfillment of the plan.[12] The decisions of the director in administra-

[11] The correspondence of wages and productivity, however, in this context is not to be interpreted rigorously. The workers in one occupation might be less productive and yet be paid higher wages than the workers in another occupation, but if *both* kinds of labor were in short supply no substitution could be made.

[12] Postanovlenie TSK VKP(b), September 5, 1929, *Izvestiia TSIK*, September 7, 1929; quoted in Kiselev i Malkin, *op. cit.*, tenth edition, p. 19.

tive, organizational, and technical matters, by declaration of the party, are obligatory for all employees of the enterprise. The factory party cell and the local organ of the trade union may appeal appointments and dismissals, and so in any case, under the labor code of the R.S.F.S.R., may a worker dismissed for unsatisfactory service.[13] But, within limits of the directives established by superior organs in the plan, the discretion of the management of a Soviet enterprise to determine the occupational, as distinct from personal, composition of the enterprise's working force appears to be unrestricted. To the extent that this is so, the adjustment of wage rates to equate supply and demand is not only a useful administrative device, but, if more important uses of labor in one plant are not to be sacrificed to less important ones in another, well-nigh indispensable.

3

Freedom of Choice of Employment. Conceivably, capitalist wage principles might prevail in the U.S.S.R. even though the occupation and place of employment of the Soviet worker were determined by administrative order rather than by individual choice. It is more than doubtful, however, that in this case money wage differentials would long continue to correspond to workers' preferences for different kinds of labor. *Per contra,* once workers are permitted to choose freely their occupation and place of employment, resort to money wage adjustments to assure that the supply of different kinds of labor approximates

---

[13] The labor code of 1922 (Kodeks Zakonov o Trude RSFSR, November 1922, article 47) permits the dismissal of a worker by the employer in case of full or partial liquidation of the enterprise, or the curtailment of work in it; suspension of work for a period of one month for technical reasons; disclosure that the employee is unsuited for the work; systematic failure on the part of the employee to fulfill the tasks placed upon him by the work agreement or by the rules of internal order; and in certain other cases (criminality, absenteeism, loss of work capacity). Dismissal for the third and fourth of the enumerated causes requires the assent of a mixed management-labor commission (*Ratsenochno-Konflictnaia Komissiia*). In substance, these provisions of the code still are in effect.

demand is avoidable only to the extent that non-pecuniary incentives may be relied on for this same purpose. The extent to which freedom of choice prevails in the Soviet labor market, thus, is of much interest in the present context.

The subject of forced labor already occupies extensive space in the literature on Soviet economics. Little will be added in these pages to the material that already has been presented.[14]

That Soviet labor was subjected to forms of compulsion in the early post-revolutionary years is a fact familiar to casual students of Russian history. Attachment of the worker to his place of employment, mobilization of able-bodied citizens for specially urgent work, administrative transfer of workers from one place of work to another — recalcitrants in every case being subject to fine, arrest, or other punishment —, all these were measures adopted in the critical period to which Soviet writers have since given the name War Communism. More recently, in two instances, it has been ascertained, a form of compulsion has been used to transfer industrial workers from one employment to another. In 1931, under penalty of criminal prosecution, but with two weeks' bonus for conformance, certain groups of skilled railway workers engaged elsewhere were required to return to their former occupation.[15] In the same year a similar requirement was decreed for skilled workers engaged in sea transport.[16] The system of contracting with collective farms to supply seasonal labor recruits, which was adopted by many Soviet industrial enterprises beginning in 1931, apparently also has been applied in certain cases without regard to the desires of the individual recruit. Involuntary recruitment has been an object of attack by the Soviet authorities themselves.[17]

---

[14] Of the studies of this subject in English which I have examined, that of Joseph Freeman (*The Soviet Worker*, New York, 1932, chapter ix) seems to me the most thorough.   [15] *Izvestiia NKT SSSR*, 1931, no. 4, p. 63.

[16] Postanovlenie STO, April 14, 1931, article 28, *B.F.Kh.Z.*, 1931, no. 12, p. 44.

[17] Postanovlenie TSKK VKP(b) i Kollegii NKRKI, August 28, 1931, *Izvestiia NKT SSSR*, 1931, no. 29.

Instances of the use of compulsory labor since the period of War Communism in fields more remote from the present study also have been recorded. The conscription of peasant labor for road work and other projects has been reported,[18] and indeed the liability of inhabitants of rural regions to limited service on such works has been established in Soviet law.[19] The use of forced labor in prison camps for canal and other construction work, which is reported by numerous travelers to the U.S.S.R., is acknowledged by the Soviet authorities.[20]

It cannot be claimed that this list of cases where the Soviet worker's employment has been determined for him by administrative action is exhaustive. At least among industrial workers, however, it is quite clear such compulsion could not have been general. A careful weighing of personal observation on this subject, it is believed, would support this view.[21] The Soviet

[18] Freeman, *op. cit.*, pp. 256–257.

[19] By a decree of the Central Executive Committee and of the Council of Commissars of the Russian Republic of August 17, 1925 (*S.U.R. RSFSR*, 1925, part I, no. 57, section 455, pp. 718 ff.), village soviets in this republic were permitted, by a majority vote of all citizens of the locality, to conscript able-bodied inhabitants for road work. The decree provides that the village soviet, on being petitioned, may permit monetary payment to replace the road work. By later all-Union decree, the period of service on this work for any one inhabitant was limited to six days. The R.S.F.S.R. decree was abolished on April 1, 1929, and at that time local administrative organs were permitted to mobilize the population for road work apparently without the sanction of an assembly of citizens. Administrative procedure may have been altered again in subsequent years, but there was still provision in Soviet law for the mobilization of the population for road work as late as 1935.

The voting of taxes by rural local assemblies, to be paid in money, goods, or labor service, also was once permitted by Soviet law, but provision for payment of the tax in labor services has been excluded from decrees on local taxes promulgated more recently.

[20] See the account of the completion of the Moscow-Volga Canal, in *Pravda*, July 5, 1937, p. 1.

[21] It is significant that such critical observers as Citrine, Monkhouse, and Chamberlin only report the use of forced labor in prison camps, for canal and other construction work (W. Citrine, *I Search for Truth in Soviet Russia*, London, 1936, p. 80; A. Monkhouse, *Moscow 1911–33*, Boston, 1934, p. 264; W. H. Chamberlin, *Russia's Iron Age*, Boston, 1935, pp. 51 ff.). W. A. Rukeyser (*Working for the Soviets*, New York, 1932, p. 155) and J. Freeman (*op. cit.*,

labor codes also are in this respect not without significance. Provision for the conscription of workers for compulsory labor service and for the administrative transfer of workers from one employment to another was incorporated in the labor code of the R.S.F.S.R. published in December 1918.[22] The code that replaced this in November 1922, however, declares explicitly that the mobilization of citizens for compulsory labor service should be restricted to exceptional circumstances: specifically, natural calamities and cases where labor is insufficient for the performance of the most important tasks of state (Art. 11).[23] The transfer of a worker from one enterprise to another or from one place of work to another, it is provided further, requires the consent of the worker concerned (Art. 37). With due notice the worker is permitted also to abrogate a work agreement concluded for an indefinite period, and, for a variety of specified causes, one concluded for a definite period (Art. 48).[24] These provisions of the 1922 labor code were still a part of Soviet labor law as late as May 1936.

The significance of Article 37, however, at least for the period immediately following December 15, 1930, is questionable. At that time the right to transfer qualified wage earners and specialists to "the most important branches of industry" from "less important ones," on request of an interested economic organization, was explicitly granted to the Commissariat of Labor by a joint decree of the Central Executive Committee and the Council of Commissars of the U.S.S.R.[25] The transfer in each

---

pp. 252 ff.) refer to the absence or insignificance of compulsory labor so far as industrial workers are concerned.

[22] Kodeks Zakonov o Trude RSFSR, December 1918, especially articles 1–5, 24, 31, 40–43. See also articles 45–53 for the provisions regarding the workers freedom to leave his employment. It is provided that a worker who leaves his employment without the approval of the factory workers' committee should be excluded from the labor exchanges (then virtually the sole legal agent through which an enterprise might secure its labor supply) for a period of one week.

[23] Kodeks Zakonov o Trude RSFSR, November 1922.

[24] See note 22 above for reference to the provisions on this subject in the 1918 code.

[25] Postanovlenie TSIK i SNK SSSR, December 15, 1930, *Izvestiia TSIK*,

case was to be by agreement with the trade union organization concerned, and with the approval of the Council of Labor and Defense. The two orders of 1931 requiring the return to their former employment of former railway and sea-transport workers clearly were applications of the principle contained in this decree, though the actions were initiated by the Central Executive Committee of the U.S.S.R. and the Central Committee of

TABLE 13

New Employment and Departures of Wage Earners in Plants of Large-Scale Industry in Relation to the Average Monthly Number of Wage Earners Employed (in per cent)

	1928	1929	1930	1931	1932	1933	1934	1935
New employment	101	122	176	151	127	125	101	92
Departures	92	115	152	137	135	122	97	86

Source: TSUNKHU, *Sotsialisticheskoe Stroitel'stvo v SSSR* (Moscow, 1936), p. 531.
Large-scale industry, with minor qualifications, includes all industrial establishments employing either more than 30 wage earners, or if motive power is used, more than 15 wage earners.

the Communist Party, in the case of the railway workers, and by the Council of Labor and Defense in the case of the sea-transport workers. The two orders have been interpreted also, by one writer, as emergency measures of the character referred to in Article 11 of the labor code.[26]

More critical evidence is available, however, on freedom of choice in the Soviet labor market. Reference is to the Soviet labor turnover itself. In 1928 the number of newly employed workers in the plants of large-scale industry was 101 per cent of the average monthly working force. Departures were 92 per cent. In the ensuing years through 1934 the rates were higher, a peak being reached in the midst of the first five-year plan when new employment was 176 per cent and departures 152 per cent of the average monthly working force. (See Table 13.) Needless to say, this labor flow was not a matter

December 17, 1930, quoted in Kiselev i Malkin, *op. cit.*, second edition, p. 62. The "most important industries" are specified in the decree as ferrous metallurgy, coal, chemicals, machinery, construction, transport, electric power.

[26] Freeman, *op. cit.*, pp. 256–257.

of indifference to the Soviet government, and after 1930 measures were taken to reduce it. Nevertheless, such a turnover is hardly the characteristic of a system where compulsory labor is used. On this account the attention that has been given it by observers to affirm the absence of forced labor in Soviet industry is more than justified.

The government measures to reduce the labor turnover were diverse. All were short of force, but they are of interest nonetheless. By a decree of the R.S.F.S.R. of September 23, 1930, individuals who voluntarily left their employment were deprived of the right to receive unemployment compensation.[27] Such individuals, it was declared, should be directed to new employment last among those registered at the state labor exchanges. At the discretion of the Council of the local labor exchanges, "drifters" (*letuny*), together with various other antisocial elements, might be dropped from the labor exchange lists altogether, or be placed in an inferior ration category. By an all-Union decree of the following January, employment through the state labor exchanges was denied for a six-month period to any worker who left his work voluntarily more than once in a year.[28] A worker who left his work voluntarily without due notice, or without awaiting a replacement, or prior to the expiration of his work agreement, was declared subject to the same penalty. The association of a worker's ration privileges with employment in a particular plant, which was anticipated in the republican decree of September 1930, was initiated in a wide sector of Soviet industry by the organization of closed shops in the latter part of 1930. This was two years after rationing was adopted. The policy was applied more rigorously after December 1932, when control over the issue of ration booklets was transferred to the management of the employing establishment. By decree of the Russian Republic of Febru-

---

[27] Postanovlenie NKT i VSNKH RSFSR, September 23, 1930, *Izvestiia NKT SSSR*, 1930, no. 26–27; quoted in Kiselev i Malkin, *op. cit.*, second edition, p. 67.

[28] Postanovlenie NKT SSSR, January 17, 1931, *Izvestiia NKT SSSR*, 1931, no. 4; quoted in Kiselev i Malkin, *op. cit.*, fifth edition, p. 99.

ary 10, 1931, it was further provided that a worker who dwelt in quarters supplied either directly by the employing establishment or by the local soviet at the direction of the employing establishment might be evicted from his quarters on the severance of his connection with the employing establishment.[29] Though the workers concerned are employees of state institutions rather than industrial workers, it is of interest to note that the all-Union, republican, and local labor organs were directed by the Council of Commissars of the U.S.S.R. in February 1933 to assure that members of the economic and administrative staff who shifted from one institution to another should receive for one year no higher earnings than they received in their previous employment.[30]

Together these measures are impressive enough, and others may be appended to the list.[31] None the less, their effect in restricting the turnover of industrial labor, at least, is open to question. The granting of unemployment compensation, it should be observed, ceased altogether after 1930. But, under the conditions of the five-year program of expansion, it is unlikely in any case that the between-jobs interval facing a worker could have been a substantial deterrent to his departure from a particular establishment. Deprivation for a six-month period of the right to find employment in industry and transport through the state labor exchanges, for a time, may have

[29] Postanovlenie VTSIK i SNK RSFSR, February 10, 1931, *S.U.R. RSFSR*, 1931, part I, no. 9, section 116, pp. 122 ff.

[30] Postanovlenie SNK SSSR, February 21, 1933, *S.Z.R. SSSR*, 1933, part I, no. 13, section 75, pp. 149 ff.

[31] Variation of the worker's social insurance disability payments with the number of years service (up to two years) in one plant has been provided for. Furthermore, the *regional* movement of labor may have been restricted by the administration of the unified internal passport system which was introduced in December 1932. The avowed objectives of the system were to improve the records of the population of cities, workers' settlements and factory sites; to discharge from these places individuals not connected with production or work in institutions or schools (excepting invalids and recipients of pensions); and "to clean out from these settlements concealed *kulak*, criminal, and other antisocial elements" (Postanovlenie TSIK i SNK SSSR, December 27, 1932, *B.F.Kh.Z.*, 1933, no. 2, p. 3).

been decidedly more severe as a penalty. The hiring of workers only through the state exchanges, which was already a stipulation of many collective agreements, was declared mandatory for all enterprises, institutions, and other employing units in December 1930.[32] Whether, under the strain of the expansion program this regulation ever was effective is questionable, but it was soon voided. In September 1931 enterprises and institutions in the socialized sector again were permitted to hire labor directly.[33]

The purpose of the reorganization of the supply system which was initiated in 1930 was not alone to reduce the labor flow. But it meant that between jobs a worker either was forced to purchase goods at open-market prices or was given the lower ration category of the unemployed. The loss of ration privileges, even though only temporary, together with the risk of eviction from his living quarters, should have been of more serious concern to the restless worker than any of the other penalties threatening him.

It is apparent from Table 13 that the labor turnover declined in the years following 1930, after the counteracting steps had been taken. But the decline continued into 1935, after the most important food products had been derationed. Furthermore, in 1934 the labor flow was little different from that of 1928 when none of the restrictive measures had yet been introduced. It could not be argued from this that the government measures played no role. But it is believed that the more important causes of the reduced turnover would have to be sought instead in the factors which were responsible for its exceptional rise. Of these, two appear of special import: the food shortage and the rapid influx of peasant labor. Both factors were of less im-

[32] Postanovlenie TSIK i SNK SSSR, December 15, 1930, *Izvestiia TSIK*, December 17, 1930; quoted in Kiselev i Malkin, *op. cit.*, second edition, p. 60. A variety of exceptions to the regulation were permitted.

The employment of labor only through state organs maintained for this purpose was mandatory as a general rule under the labor codes of 1918 and 1922. By decree of January 2, 1925, however, this requirement had been voided.

[33] Postanovlenie TSIK i SNK SSSR, September 13, 1931, *S.Z.R. SSSR*, 1931, part I, no. 60, section 385, pp. 693–694.

portance after 1932. In particular, the annual increase in the working force of large-scale industry, which was 12, 38, and 28 per cent in the years 1930–32, fell to 1, 0, and 7 per cent in the next three years.

While the statistics on Soviet labor turnover must be acknowledged as striking evidence that the Soviet worker has not been seriously restricted in his choice of employment, it might be suggested that this data is relevant only to the worker's freedom to choose his *place* of employment, as distinct from his *occupation*. On the import of this logical stricture, the writer has only this to say. A study of the reasonably accessible materials reveals but one case — a not unimportant one — aside from the instances of compulsory labor already referred to, where a worker may not leave his occupation for another which he is competent to perform. Since as early as 1926 the graduate of a Soviet university or technicum has been required to work for a limited period at his specialty. By decree of September 16, 1933, this period of service was fixed at five years, which must be devoted to directly productive (*na proizvodstve*) as distinct from administrative work.[34] During this period, however, the young specialist may not choose his place of employment either. He is presumably directed to work by the commissariat which administers the educational institution where he studied, though in practice it appears that the personal distribution of graduates among available places in some measure has been performed by the educational authorities themselves. By decree of September 15, 1933, the graduates of factory apprentice schools are required to serve three years in directly productive work at their specialty.[35]

[34] Postanovlenie TSIK i SNK SSSR, September 15, 1933, *SZ.R. SSSR*, 1933, part I, no. 59, section 356, pp. 650 ff. This decree also required the Soviet commissariats to transfer to operating enterprises for work in their specialties not less than half the young specialists who were employed in administrative organizations, and who had graduated from the educational institution within the preceding five years — if they had not in the meantime spent three years in directly productive work.

[35] Postanovlenie TSIK i SNK SSSR, September 15, 1933, *S.Z.R. SSSR*, 1933, part I, no. 59, section 357, pp. 652 ff.

4

Clearly the framework within which the director of a Soviet factory organizes his labor force and the Soviet worker chooses his employment differs in numerous particulars from that which confronts their counterparts in a modern free-enterprise economy. The Soviet factory director and his associates undoubtedly are able to exercise less discretion over the composition of their working force than the management group of a capitalist enterprise. The limitation on the departure of the newly trained worker from his specialty, and the loss of housing and, until recently, rationing privileges which have faced the worker leaving his place of employment in the Soviet Union, however, should be contrasted with the trade union restrictions on entry into various skilled occupations and the costs of education incident to entry into the professions in a capitalist economy. Quite possibly, if the risk that his employment will be determined in any case by administrative action is reckoned with, the institutional limitations on the Soviet worker's choice of employment have on the average been more substantial than those confronting the capitalist worker. The comparison, needless to say, is not very meaningful, but if it is made, it must be observed in the same breath that the restrictions on labor's freedom of choice in the Soviet Union, in contrast with those prevailing in a capitalist economy, do not operate consistently to favor any one sector of the working force.

The limitations on freedom of choice in the Soviet labor market, it appears in any case, could not have extinguished the tendency, usually attributed to a capitalist labor market, of workers to distribute themselves among the different occupations which they are competent to perform according to the relative rewards of the diverse tasks and their preferences for them. The further tendency, characteristic of a capitalist economy, for workers to be distributed among different employments so that their relative productivity corresponds to their relative money wages, requires only that money costs be economized, a behavior pattern which clearly prevails in the Soviet Union. The upshot is that the forces of supply and demand which operate in a capitalist labor market are also active in the Soviet labor market.

It would be tempting to conclude from this evidence alone that Soviet wage differentials are determined by capitalist principles. The fact that the forces of supply and demand are operative, however, does not establish that the Soviet authorities adjust wages in response to these forces. Wilful planners, contemptuous of capitalist mores, might consult only their consciences and political fences to fix wage differentials. Wages, then, could be expected to correspond but not necessarily to be proportional to the productivity of different workers; and workers attracted to a particular occupation would have no assurance of employment in it. The consequences of such a course should not favor its continued pursuit. At least a presumption that capitalist principles prevail in a labor market such as has been described would be warranted.

But it remains to inquire, in the next chapter, how, within the institutional framework that has been described, Soviet wage differentials are determined. Certain broad policies as to wage differentials which have not crystallized into administrative practice are discussed in a subsequent chapter on Soviet equalitarianism.

CHAPTER XII

WAGE ADMINISTRATION (Continued)

Wage Scales. Since shortly after the Revolution the major constituent of the wages of industrial wage earners and, until 1931,
of industrial salaried workers in the Soviet Union has been
determined through the use of a system of wage scales. A
Soviet wage scale consists simply of a series of coefficients relating the basic wage rate of workers in any given wage category to the basic wage rate of workers in the lowest wage
category.

The system of wage scales applied to industrial workers in
the U.S.S.R. has been subject to not infrequent revision. At
the time to which our first set of detailed wage statistics relate,
March 1928, a wage-scale reform which had been initiated by
the seventh congress of trade unions in December 1926 still
had not been extended to a substantial minority of industrial
workers. Where the new system had been adopted, however,
workers were classified for purposes of wage regulation into
four categories: "ordinary laborers" (*rabochie*), apprentices,
engineers and technical workers, and salaried workers other
than engineers and technical workers.[1] Each group of workers

---

[1] Foremen were classified with engineers and technical workers, but skilled
workers were included in the class of ordinary laborers.

The term "wage earner" has been used in the present study and will continue
to be used to include apprentices, ordinary labor, and a third class of labor
which is distinguished in Soviet wage statistics, and which is composed of janitors, scrubwomen, watchmen, etc. It is uncertain whether, for purposes of wage
regulation, workers of this third class were grouped with ordinary laborers, or
whether their wages were regulated separately.

In the wage-scale system described in the text, salaried workers other than
engineers and technical workers are designated by the Russian term *sluzhashchie*.
This term is sometimes used in Russian, however, to refer to all salaried workers,
including engineers and technical workers.

was distributed in turn by industries among the graduated classes of an established wage scale. The number of wage rate classes and the values of the coefficients in each scale varied as between industries and occupational groups. Among the ordinary labor scales adopted after December 1926 the range of basic wage rates was greatest in the glass industry, the extreme coefficient being 4.2:1. The largest extreme coefficient among the engineer and technical-worker scales was 5.0:1, in the textile industries; and among the scales for other salaried workers, 8.0:1, in the metals industries.[2]

Changes in the range of basic wage rates in the Soviet wage scales have been numerous; they provide an illuminating trace of the equalitarian policies which are studied in the following chapters. Certain principles observed in the construction of the scales, however, have survived the revisions.

In the first labor code of the R.S.F.S.R., promulgated in December 1918 by the Central Executive Committee of the Soviets, it is declared that in determining the remuneration of different kinds of work the following factors should be taken into account: the arduousness of the labor; its riskiness, complexity, and exactness; the degree of independence of and the responsibility borne by the worker; and the education and experience required (Art. 59). This directive was not repeated in the labor code promulgated in November 1922. The latter code provides only that wages are to be determined by the collective and individual work agreements (Art. 22). The criteria which avowedly were used in classifying occupations into the categories of the new wage scales adopted after the most recent turn in Soviet wage policy, in June 1931, however, are essentially the wage principles set forth in the 1918 code. According to a Soviet text on labor economics, published in 1934, the factors which ought to be and in a majority of cases are considered are the complexity and exactness of the work, the

---

[2] *Professional'nye Soiuzy SSSR, 1926–28, Otchet VTSSPS k VIII S'ezdu Professional'nykh Soiuzov* (Moscow, 1928), p. 326.

responsibility associated with it, and the working conditions.[3] The necessary training period is not separately specified.[4]

Continued reference to the wage-determining factors enunciated in the 1918 code is not surprising in view of their generality. The criteria are interesting none the less. Clearly all are factors which, in a free labor market, directly affect the supply of labor in different occupations. They are the factors which determine the attractiveness or unattractiveness of different occupations to the workers engaged in them. At least in classifying workers in a particular wage category, and presumably also in determining the relative wages of workers in different categories, the Soviet administrators apparently reckon with the same factors that influence the supply of labor in a capitalist economy. The criteria enumerated in the 1918 Soviet labor code, indeed, might serve well enough a capitalist employer in the construction of his wage scales.

2

"Supplements." As is implied by the qualification "basic," the Soviet worker's basic earnings are not exhaustive of his actual earnings. The difference, prior to 1931, consisted in part of a number of "supplements"[5] which were only formally distinct from the basic rates themselves. Probably most important were the supplements paid piece workers. These were introduced for a variety of reasons, among them to make the piece system more palatable to the workers. The supplements to piece workers often were accompanied by a supplement to auxiliary time workers, usually a percentage of the excess of actual over basic earnings of the piece workers served by them.

[3] M. M. Krivitskii, editor, *Ekonomika Truda*, second edition (Moscow, 1934), pp. 192 ff. This study contains an interesting account of how, on the basis of the enumerated criteria, points are assigned to the different occupations so that they may be classified in a wage scale.

[4] See also A. G. Titov, *Itogi Bor'by s Uravnilovkoi v Oplate Truda Rabotnikov Sviazi* (Moscow, 1933), pp. 56 ff.; V. I. Val'kov, *Perestroika Zarplaty v Lesopil'nom Proizvodstve* (Moscow, 1935), pp. 11 ff.

[5] The constituents of wages which are labelled "supplements" here are referred to variously in Soviet writings as *raschetnye prirabotki, protsent nadbavki*, etc.

The extras were a separate category in the Soviet wage accounts, even though those paid to piece workers were included with the basic wage in calculating a worker's piece rate.

Such extras as these were grafted on the Soviet wage scales during the 'twenties largely through the independent actions of the different organs in the trade union and management hierarchy.[6] Together they came to form a sizeable constituent of a worker's wage, a phenomenon of no little concern to the Soviet authorities. In accord with a resolution adopted by the seventh trade union congress in December 1926, the total excess of actual over basic earnings was reduced substantially. This was accomplished in part by an appropriate adjustment of basic wage rates. In those plants in which the overall changes in the wage-scale system directed by the seventh congress had been accomplished by March 1928, the excess of actual over basic earnings at that date amounted to 40 per cent for piece workers and 15 per cent for time workers.[7] Complete liquidation of extras was one objective of the wage scale revision undertaken in 1931.[8] Supplements still were paid thereafter, however, at least to workers in the so-called "leading professions" — usually understood as occupations having a decisive role in the fulfillment of the plan.[9] The liquidation of

[6] By one union central committee at least the supplements were regarded as an appropriate corrective to the system of wage scales, which at the time was constructed in its entirety by the Central Council of Trade Unions (S. L. Rabinovich-Zakharin, *Zarabotnaia Plata po Sovetskomu Pravu*, Moscow, 1927, p. 71). Beginning in December 1926, the union central committees were able to participate in the construction of the wage scales themselves.

[7] *Professional'nye Soiuzy SSSR, 1926–28, Otchet VTSSPS k VIII S'ezdu . . .*, p. 331.

[8] Krivitskii, *op. cit.*, pp. 195, 196.

[9] See Primernyi Koldogovor na 1932 god . . . , *Trud*, January 6, 1932, quoted in Kiselev i Malkin, *op. cit.*, fourth edition, p. 161; Krivitskii, *op. cit.*, p. 195; also, for an example of the use of such supplements in a specific case, Postanovlenie NKLP, September 10, 1935, *B.F.Kh.Z.*, 1935, no. 36, pp. 34–35.

The "leading professions" are referred to by Krivitskii (*op. cit.*, p. 195) as the "leading 'deficit' groups of labor." But it is indicated that in practice the category is interpreted with sufficient discretion to embrace as many as 45 per cent of the workers of some plants and as few as 1 per cent in others.

special supplements to piece workers has been associated with the introduction of separate wage scales for time workers and piece workers.[10]

Piece Work. But the excess of actual over basic earnings of the Soviet worker has not been entirely an accounting fiction. One element in the excess, of special concern here, is that arising from the operation of the piece system itself.[11] Under Soviet piece work, as under capitalist piece work, output in excess of an established norm is rewarded by higher earnings. Recent wage-scale reforms in the U.S.S.R. have reduced not at all the size of this wage component.

Contrary to a popular view, piece work is not a recent innovation in Soviet wage administration. Instances of its use prior to April 1922 are recorded.[12] As early as March 1926, piece systems of one sort or another already were applied extensively in Soviet industry. Of the wage earners in large-scale industry, 58 per cent were remunerated at piece rates at that time. The number of piece workers was 84 per cent of the total in the rubber industry.[13] The scope of piece work, nevertheless, has since been extended. The number of working hours remunerated at piece rates in large scale industry, which was 59 per cent of total hours worked in December 1926,[14] had

[10] Krivitskii, *op. cit.*, p. 196; also, A. G. Titov, *op. cit.*, p. 59; and V. I. Val'kov, *op. cit.*, p. 13.

[11] To the extent that the supplements to earnings of auxiliary time workers depend on the degree to which the piece workers they serve exceed the production norms, these supplements, of course, are analogous to the extra earnings of piece workers arising from the same source, and are not to be dismissed as being only formally distinct from the basic rate.

[12] *Otchet Vserossiiskogo Tsentral'nogo Soveta Professional'nykh Soiuzov, c Maia 1921 g. po Aprel' 1922 g.* (Petrograd, 1922), p. 212.

[13] *Professional'nye Soiuzy SSSR, 1924–26, Otchet VTSSPS k VII S'ezdu Professional'nykh Soiuzov* (Moscow, 1926), p. 214. Here and in the following pages data on the coverage of piece work are understood to refer to the Russian category *rabochie*, which does not quite correspond in content with the category "wage earners" referred to elsewhere in the text.

[14] *Professional'nye Soiuzy SSSR, 1926–28, Otchet VTSSPS k VIII S'ezdu . . . ,* p. 323.

risen to 64 per cent by 1932, and was 72 per cent in 1937.[15]

Needless to say the apparent anomaly of a socialist state appropriating a wage system so often identified as an implement of capitalist exploitation has not escaped the notice of Soviet theoreticians. In the face of a still vocal opposition, the communist fraction of the Second All-Russian Congress of Trade Unions, convening in January 1919, took pains to resolve the paradox. The use of incentive wage systems of both the piece and premial type was defended at length at the Congress by Shmidt, in the name of the communist fraction:

> . . . all of our industry is nationalized, and in the regulation of wages as well as in the work of increasing the productivity of labor participate the very trade unions which themselves establish the necessary norm in accord with the food problem and with the general position of the country. But once they establish this norm,[16] once they control it, then all objection that such a system can be understood or interpreted as excessive exploitation of the workers or as a return to old forms of wage payment — as the establishment of a sweating system — without question fall to the ground.[17]

More recently, the existence of a six and seven-hour working day; the concern of the party, trade union, and management for the health of the laborer; and finally the fact that the gains from increased productivity are reaped by the working class rather than by capitalist exploiters — all have been cited by Soviet writers as circumstances attendant on the use of piece work in the Soviet Union which warrant its interpretation in altogether a different light from the use of piece work under capitalism.[18]

Significantly the piece system as first applied by the Soviets was subject to certain limitations. The General Law on Wages promulgated on June 17, 1920, by the Council of Commissars (over Lenin's signature) required that piece remuneration for

[15] E. L. Granovskii i B. L. Markus, editors, *Ekonomika Sotsialisticheskoi Promyshlennosti* (Moscow, 1940), p. 484.

[16] Shmidt does not specify the precise content of the "norm."

[17] *Vtoroi Vserossiiskoi S'ezd Professional'nykh Soiuzov, 16–25 Ianvaria 1919 goda, Stenog. Otchet* (Moscow, 1921), part I, p. 151.

[18] Krivitskii, *op. cit.*, pp. 199–200; A. G. Titov, *op. cit.*, pp. 62–63.

output in excess of the established norms should not in any case exceed 100 per cent of normal earnings (Art. 68). It was decreed also that actual earnings be not less than two-thirds of the remuneration paid for the fulfillment of the established norms.[19] The latter requirement was retained in the second Russian labor code promulgated in November 1922 (Art. 57). But the first requirement was omitted. The assurance of a minimum of two-thirds the normal rate of pay remained a provision of Soviet labor law until March 17, 1934, when it was decreed that only where the worker's output is unduly low through no fault of his own is he to receive a minimum of two-thirds of normal earnings.[20]

More notable than the removal of these limitations is a change that has occurred recently in the form of the piece system itself. In September 1931 was projected for the first time in the Soviet Union an extensive application of progressive piece work. The Supreme Economic Council and the Central Council of Trade Unions at that time jointly directed that all wage earners directly engaged in production in metallurgy shops and 20 per cent of the workers serving them be placed under a progressive piece system.[21] Progressive piece work was likewise ordered introduced among wage earners in a list of specified occupations in the coal industry. The degree to which this projected change in wage system was realized in practice is uncertain. It does not appear in any case that progressive piece work enjoyed for more than a brief interlude any wide application.[22] Since 1935, however, the scope of the new system has been extended substantially. The Stakhonovite movement to increase the productivity of labor, which was initiated in the latter part of the year, was doubtless a major stimulus.[23]

---

[19] Dekret SNK, June 17, 1920, *S.U.R.*, 1920, no. 61–62, section 276, pp. 285 ff.

[20] Postanovlenie TSIK i SNK SSSR, March 17, 1934, *S.Z.R. SSSR*, 1934, part I, no. 15, section 109, p. 208.

[21] Postanovlenie Plenuma VSNKHA SSSR i VTSSPS, September 20, 1931, *Za Industrializatsiiu*, September 22, 1931.

[22] V. Zasetskii, *Progressivnaia Sdel'shchina* (Moscow, 1936), pp. 5–6.

[23] Data available on the scope of the progressive piece system are more recent

Piece work, as Soviet writers imply, may well be accorded a more cordial reception by Soviet workers than by capitalist workers. So far as the determination of wages is concerned, however, the results are the same. The earnings of workers in the same occupation are proportional to their productivity. There is good reason to believe that, as in a capitalist economy, the use of progressive piece rates in the Soviet Union merely represents an attempt to reckon with overhead cost economies as well as physical productivity in determining wages. Extensive use of a piece system, more than any other aspect of Soviet wage administration, evidences the prevalence of capitalist wage principles in the U.S.S.R.

Premiums. Scarcely less significant in this respect is a remaining element in the excess of the Soviet worker's actual over basic earnings. The extent to which premium systems were applied in the Soviet Union in the early post-revolutionary years is not known to this writer. The General Law on Wages of June 17, 1920, however, authorized the management of operating enterprises and of institutions to introduce premium systems as well as piece work in their establishments whenever they found this "expedient" (Art. 53). All forms of additions to earnings were limited by law to 200 per cent of the basic wage rate (Art. 78). The various funds for the payment of premiums which were established in the Soviet Union beginning in 1927 have already been referred to.[24] But it should be observed that it was not until August 1931 that the establishment of a fund for the payment of individual premiums for distinguished attainments by workers in general, and not

---

than the boundary date of our investigation. According to a sample study, 32 per cent of the wage earners of large-scale industry on January 1, 1938, were remunerated at progressive piece rates, while 43 per cent were paid at proportional piece rates. Of all piece workers — 75 per cent of the total number of workers — 30 per cent were engaged in brigade or other collective piece work and 70 per cent were paid in accordance with their individual product. *Ekonomika Sotsialistickeskoi Promyshlennosti*, p. 484.

[24] Above, Chapter XI, section 2.

merely one for the rewarding of inventors or for the payment of bonuses to administrative personnel, was mandatory for all state enterprises. More recently, by decree of April 1936, the sum of 4 per cent of the planned profits and 50 per cent of the unplanned profits realized through its own actions by a state enterprise engaged in production is set aside for the improvement of working and living conditions and for the payment of premiums other than for inventions, technical improvements, and rationalization proposals. Achievements in the latter sphere still are rewarded from a separate fund.

The specific attainments for which premiums should be paid the Soviet worker has been a subject of legal pronouncement at various times, but with no essential variation. For workers engaged directly in production a decree promulgated by the Council of Commissars on October 13, 1929, perhaps, lists the meritorious achievements in as great detail as is done elsewhere. Special attainments in the following spheres are noted as meriting premiums:

Economy of fuel, raw materials and [other] materials; . . . reduction in cost of finished products as well as of semi-finished products . . . ; increase in output, improvement in quality; improvement in safety and sanitary techniques; . . . other technical and economic improvements.[25]

The same decree declared that in the application of the premium system the establishment of exact norms of work was obligatory.

3

Minimum Wages. The minimum-wage scales which were promulgated periodically in the Soviet Union in the first decade after the Revolution are without practical import for the determination of relative wages during the years concentrated on in the present investigation. Their application for a lengthy period, however, is reason enough for studying them here.

---

[25] Postanovlenie SNK SSSR, October 13, 1929, *S.Z.R. SSSR*, 1929, Part I, no. 66, section 620, p. 1280.

They are, furthermore, an illuminating precedent for recent Soviet legislation boosting the earnings of low-paid workers.

The principle that no wage should be lower than a minimum fixed by proper government authority is introduced in both the 1918 and 1922 labor codes of the R.S.F.S.R. Minimum wages were established, however, beginning in January 1918, and a regional scale of minima was published for the first time in September of the same year.[26] The early minimum wage scales were differentiated also on other accounts, but from March 1923 only the regional differentials were retained.[27] These differentials avowedly were determined not only from a consideration of local differences in living costs, but also of the industrial importance of different regions, as well as of differences in climatic conditions.[28] Until 1926 the scale of minimum wages was revised periodically — for a time as often as once a month — apparently in accord with changes in the cost of living.[29] The scale promulgated for the quarter-year beginning in October 1925, however, was extended to succeeding intervals without revision, except for an occasional re-shuffling of the localities in different regional categories. Five regional categories are distinguished in the scale, with the minimum wage varying from 7 rubles a month in Region V to 10 rubles a month in Region I.[30] Moscow and Leningrad, as of October 1925, were classified in Region I. The October 1925 scale, like nearly all others, was promulgated by the Commissariat of Labor.

The *raison d'être* of minimum-wage legislation in a community such as the Soviet Union is by no means patent. Pre-

[26] Dekret VTSIK, September 22, 1918, *S.U.R.*, 1918, no. 69, section 747, p. 848.

[27] The first scale, published in January 1918, incorporated differential minima for adult males, adult females, and youths of both sexes. For some time prior to March 1923, the minimum was differentiated in accord with a worker's supply category. See Rabinovich-Zakharin, *op. cit.*, pp. 35, 45.

[28] *Ibid.*, p. 45; also I. S. Voitinskii, editor, *Azbuka Sovetskogo Trudovo Prava*, fifth edition (Moscow, 1929), p. 116.

[29] Rabinovich-Zakharin, *op. cit.*, pp. 44, 45.

[30] Postanovlenie NKT SSSR, October 29, 1925, *Izvestiia NKT SSSR*, 1925, no. 45, pp. 6 ff. See also Voitinskii, *op. cit.*, pp. 115, 116.

sumably, the fact that even after widespread nationalization there were numerous workers — those in handicraft industry, for example — who were not reached by other regulation was one consideration prompting enactment of the legislation.[31] It is also relevant, perhaps, that Soviet wages are and have been administered not, as might be supposed, by one central authority, but by numerous agencies with varying degrees of autonomy.[32] A minimum wage obligatory on all is thus not without point.

The effect of the Soviet minimum-wage legislation on the earnings of workers whose wages were not otherwise regulated, in any case, should have been much the same as that of the like legislation of a capitalist economy. Since such workers might have been exploited in the U.S.S.R. no less than in a capitalist economy, the fixing of a minimum wage may well have resulted in their earnings being more rather than less proximate to their productivity. Of primary concern here, however, are the workers who were embraced by the Soviet wage-scale system. If the minimum wage legislation had any point at all with respect to these workers, it is easy but not very illuminating to conclude that in some industries the general level of wages should have been higher, or wage differentials less, or both, because of the minimum-wage legislation. Whether in consequence there was a departure from capitalist wage principles the reader is free to conjecture.

For at least the workers in large-scale industry, however, it is clear that such effects could have been significant only in the early post-revolutionary years. The average earnings of workers in industries covered by the March 1928 wage investigation [33] were 76.45 rubles in that month, or 9.2 times the average minimum wage of 8.3 rubles effective at the time. Only 5.6 per cent of the workers studied earned less than 30 rubles in March 1928. This number doubtless included many who

[31] Compare the remarks of Rabinovich-Zakharin (*op. cit.*, pp. 49 ff.) on the significance of the minimum-wage scales as of 1927.

[32] See below, section 4.

[33] Workers in the industries listed in Table 7, p. 101, are referred to.

worked less than the full-time month to which the minimum wage applied.[34]

The revision — the last one to occur — in the minimum-wage scales in October 1925 was substantial, the previous range of the scale being 4.50 to 6.50 rubles. Even for the period immediately following October 1925, however, the minimum wage is evaluated by a contemporary Soviet critic as "insufficient." [35] The evidence cited is that the average monthly earnings of an unskilled laborer (*chernorabochii*) in October 1925 amounted to about 30 rubles a month, and that the average earnings of a youth (*podrostok*) in the linen industry were 18.78 rubles in March 1926, while in other industries it was higher.

In September 1928 the existing minimum-wage scale was extended — subject to the execution of a contemplated reform in the minimum-wage system itself — "temporarily," "to the coming economic year." [36] There is no record that the scale was either extended thereafter, or abolished.[37] In June 1934, however, in association with an increase in the price of bread, a substantial boost in wages was granted low-paid workers. In the rubber industry, for example, piece workers were granted an increase in their basic rates varying from 18 per cent, for workers in the first, or lowest, category of the piece-wage scale, to 7 per cent for workers in the fourth category. The increases for time workers in corresponding categories of the time-wage scale varied from 20 to 9 per cent.[38] These increases were

---

[34] However, the excess earnings of piece workers due to the excess of their output above the output norms, and presumably premiums paid to all workers, were not taken into account in reckoning whether a worker's earnings exceeded the minimum.

[35] Rabinovich-Zakharin, *op. cit.*, pp. 50–51.

[36] Tsirkuliar NKT SSSR, September 13, 1928, *Izvestiia NKT SSSR*, 1928, no. 42, p. 645.

[37] Writing in 1936, Z. Grishin (*Sovetskoe Trudovoe Pravo*, Moscow, 1936, p. 186, n. 49) refers to the minimum-wage scales promulgated on December 5, 1927, as being without "practical significance." It is implied, thus, that they were still *formally* in effect.

[38] Postanovlenie NKTP i VTSSPS, May 29, 1934, *B.F.Kh.Z.*, 1934, no. 16–17, pp. 73 ff. See also the other directives in the same number, pp. 70 ff., and in

granted low-paid "ordinary laborers" (*rabochie*), but the earnings of other low-paid workers also were boosted. Though it was more than offset by other factors, the June 1934 boost in the pay of low-paid workers was doubtless one of the more important forces affecting the inequality of earnings between March 1928 and October 1934.

Prior to November 1923, Soviet earnings were subject to maximum as well as minimum wage legislation. In June 1923 the prevailing maximum wage for workers in all state enterprises and institutions, depending on the region of employment, was 6,000 to 7,200 rubles a month — in the inflated currency of the time.[39] These limits are to be compared with the minimum rates of 110 to 180 rubles which were promulgated for the same month.[40]

4

Occupational Rates (Dolzhnostnye Oklady); Personal Rates (Personal'nye Oklady). While wage scales, such as have been described as prevailing in March 1928, continue to be used in the fixing of wages in Soviet industry, salaries are now determined more directly. Scales of relative basic rates for salaried workers have been replaced since 1931 by lists of absolute basic rates, specified for particular occupations. Such lists of "occupational rates" (*dolzhnostnye oklady*)[41] are formally the same as those which since 1925 have been published for the employees of government institutions.[42]

---

ensuing numbers. The overall increase in pay was ordered initially in a joint decree of the Council of Commissars and the Central Committee of the Communist Party of May 27, 1934.

[39] Postanovlenie NKT SSSR, June 2, 1923, *Izvestiia NKT SSSR*, 1923, no. 20, p. 7. For the decree abolishing the maximum scale, see Postanovlenie STO SSSR, November 2, 1923, *Izvestiia NKT SSSR*, 1923, no. 11/35, pp. 3-4.

[40] Postanovlenie NKT SSSR, June 2, 1923, *Izvestiia NKT SSSR*, 1923, no. 20, pp. 6-7.

[41] The translation *occupational rates* is at best an awkward one, but no better occurs to me.

[42] The system used in the U.S.S.R. to determine the wages of employees of state institutions, and quite recently, of certain salaried workers in industry, is

The occupational rates published from 1931 for salaried workers, furthermore, usually have set limits rather than specific rates for particular occupations. On occasion, at least, the setting of specific rates for different workers within the stated limits has been left to the management of the individual enterprise. In one of two salary lists — perhaps the earliest of the revised type — published in September 1931, that for supervisory and technical personnel in metallurgy, for example, the monthly earnings of shop superintendents were fixed at 450 to 650 rubles; of foremen, at 250 to 350 rubles; and so on.[43] Plant managers were instructed to determine the salaries of individual workers within these limits from a consideration of each worker's qualifications and experience, and record of continuous service. The other salary list related to workers in coal mining. Here it was declared that salaries *exceeding* the limits established in the list of occupational rates might be paid "specially qualified" specialists and technicians, on agreement between the pit superintendent and the mine administration.

In so far as wage decrees of 1931 and more recent years direct or, as has been more often the case, permit the fixing of basic rates which vary with the qualifications of different salaried workers in the same occupation,[44] they must be regarded as supplementing earlier Soviet legislation expressly permitting the remuneration of individual workers at rates above those fixed in the wage and salary scales for persons in the same occupation. Such "personal rates" (*personal'nye oklady*) apparently were designed to be exceptional. As of March 1928 the various departments and administrative agencies of the central, republican, and local Soviet govern-

---

usually designated "government regulation" (*gosudarstvennoe normirovanie*). This is distinguished from the so-called "collective agreement" system by which the wages of most industrial workers are determined (see below, section 5).

[43] Plenum VSNKH i VTSSPS, Postanovlenie, September 30, 1931, *Za Industrializatsiiu*, September 22, 1931. Absolute, rather than relative, basic rates were published for wage earners also in this decree.

[44] For recent decrees promulgating lists of occupational rates, see *B.F.Kh.Z.*, 1934, nos. 10–11, 13, 15; 1935, no. 36.

ments derived from a decree of November 2, 1923, authority either to fix personal rates for their employees and for employees of subordinate agencies, or, on their responsibility, to permit administration of subordinate agencies to exercise such authority.[45] Funds used for extra wage-scale payments, however, were subject to the sanction of one or another of the labor departments and organs — central, republican, and local — in the Soviet administrative hierarchy.[46] All personal rates in excess of 360 rubles a month required the approval of the Union Commissariat of Labor and had to be registered individually with the Commissariat. Periodic reports of agreements to pay personal rates of 360 rubles or less also were required.

Regulations concerning the payment of personal rates have been subject since March 1928 to occasional revision. By a as late as 1934, the administration of industrial enterprises decree of July 19, 1930, which it is believed was still in effect was given directly the authority to fix personal rates for administrative workers, engineers, and technical workers.[47] Such rates could not exceed by more than 30 per cent the maximum rate fixed in the salary scale for workers in the same occupation, and the number of workers so rewarded could not exceed 15 per cent of the total number paid under the salary scale.

The differentiation of the basic rates of workers in the same

---

[45] Postanovlenie STO, November 2, 1923, *S.U.R. RSFSR*, 1924, part I, no. 11, section 90, pp. 142–143; quoted in Danilova, *op. cit.*, I, 363. See also Instruktsiia NKT SSSR, December 6, 1923, *Izvestiia NKT SSSR*, 1923, no. 13; quoted *ibid.*, p. 364. The decree of November 2, 1923, also abolished the maximum wage.

[46] Postanovlenie NKT SSSR, July 5, 1927, *Izvestiia NKT SSSR*, 1927, no. 30, p. 435. This decree did not apply to those workers — mainly employees of state institutions — whose wages were determined by the so-called system of "state regulation" (*gosudarstvennoe normirovanie*).

[47] Postanovlenie NKT SSSR, July 19, 1930, *Izvestiia NKT SSSR*, 1930, no. 22; quoted in Kiselev i Malkin, *op. cit.*, fourth edition (Moscow, 1932), p. 66.

This law, more accurately, applied to all workers, in both industrial enterprises and government institutions, whose salaries were determined from a salary scale, — as distinct from workers whose salaries were determined under the system of "state regulation" referred to on p. 166, n. 42, above.

occupation, whether through the payment of personal rates, legally so called, or through the variation of individual basic rates within limits fixed in a published salary list, is one further evidence that the Soviet wage system is oriented in the interests of production. The possibility that Soviet administrators succumb occasionally to petty favoritism in fixing such personal or other individual rates is not to be excluded. But in view of the incentives provided in the U.S.S.R. for the realization of cost economies, it might be expected that, among workers in the same occupation at least, a closer correspondence than otherwise between a worker's contribution and his reward would generally be established. In this respect the effect is similar to that of the application of piece and premium systems. The use of personal and other individual basic rates, of course, directly affects the relation of earnings and productivity among workers in different occupations in the same way as it affects this relation among workers in the same occupation. Conceivably, however, the limited discretion of Soviet plant management in fixing basic rates might be exercised in a manner unfavorable to workers whose skills are specialized to one or a few plants. Under propitious circumstances bargaining as well as production might well be the concern of the Soviet manager seeking economy. In this event, interestingly enough, he should behave no differently from a monopolistic employer in the capitalist labor market. Workers at a bargaining disadvantage in the Soviet Union might be comforted only by reflection that their loss was the common gain.

5

Administrative Agencies. Our study of Soviet wage administration has proceeded so far with little reference to the organs exercising this function. The deficiency may be repaired in good part if we complete a sketch, for which a few strokes already have been provided, of the apparatus administering relative wages in the U.S.S.R. as it was in March 1928 and thereabouts.

At this time, it will be recalled, Soviet wage regulation encompassed the construction, for every industry, of four wage scales for as many categories of workers.[48] The maximum number of wage-rate classes and the maximum percentage difference in the basic wage rates of the highest and lowest class in each wage scale were established by the Central Council of Trade Unions. This council was an elected executive body administering trade union affairs between meetings of the congress of trade unions.[49] The congress itself had established in 1926 the main outlines of the classification of workers used in 1928, and had established also general directives for the construction of wage scales. The maximum number of wage-rate classes which the Central Council fixed and the maximum range of basic rates permitted for workers in a given group were the same for all industries, though exceptions in certain cases were permitted by the Central Council. The actual number of wage-rate classes and the relative basic wage rates for each class, within the limits set by the Central Council, were determined for each industry by the central committee of the union of workers in that industry. With the participation of the industrial administrators, the central committee also classified the different occupations in the industry into the various wage-rate classes. This classification was included, or cited as operative, in the collective agreements to regulate wages and conditions of work which were concluded between the union locals and the management of the corresponding industrial units. In some cases the detail of the classification of occupations was left to a local commission representing the plant management and the workers — the so-called Valuation and Conflict Commission (*Ractsenochno-Konfliktnaia Komissiia*). The plant management itself classified the workers employed in the given

---

[48] The four classes of workers were "ordinary laborers," apprentices, engineers and technical workers, and salaried workers other than engineers and technical workers. (See above, p. 154, n. 1.)

[49] A smaller body, the Presidium, in turn met more frequently than the Central Council.

plant into the different occupations. This was subject, however, to the limitation that complaints could be taken, by workers, to the mixed commission for arbitration.

Norms of work for piece workers, *circa* March 1928, were established in preliminary form by the factory management. They became effective either on being embodied in the collective agreement with the union local, or, if such were provided in the collective agreement, on being approved by the Valuation and Conflict Commission. General directives or norms of work apparently were issued jointly by the Central Council of Trade Unions and the Supreme Economic Council.[50] Premiums, to the extent that they were paid in 1928, were the sphere of the factory management, or, where the management itself was to be rewarded, of superior administrative organs. The broad objectives of the premiums, the size and source of the funds from which they were paid, and, in the case of bonuses to inventors, the scale of payment, were the subject of directives of the central government and of other superior organs and agencies. The agencies responsible for the establishment of "supplements" to basic wages,[51] minimum wages, and personal rates already have been noted.

While their sphere was not all-inclusive, it is evident that at the time considered the role of the trade union organizations in the determination of wages was a large one. Perhaps also it is a surprising one. But it should be remarked that the Soviet trade union organizations themselves are and for long have been controlled by the Communist Party. At the seventh trade union congress 72.5 per cent of the delegates were party members. M. P. Tomsky, the president of the central council of Trade Unions, shared with Stalin, Bukharin, Voroshilov, and

[50] See, for example, the Tsirkuliar VTSSPS i VSNKH SSSR, *Trud*, April 3, 1929, quoted in G. Melnichanskii, editor, *Sbornik Profrabotnika* (Moscow, 1930), p. 32.

[51] The writer has not unraveled in detail the different administrative participants in the determination of supplementary earnings. But it should be noted that certain of the supplements at least were fixed in the collective agreements concluded between the union local and the plant management.

Molotov membership in the party's powerful Political Bureau.

That the Soviet wage structure, nevertheless, was given a peculiarly trade-unionist orientation, and a deleterious one at that, has recently been charged by Soviet writers and officials. Whether such was the case is one of the questions which is examined in the following chapters. It is to be observed here, however, that the influence of Soviet trade unions on the wage structure could have resembled little that of trade unions in a capitalist economy. For the Soviet unions, in industry at least, were without exception industrial rather than craft unions. At the same time, absolute, as distinct from relative, wage rates were established by the unions and industrial administrators together — and within the limits of funds allocated, with the participation of the unions, by the government organs — rather than by the unions alone.

In the decade prior to March 1928, there were occasional changes in the organs responsible for particular aspects of Soviet wage regulation — the determination of work norms, for example — and there was some reshuffling of functions within the union hierarchy itself. In addition, certain wage categories (personal rates, "supplements") may not have been in existence during the entire period. The role of the trade unions in establishing wage scales, however, was substantially the same as that occupied by them in March 1928.[52] And so it continued to be in the three years subsequent to that date.

Since 1931, however, the position of the trade unions has significantly changed. In a speech delivered in June 1931, Stalin vigorously attacked trade union wage policy, and at the same time called for a large reconstruction in prevailing wage scales.[53] Stalin's speech was implemented immediately thereafter, without pause for the convening of the trade union congress. The congress, which had assembled for the eighth time

---

[52] Until 1921 the Soviet wage scales were subject to the confirmation of the Commissariat of Labor. It is questionable, however, whether this was of more than formal significance. (See below, p. 189.)

[53] See below, p. 178.

in December 1928, did not meet again until April 1932, when the new wage policy initiated by Stalin was approved without dissent.

Significantly, the decree of September 20, 1931, establishing new wage scales and new lists of occupational rates in the coal and metallurgy industries, was promulgated jointly by the Supreme Economic Council and the Central Council of Trade Unions, rather than by the latter organ alone. More recently directives on wage scales and occupational rate lists have been published variously. On occasion decrees have been issued, as was that of September 1931, jointly by a trade union organ and an organ or agency of the government, properly so called — the Central Council of Trade Unions and an industrial commissariat are a usual team.[54] But more often recent decrees on wage scales and occupational rate lists have been published by a government organ or agency alone — frequently by an industrial commissariat, and sometimes a superior organ.[55] In certain instances, as in the case of two decrees of the Commissariat for Light Industry of September 10, 1935, an order directing the revision of wage scales and occupational rate lists has been accompanied by explicit instructions to subordinate administrators to conclude with an appropriate trade union organ a collective agreement embodying the directed revisions.[56]

While the general drift of these changes is clear, it must be acknowledged that the precise role of the various agencies which since 1931 have become participants in wage-scale construction is by no means easy to delineate. While in certain cases the various commissariats are clearly acting in accord with the di-

---

[54] See, for example, the decrees of May 29, 1934, and after, boosting the earnings of low-paid workers (*B.F.Kh.Z.*, 1934, nos. 16–17, and ensuing numbers).

[55] See Prikaz NKTP, March 17, 1934, *B.F.Kh.Z.*, 1934, nos. 10–11, p. 353; Prikaz NKPS, 14, 1934, *B.F.Kh.Z.*, 1934, no. 13, p. 38; Postanovlenie NKLP, April 23, 1934, *B.F.Kh.Z.*, 1934, no. 21, p. 39; Rasporiazhenie NKTP, March 9, 1936, *B.F.Kh.Z.*, 1936, no. 11, p. 28; Postanovlenie STO, April 5, 1936, no. 164, *B.F.Kh.Z.*, 1936, no. 15, p. 34; the two decrees referred to in n. 56, below.

[56] Postanovleniia NKLP, September 10, 1935, *B.F.Kh.Z.*, 1935, no. 36, pp. 34 ff. These two decrees relate to the hemp-jute and linen industries.

rective of a superior organ (the Council of Commissars, or the Council of Labor and Defense), in other cases they are to all intents and purposes acting autonomously.[57]

Evidently there also has been a shift in authority recently with respect to norms of work. A revision in output norms in the coal industry, for example, was initiated in May 1933 by a joint decree of the Central Committee of the Communist Party and the Council of Commissars.[58] The decree obliged the Commissariat of Heavy Industry to carry out the revision, and at the same time defined the responsibility for this task of various subordinate administrators in the coal industry. The supervisor of a "section" (*uchastok*), it is worth noting, was given permission in the future to revise norms of work up to 10 per cent in accord with changes in work conditions. A similar decree was promulgated for transport workers by the same authority in July 1933.[59] Work norms established in accord with these decrees may well have been a subject of collective agreement, but it is doubtful in the circumstances that the approval of the trade union organs could have amounted to more than a formality.

Since the administrative changes that have been described were inaugurated in association with a new and clearly defined wage policy, their import for the Soviet wage structure cannot be assayed readily from the facts as to the change in the wage structure itself. That there should have been a reorientation of the wage structure on their account alone, however, is on the face of it at least not implausible. Whatever might be said as to the unionist outlook on relative wages, trade unions should be less concerned for the adequacy of the supply of skilled labor than the agencies employing such labor. Accordingly, the greater participation of the industrial commissariats in wage

---

[57] See the decrees referred to in n. 55, above.

[58] Postanovlenie SNK SSSR i TSK VKP(b), May 21, 1933, *S.Z.R. SSSR*, 1933, part I, no. 31, section 183, pp. 335 ff.

[59] Postanovlenie SNK SSSR i TSK VKP(b), July 8, 1933, *S.Z.R. SSSR*, 1933, part I, no. 41, section 242, pp. 462 ff.

regulation after 1931 should in itself have been a force for the widening of wage differentials. The fact that the commissariats on occasion acted in accord with explicit directives of superior government organs perhaps requires, however, that this conclusion be qualified.

The changes in Soviet wage administration which have occurred since 1931 have affected little the authority over wages of agencies concerned directly with production. The managements of factories and other enterprises at the operating level, as has been observed, now have greater discretion to determine the salaries of supervisory and technical workers. Their autonomy in the determination of output norms and in certain other spheres also has increased.[60] Accordingly the Soviet management, in fixing wages, is able more nearly than hitherto to emulate the monopolist employer in a capitalist labor market. But it is no less important to note that even so the management's discretion over relative wages still is decidedly limited. Wage scales and occupational rate lists, the framework of the wage structure, continue to be the spheres of other authorities. The scope and character of the piece and premium systems applied are the subject of detailed directives from above. The further reduction in the amount of "supplements" after 1931 may have resulted in a narrowing of the management's sphere, though what authorities were responsible for the supplements in the first place is not altogether clear. In its search for economy, the management of a Soviet enterprise doubtless is on the average more narrowly limited than its capitalist counterpart to productive as distinct from bargaining activities.

Conceivably, of course, the various commissariats might themselves give the Soviet wage structure a monopolistic imprint. Since each commissar administers a vast sector of the

[60] In a series of decrees, which may have counterparts elsewhere, the Commissariat for Light Industry in August 1931 gave the management of individual enterprises in a number of industries discretion to classify wage earners in a given occupation in either the next higher or next lower wage-scale class to that to which their occupation was assigned (Postanovleniia NKLP, August 27, 1935, August 31, 1935, *B.F.Kh.Z.*, 1935, no. 30, pp. 29 ff.).

Soviet economy,[61] his monopoly power in this respect is great. The size of the commissar's domain, however, doubtless also ensures that he will be much concerned with the supply of skilled labor. Further, the commissar would have to reckon that an unduly depressed wage for skilled labor might result in the wasteful use of such workers. In particular, more important uses for such workers in one firm might be sacrificed for less important uses in another.

[61] As of July 1934 the Commissariat for Heavy Industry employed 3.5 million, and the Commissariat for Light Industry employed 1.4 million of the 6.4 million workers in large-scale industry.

CHAPTER XIII

SOVIET EQUALITARIANISM: A CRITIQUE

MANY among those who seek and who have sought to reconstruct society hold that the inequality in income which exists in a capitalist economy is unjust. Capitalist differences in earnings even among wage earners, it has been urged, are inequitable. Concomitant with this view there prevails a belief and a hope that with the advent of a new society the injustice will be reduced, perhaps eliminated. It would not be surprising if these were the ideals, too, of the Russian revolutionaries, and of those who have administered the Soviet state. To broach this possibility is to suggest immediately an answer to a question which this investigation has raised. What motivated the reduction in the inequality of earnings in Russia between 1914 and 1928? Was this simply an expression of a desire for justice on the part of the early Soviet administrators? And, if so, how explain the increase in inequality which occurred after 1928? Was the just-wage policy discredited, and hence abandoned, after a decade of practice?

The motives of man are surely an elusive subject. But efforts to probe them, rightly enough, are not dissuaded on that account. The answers to the questions that have been raised have interest much beyond their present context. They reflect directly on the general and much-discussed problem of the relation between socialism and equalitarianism.

2

The problems that have been raised can best be approached by turning again to the address delivered by Stalin at the meeting of factory managers on June 23, 1931. Stalin was concerned in his speech not only with the position of Soviet engineers and technical personnel. He turned his attention also to the wage policy effective in the Soviet Union up to that time. His address clearly portended a new one.

The subject under immediate consideration was the cause of the high and increasing Soviet labor turnover:

> In what lies the reason for the flow of labor?
>
> In the incorrect wage scales, in the "left" equalitarianism [1] in the sphere of wages. In a number of establishments the wage rates are established in such a manner that the difference almost disappears between qualified labor and unqualified labor, between heavy labor and light labor. Equalitarianism leads to this, that the unqualified laborer is not interested in becoming a qualified laborer and is deprived thus of the prospect of advancement, in view of which he feels himself a "summer resident" in industry, working only temporarily in order to earn a little and then go away somewhere in another place to "seek his fortune." Equalitarianism leads to this, that the qualified worker is forced to move from plant to plant in order to find finally such a plant as values qualified labor in the proper manner. . . .
>
> In order to destroy this evil it is necessary to abolish equalitarianism and to destroy the old wage-scale system. In order to destroy this evil it is necessary to organize such a system of wage scales as will take into account the difference between qualified labor and unqualified labor, between heavy labor and light labor. . . . Marx and Lenin say that the difference between qualified and unqualified work will exist even under socialism, even after the destruction of classes, that only under communism must this difference disappear, that in view of this "wages" even under socialism must be paid according to work done,[2] and not according to need. But our equalitarians among the managers and trade unionists do not agree with this and suppose that this difference already has disappeared in our Soviet system. Who is right — Marx and Lenin or the equalitarians? [3]

Stalin's speech was the signal for a broad attack on equalitarianism and on equalitarians. In April of the following year a reconstituted congress of trade unions (the ninth) lost no time in echoing Stalin's words. A decisive liquidation of "petty-

---

[1] *Uravnilovka.*

[2] Literally, the Russian word *trud* should be translated as "labor" rather than as "work done."

[3] I. V. Stalin, *Voprosy Leninizma*, tenth edition (Moscow, 1934), pp. 451–452.

bourgeois equalitarianism" was called for by the congress.[4] By other Soviet writers the term was used in less pleasant association.[5]

Stalin's address was followed also by a widespread readjustment of the Soviet wage scales in the direction of a wider differential between the pay of skilled and unskilled labor. In metallurgy an increase from 1:2.8 to 1:3.7 in the ratio of the basic wage rates in the two extreme classes of the ordinary labor scale was decreed in September 1931.[6] The wage scales in use in the coal industry were revised by the same decree. In the following April the Central Council of Trade Unions was instructed by the ninth congress to complete the reconstruction of the wage scales in all branches of industry as well as in transport and in agriculture. The avowed purpose was to realize in fact

the socialist principle of remuneration according to the quantity and quality of work done (*truda*) and to stimulate the worker to improve his qualifications.[7]

The extent to which Soviet differentials were widened to effect the new wage policy is reflected in part in the changed values of the quartile ratios in Table 7 (p. 101) and Table 10 (p. 118).

Stalin's speech suggests an answer to the questions we have raised, but it also raises additional ones. How much did the reduction in wage differentials, accomplished prior to the time of Stalin's address, contribute to the admittedly high Soviet labor turnover? And was the supply of skilled labor affected? Stalin's indictment of the equalitarian wage policy certainly deserves close scrutiny. But first, what of the equalitarianism itself?

[4] *Deviatyi Vsesoiuznyi S'ezd Professional'nykh Soiuzov SSSR, Stenog. Otchet* (Moscow, 1933), p. 705.

[5] By at least one writer, in 1934, the terms were identified with "Trotskyism" and "right opportunism." Cf. *Voprosy Zarabotnoi Platy i Zadachi Profsoiuzov* (Moscow, 1934), p. 38.

[6] Postanovlenie Plenuma VSNKH i VTSSPS, September 20, 1931, *Za Industrializatsiiu*, September 22, 1931.

[7] *Deviatyi Vsesoiuznyi S'ezd Professional'nykh Soiuzov SSSR*, p. 705.

3

Stalin's attack, it is probable, referred primarily to the wage policy prevailing in the period immediately preceding his speech, and in particular to that formulated by the seventh congress of trade unions in December 1926. It will be profitable, however, to probe the earlier years as well. Since our interest is in the motivation of Soviet wage policy, it will suffice for the moment to concentrate on the activities of the seventh congress and on two earlier ones, the second and third. These together mark or approximate the turning points in Soviet policy on relative wages for the period between the revolution and Stalin's speech.

The second and third trade union congresses projected in skeleton form two sets of wage scales which were the earliest, but one, of the predecessors of the wage-scale system which has been described as operating in March 1928.[8] The relation of the early Soviet scales to practice was at best a tenuous one. The aftermath of revolution and the succession of civil war, famine, and economic collapse, which occupied the years in which they were constructed, were unfavorable to the realization of any wage policy. That the particular wage policies projected could have been realized under more favorable circumstances is questionable. But in any case it is not surprising that in the reports on the operation of the wage scales which were presented at the second and third trade union congresses departures from the scales were acknowledged to be general.[9]

---

[8] Reference is to wage scales of more than local or single-industry scope. There were also early — and highly interesting — wage scales applying to a single industry. Examples are the one promulgated for railroad workers in December 1917, and that promulgated in January 1918 for the metal workers of Petrograd and its environs (Dekret SNK, VTSSPS, NKPS, NKT, December 11, 1917, *S.U.R.*, 1917–18, no. 8 section 116, pp. 121 ff.; Postanovlenie (?) NKT, January 19, 1918, *S.U.R.*, 1917–18, no. 16 section 242, pp. 252 ff.).

[9] *Vtoroi Vserossiiskii S'ezd Professional'nykh Soiuzov, 16–25 Ianvaria 1919 goda, Stenog. Otchet* (Moscow, 1921), part I, p. 153; *Tretii Vserossiiskii S'ezd Professional'nykh Soiuzov, 6–13 Aprelia 1920 goda, Stenog. Otchet* (1921), part I,

The reporter for the Central Council of Trade Unions at the third congress, V. Shmidt, was put to much pain to demonstrate that, contrary to the assertion of certain unionists, a wage policy did exist.[10] As to the wage scales which the third congress in turn launched, the writer has been able to obtain no evidence that the skeleton itself ever was completed. What information there is is to the contrary.[11] But by the time of the third trade union congress efforts to regulate money wages in any case were of little import. Rationed goods, together with services distributed free of charge, by 1920 were almost the sole source of the wage earners' real income.[12] As we shall see, the early Soviet wage scales would have involved a considerable leveling of wage differentials. But the consequence of the rationing system employed was an equalization of real income far beyond that.[13]

The early wage scales clearly had a very limited success. But they do illuminate a wage policy which Soviet administrators at least attempted to apply. Even the abortive set of scales, which was adopted by the third trade union congress, marks a course from which later and more successful scales did not deviate.

The writer has been unable to obtain satisfactory information on the earliest set of Soviet wage scales. But it is believed

---

pp. 110 ff. Cf. also A. Goltsman, "Tarifnaia Rabota," *Vestnik Truda*, Oktiabr' 1920 g., pp. 35 ff.

[10] *Tretii Vserossiiskii S'ezd Professional'nykh Soiuzov*, part I, p. 110.

[11] A. Andreev ("Profsoiuzy za 4 Goda Proletarskoi Revoliutsii," *Vestnik Truda*, October–November 1921, g., p. 11) states that the resolution of the third congress that an overall range of basic rates of 1:8 (wage earners and salaried workers included) be established was not realized. I have come across references which imply also that the second set of scales continued in operation after the third congress.

[12] S. G. Strumilin, "Zarabotnaia Plata v Russkoi Promyshlennosti za 1913–1922 gg.," p. 108 (in the volume STO RSFSR, *Na Novykh Putiakh*, part III, Moscow, 1923).

Among the services distributed without charge were those of apartments, theaters, tramways. Payment ceased for rations, too, in Petrograd in 1920.

[13] The rations were distributed equally among wage earners within any one undertaking. There was discrimination as between enterprises and industries.

that the second set, which was projected by the second trade union congress in January 1919, will serve to indicate the first course taken by Soviet wage policy. It was resolved by the congress that for purposes of wage regulation all *wage earners* were to be classified into four industry groups and, within each industry group, into a twelve-class wage scale.[14] The different types of salaried workers were to be classified similarly, but for them there were to be two twelve-class scales, rather than one.[15] *Within each twelve-class scale the ratio of the basic wage rates of the two extreme classes was fixed by the congress as 1 to 1.75.* If the reader will turn again to Table 3, p. 69, the import of this figure will be apparent. The ratio of the lower to the upper extreme basic wage rate fixed by the congress, 57 per cent, is less than the quartile ratio in all but one of the industries studied in 1914. The result, if the wage scale had been realized, would have been a drastic reduction in the pre-war differentials.

The report in which the new wage scales were proposed to the second congress is regrettably brief. On the motives prompting the proposal there is only a concise statement, and this with reference to the change from the previous set of scales:

> It is impossible to forget that the kernel of the establishment is the laborer of average qualification, at work of average injuriousness and intensity. Chief attention must be turned on this, that this . . . kernel of laborers be paid more justly.[16]

Though it hardly can be doubted that the unionists were aware of the rough magnitude of the adjustment from the pre-revolutionary position which was involved in the application of the new scales, there is no appraisal of this aspect of

[14] *Vtoroi Vserossiiskii S'ezd Professional'nykh Soiuzov*, part I, pp. 153–154.

[15] One of the scales was to apply to the "highest technical, commercial, and administrative personnel," and the other to "average technical and administrative personnel," and to ordinary office workers.

[16] *Vtoroi Vserossiiskii S'ezd Professional'nykh Soiuzov*, part I, p. 152. See also p. 154. The Russian word translated as "justly" is *spravedlivo*.

the scales in the report to the congress. In the discussion which followed the presentation of the report, however, one unionist, in the course of a general criticism, affirmed that the leveling of wages already "presses on the qualified class of the proletariat, for whom the decreed wages are lower than they ought to be." [17] This unionist spoke for the unattached members of the congress. The report itself was submitted by V. Shmidt, a member of the Central Council, in the name of the communist fraction of the congress.

The wage scales projected by the third trade union congress in April 1920, like those constructed by the second, would have involved a leveling of the pre-war differentials. But the extent of the leveling was less, and accordingly the scales mark a turn in Soviet wage policy. It was resolved by the third congress that an eight-class scale be established for wage earners, and that the ratio of the basic wage rates of the extreme classes be 1:2.[18] With the approval of the Central Council of Trade Unions, up to a twelve-class scale was to be permitted in exceptional industries, and the ratio of extremes in these industries could be as high as 1:2.8. The report proposing the new scales again was submitted by Shmidt in the name of the communist fraction. Among the considerations prompting the change from the scales established by the second congress, according to Shmidt, was the desire to include in the scales certain categories of workers, "specialists," who had been excepted from the old scales and had been paid special rates.[19] Whether wage earners were among those classed as "specialists," and thus whether this consideration led to the broadening of the differentials within the wage earners' scale alone,

---

[17] *Ibid.*, p. 157.

[18] *Tretii Vserossiiskii S'ezd Professional'nykh Soiuzov*, part I, p. 114.

[19] *Tretii Vserossiiskii S'ezd Professional'nykh Soiuzov*, part I, p. 112. The *overall* ratio that was proposed in the new scales — from the first class in the wage earners' scale to the last in the administrators' scale — was 1:8. How this compared with the previous overall ratio I do not know. The latter ratio was not fixed by the second congress, but apparently was left to the trade union executive organs.

Shmidt does not say. But the extra-scale payments to which he referred were important enough to be described later by one unionist as taking on the dimensions of an avalanche after January 1919.[20] On the changes in the wage earners' scale, a general statement, which Shmidt proposed in the form of a resolution as a guide to the construction of the new scales, is more clearly relevant. It was proposed that

the change in the construction of the wage scales have the aim of attracting into industry a qualified working force.[21]

The importance of this consideration for the change in wage scales was stated at greater length by another member of the Central Council of Trade Unions, Andreev, some months after the third congress had adjourned. In an article in the organ of the Central Council, Andreev affirms that the "huge insufficiency in the qualified working force" is one of the two basic facts from which Soviet wage policy must depart. The other is the great scarcity of material resources. On account of the insufficiency of qualified workers, Andreev continues,

wage-scale policy . . . for the present moment, and apparently still for a very long time to come, must be a system of maneuvering, and not some sort of system of "justice." [22]

By "maneuvering" Andreev makes clear he means, among other things, that the greater the insufficiency of qualified labor, the more privileged must be the position of workers in the highest classes of the wage scales.[23] The view that the income of qualified workers was insufficient was expressed elsewhere. By one writer it was asserted that the old wage scales, where effective, had caused a flow of qualified labor from the factories, and a decline in Soviet industry.[24]

[20] A. Andreev, *Vestnik Truda*, October–November 1921, pp. 10–11.

[21] *Tretii Vserossiiskii S'ezd Professional'nykh Soiuzov*, part I, p. 112.

[22] A. Andreev, "Ocherednye Zadachi Soiuzov," *Vestnik Truda*, October 1920, p. 7.

[23] *Ibid.*, p. 8.

[24] V. Verzhbitskii, "Promyshlennost' i Tarify," *Vestnik Truda*, October 1920. p. 43.

The increase in wage differentials, which was initiated by the third congress in April 1920, was continued by its successors. In the important set of wage scales which was promulgated in complete form in 1922 all workers were classified in seventeen wage classes. Of these, wage earners occupied the first nine. The ratio of the basic wage rates of the extreme classes in the wage earners' division was fixed at 1:3.5.[25]

The 1922 wage scale had a longer life than any of its predecessors, remaining in effect through 1926. It is likely also that among the early scales it was approximated more closely in practice than any other. In the early recovery years, with the valuation and inclusion in wages of goods distributed to the workers *in natura,* and with the rapid diminution in the share thus distributed,[26] money wages soon regained significance. There remained, however, as a cause of departures from the wage scale, the supplements to earnings which were referred to in Chapter XII. These earnings had been grafted on the wage scale largely through the independent actions of the different administrative organs in the trade union and industrial hierarchy.[27] It was not until after the seventh congress assembled in December 1926 that a serious effort was made to reduce and control them. The effect of the supplements on

[25] In practice certain wage earners later were included in the tenth class (ratio 1:4.2), and in certain industries the ratio of extremes was slightly higher.

In a scale which preceded, and for a time coexisted with the 1922 scale, the ratio of extremes was midway between that of the latter and the ratio fixed by the third congress. Cf. *Otchet Vserossiiskogo Tsentral'nogo Soveta Professional' nykh Soiuzov, 5 Maia 1921 g. po Aprel' 1922 g.* (Petrograd, 1922), pp. 184, 185.

[26] The share of goods wages in total wages declined from more than two-thirds in the early part of 1922 to less than 10 per cent in the fourth quarter 1923. (A. G. Rashin, *Zarabotnaia Plata za Vosstanovitel'nyi Period Khoziaistva SSSR, 1922/23–1926/27 gg.,* Moscow, 1928, pp. 58, 59.) The use of ration cards was abandoned in the months following October 1921, but goods continued to be distributed directly to the workers — no longer necessarily in equal amounts.

[27] By one union central committee at least the supplementary earnings were regarded as an appropriate corrective to the system of wage scales, which at that time was constructed in its entirety by the central council of trade unions. (Cf. Rabinovich-Zakharin, *Zarabotnaia Plata po Sovetskomu Pravu,* Moscow, 1927, p. 71.)

relative earnings cannot be measured separately from that of other additions to basic rates, mainly piece work bonuses. It is significant, however, that where these elements in earnings did exhibit a consistent tendency they acted to increase the inequality of earnings beyond that which would have resulted from the operation of the wage scales alone. Among members of the metal workers' union in Leningrad, for example, the ratio of actual earnings of workers in the third and ninth categories in the wage scale (there were only an insignificant number of workers in the first two wage classes) in March 1926 was 1:2.87, while the ratio of basic wage rates was 1:2.33.[28]

4

By the time the seventh trade union congress convened, Soviet industry had virtually reattained its pre-war position. That this recovery should be associated with a change in wage policy was suggested by a contributor to the journal of the central trade union council some months before the meeting of the congress. The writer argued in particular that in the future a decline in the rate of increase of wages was to be expected, and that in consequence more attention should be turned to the distribution of the wage bill.[29]

To what extent this argument was influential in determining the action taken by the seventh congress with respect to wage differentials is uncertain. But a new course was set. The change in policy was proposed to the congress in a report by M. P. Tomsky, for the central council. Tomsky referred again to the probable decline in the tempo of growth of the wage bill. But this change was considered in relation to the problem of future adjustments in the general level of wages, rather than in the differentials.[30] On the reasons for the submission of his proposal on wage *differentials* at the particular time selected

[28] Rashin, *op. cit.*, pp. 51–53.

[29] P. Revzin, "K Probleme Regulirovaniia Zarplaty," *Vestnik Truda*, May 1926, p. 67.

[30] *Sed'moi S'ezd Professional'nykh Soiuzov SSSR, 6–18 Dekabria 1926 g., Stenog. Otchet* (Moscow, 1927), p. 50.

Tomsky did not dwell. Nevertheless, his report does illuminate the general considerations prompting the proposal:

The direction of our wage policy must be along the line of a leveling [31] of wages, on the one hand of the low-paid workers of separate industries and branches of the economy, and on the other hand, within the working class itself in the direction of a leveling of the increasingly incongruous gap between the wage of qualified labor and the wage of simple, unqualified labor. In truth, when foreigners travel here they are surprised most of all by the circumstance that under a dictatorship of the proletariat in our revolutionary unions . . . the difference between the pay of qualified and unqualified labor is of such a colossal magnitude as does not exist in western Europe. Of course this is explained by . . . the fact that we are too backward technically, that too large a role is still played by individual skill, handicraft practice, etc. . . . But the explanation is one thing, and elementary class justice is another. In the future we must reduce the gap in wages between qualified and ordinary labor.[32]

The foreigners' estimate of the extent of Soviet differentials which Tomsky cites and apparently accepts, there is no doubt, was an exaggeration.[33] This was true as well of the impression given by Stalin's speech in June 1931, though in the reverse direction. But the direction pointed out by Tomsky, like the reverse one later set by Stalin, was the one followed. At the close of the seventh congress his proposal to reduce the inequality of wages was embodied in a resolution and adopted by the assembly.[34] Thereafter a widespread revision of wage scales was undertaken under the supervision of the Central Council. At the same time, in accord with the directives of the congress, there was a revision in the form of the scales, in the administrative procedure of constructing them, and in the role of supplementary earnings. The result was the regulative system which was described in the previous chapter.

[31] *Vyravnivaniia.*

[32] *Sed'moi S'ezd Professional'nykh Soiuzov SSSR*, p. 51.

[33] Our later wage comparisons do not include a western European country of the period to which Tomsky referred. But they establish plausible limits for the magnitude of the discrepancy between differentials in such a country and in the U.S.S.R.

[34] *Sed'moi S'ezd Professional'nykh Soiuzov SSSR*, p. 735.

Because of the change in the form of the new wage scale, the ratio of the basic rates of the extreme classes in the new scale is not comparable with that of its predecessor.[35] It is possible, however, to determine the effect of the seventh congress' decision more directly. I have calculated, for three of the industries and industry groups which are studied in Table 3 (p. 69), quartile ratios of wage frequency distributions for March 1926, March 1928, and March 1930.[36] The statistics used were gathered in the annual March investigations of wages, which were conducted by the Central Bureau of Statistics of Labor.[37] The three industries considered are metal products, machinery, and equipment;[38] woolen and worsted goods; and leather and shoes. In all of them the quartile ratios increased from March 1926 to 1928. The increases were respectively 5.1, 5.2, and 4.2 per cent. From March 1928 to March 1930 there was an additional increase in the first two industries of 2.1 and 1.5 per cent respectively. In the third industry there was a decrease of 2.8 per cent. What further increase the ratios exhibit from 1928 to 1930, however, may have been due partly to the fact that certain apprentices are excluded from the wage earners for which there are statistics in March 1930, while they are included in March 1928.

Of the reduction in Soviet wage variation from 1914 to 1928, which is exhibited in Table 3, a considerable part, thus, oc-

---

[35] Apprentices, who were classified with other wage earners in the lower classes of the earlier scale, were given a separate wage scale in the new one. The ratio of extreme rates was fixed by the Central Council at 1:2.5. For other wage earners the ratio was fixed at 1:3. Under the administrative system adopted, the reader will recall, these ratios were maximum ratios.

[36] The leveling policy initiated by the seventh congress was confirmed as still operative by the eighth in December 1928 (*Vos'moi S'ezd Professional'nykh Soiuzov SSSR, 10–24 Dekabria 1928, Stenog. Otchet*, Moscow, 1929, pp. 521–522).

[37] In the present comparisons, as distinct from those of Chapter V, the statistics used relate to monthly earnings, and the third group of wage earners referred to in footnote 1, p. 154 is excluded. Also certain apprentices are excluded in all three years, and all apprentices are excluded in 1930.

[38] Ferrous metallurgy is included with full weight in all three years (compare Chapter V, p. 68).

curred between March 1926 and March 1928 in response to the wage policy initiated by the seventh congress of trade unions. Allowing for statistical factors, perhaps more than a half of the total change in the quartile ratios occurred in the two-year interval. The rest of the reduction in wage variation, accordingly, may be regarded as the residue of the wage leveling which was accomplished by the early trade union congresses, and which was not overcome by their successors and by changes in supplementary earnings.

5

In Chapter XII it was indicated that the seventh trade union congress was controlled by the members of the Communist Party, and it has been remarked that the wage scales adopted by the second and third congresses were proposed to them by the communist fraction. But the materials thus far presented leave in doubt a question which should be clarified before we proceed. Granting that the communist trade unionists controlled wage policy, were their actions autonomous, or were they in response to (say) general directives of the Communist Party *as such?* Stalin's attack on *unionist* equalitarians rather than on *communist* equalitarians would imply the former. Much beyond this, it has been asserted that the leveling initiated by the seventh trade union congress in December 1926 was in fact a *violation* of the established party line.[39] As an alternative to the implication of Stalin's attack, one might suspect at least an informal direction of the trade union communist fraction by non-unionist party officials. On such a relation, however, informatioin is not available, and it is necessary to turn to the formal directives of the party on wages.

The same problem that arises as to the relation of party policy to union wage policy arises in reference to the relation of the government to that policy. Until 1921 the Soviet wage scales were subject to the confirmation of the Commissariat of

[39] A. G. Titov, *Itogi Bor'by s Uravnilovkoi v Oplate Truda Rabotnikov Sviazi* (Moscow, 1933), p. 35.

Labor.[40] How much significance can be attached to this fact alone, however, it questionable. The executive personnel of the commissariat itself was nominated by the Central Council of Trade Unions, and the relation between the government department and the union organizations was close. It is not surprising, therefore, that before the abandonment of the practice, the commissariat's approval of the wage scales had become a formality.[41]

A concrete indication of early government — as distinct from unionist — policy on wages is provided, however, by the wage scale which the Council of Commissars itself established in June 1918 for employees of the state apparatus. The scale was promulgated over the signature of Lenin. It continued in operation until March 1919, when the task of fixing the salaries of government employees, except for those of the commissars and the highest administrative personnel, was taken over by the trade union organizations. *The salaries fixed by the scale ranged from that of the commissars themselves, which was fixed at 800 rubles a month (it was declared that there were to be no extras), to that of the lowest office worker, without previous experience, who was to receive 350 rubles a month.*[42] There was a provision that specialists, who were called to do special work, might be paid up to 1,200 rubles, with the approval of the respective commissariats.

The writer has found no specific declaration by either the government or the party which anticipated the leveling wage scales established by the second trade union congress in January 1919. But in the light of the scale for government em-

---

[40] At the third congress the task of completing the skeleton wage scale constructed by the congress was placed in the hands of an organ of the commissariat and of the central trade union council. At the second congress it was resolved that the Central Council should complete the scale and that it should be submitted to the Commissar of Labor for confirmation. The latter step was required by a law of July 1918 in any case.

[41] A. Andreev, *Vestnik Truda*, October–November 1921, p. 10.

[42] Postanovlenie (?) SNK, June 27, 1918, *S.U.R.*, 1917–18, no. 48, section 567, pp. 577 ff. Cf. also the earlier decree on salaries of the higher officials, Postanovlenie SNK, November 23, 1917, *S.U.R.* 1917–18, no. 3, section 46, p. 46.

ployees which has just been referred to *it would appear that the drastic equalization projected by the second congress was quite in accord with declared government policy on wages.* There is a qualification, however, that the equalizing scale for government employees may have been prompted by such a special consideration as (say) the desire to prevent the formation of a bureaucratic government caste.

The first statement of policy on relative wages by the Communist Party as such, which the writer has found, is in a party program which was drawn up by a commission established by the seventh congress of the party in March 1918. The program was adopted by the succeeding congress in March 1919. The subject under immediate consideration was the pay of specialists, but the statement is framed in more general terms.

Aspiring to equality in reward for every kind of labor and to full communism, the Soviet power cannot regard as its task the immediate realization of this equality in the given moment, when only the first steps in the transition from capitalism to communism are being taken. Therefore it is necessary still to preserve for a certain time the higher rewards of specialists in order that they can work not worse but better than before, and for the same purpose it is impossible to turn away from the system of premiums for the most successful and special organizing work.[43]

Some amplitude for interpretation is allowed by this declaration. But, following as it did the second trade union congress, it could be expected to call a halt to the further equalization of earnings, if not to anticipate and direct the policy reversal initiated at the third trade union congress in April 1920.

Without restriction to the earnings of specialists, the policy declaration in the party program was affirmed by a decree which was issued in September 1921 by the Council of Commissars. The decree was entitled "The Basic Law on the Wage-Scale Problem." The provision in it which concerns us declared simply that in the establishment of wage rates for wage

---

[43] *Vsesoiuznaia Kommunisticheskaia Partiia (b) v Rezoliutsiiakh ee S'ezdov i Konferentsii (1898–1926 gg.)*, third edition (Moscow, 1927), p. 229.

earners, as well as for office workers and administrative workers, "any thought of equalitarianism must be discarded." [44]

The only clear presage of the new turn in policy initiated by the *seventh* trade union congress in 1926 which has been found is in a resolution adopted by the fifteenth conference of the party. The conference assembled in October 1926, shortly before the meeting of the seventh congress.[45] The resolution is not meaty, but it indicates clearly that *the action of the seventh congress was not in the least a violation of the party line, but quite in accord with it*. The conference resolved to confirm a resolution on an increase in wages issued the previous September by the Central Committee of the party and the Council of Commissars, and at the same time to confirm a general directive

on the raising of the wages of the lowest-paid group of workers, and the wages of the low-paid branches [of industry] in general, as a first and important step in the direction of overcoming the clearly abnormal difference in the pay of different categories of workers.[46]

6

Declarations as to motives are not generally the most reliable explanations of behavior. Nevertheless it is believed the ma-

---

[44] Dekret SNK, September 10, 1921, *S.U.R.*, 1921, no. 67, section 513, pp. 628 ff.

A resolution on wage policy was adopted also by the tenth party congress (March 1921). It is ambiguous, but at the same time it discloses the possibility that the course between the eighth congress and the action of the Council of Commissars in September 1921 was not smooth. While the congress recognized that "the difference in pay between qualified and unqualified labor must be temporarily preserved," it declared nevertheless that "wage-scale policy must be constructed on the possibility of a greater equality between the basic wage rates. . . ."

[45] The party conference was a smaller body than the party congress, but ordinarily did not meet more frequently than the latter.

[46] *Vsesoiuznaia Kommunisticheskaia Partiia (b) v Rezoliutsiiakh* . . . , third edition, p. 667. See also the resolution of the thirteenth party conference of January 1924, p. 508.

Whether the directive referred to in the text was issued also by the party central committee and the Council of Commissars, and what its contents were, I have been unable to ascertain.

terials that have been presented — those containing explicit statements of motives as well as those bearing on them — when taken together with general information on socialist ideals, do explain the reduction in wage variation in the U. S. S. R. up to 1928 and immediately after. In particular it appears that the reduction in wage variation was largely the result of a considered policy to reduce inequality, and the consideration was that greater equality was just, or, more generally, that it was *per se* a socially desirable aim. To this extent Stalin's labeling of those responsible for wage policy as "equalitarians" clearly was appropriate.[47]

The fixing of sole responsibility on the trade unionists, however — and on the factory managers — appears a quite disingenuous maneuver on Stalin's part. The close connection between the union organizations, the party, and the government, and the parallelism exhibited by the policy declarations of the three organizations, leaves no doubt that each was responsible in some measure for the equalitarian wage policy.

It is apparent, finally, that Soviet equalitarian policy was applied with less persistence than is popularly supposed. Two cycles of equalitarianism and its opposite, rather than one, are revealed.

[47] The possibility suggests itself here that those who formulated wage policy responded not to the conviction of the social desirability of their activity, but to political pressure, the pressure being exerted by low-paid workers. On this possibility I am able only to refer again to the evidence in the text on the convictions of those responsible for policy, and on the *a priori* likelihood, testified to by the fluctuation in policy, that there were fairly wide limits within which the policy formulators could maneuver. Granting the possibilities of such maneuvering, however, would not deny that ordinarily, in any weighing of the desirability of an adjustment, the political support of the low-paid workers as well as their own convictions would be taken into account by the policy formulators.

CHAPTER XIV

SOVIET EQUALITARIANISM: A CRITIQUE
(Continued)

To LABEL a wage policy "equalitarian," however, does not discredit it. It would be tempting to suppose that those responsible for the formulation of Soviet wage policy, in their zeal to realize a greater equality of income, ignored completely the fact that income differentials are also incentives to work, to acquire skill, and to increase productivity. It would be tempting to suppose, too, that a shortage of skilled labor consequent upon the adoption of the equalitarian policy was the immediate reason for its abandonment. These views indeed are implied by Stalin's attack. If correct, they would offer truly striking evidence that the demands of production cannot long countenance a departure from the wage principles of demand and supply even in a socialist economy. The first hypothesis, however, is not supported by the available evidence, and the second, and very tempting one, must be bracketed with a question mark.

The fact that even the drastic equalization of wages projected by the second trade union congress in January 1919 was only a *partial* equalization might in itself betoken that those responsible for wage policy were aware that in some measure an incentive wage differential is necessary. The failure to equalize wages completely, however, might have been dictated also by a political rather than an economic consideration, to wit, an unwillingness to risk the consequences of a complete liquidation of the vested interests of workers who had already acquired their skills. The declaration in the program of the Communist Party, adopted in March 1919, that the differentials for specialists, and premiums as well, must be retained in order that the specialists will work "not worse, but better than before" patently connotes an awareness of the incentive role of differentials. But the declaration might be motivated, too, by a concern for the loyalty of the specialists and a fear of sabotage.

However, there is more conclusive evidence that those responsible for even the first leveling of wage differentials, far from ignoring the relation of wage incentives to the supply of skilled and arduous labor, and to productivity, attached a significant weight to this relation. The criteria for the determination of the wages for different kinds of work enumerated in the first Soviet labor code in December 1918 already have been referred to.[1] Significantly, the labor code contained, too, provision for the application of the piece system. Far from prohibiting its use, as an equalitarianism motivated *only* by justice surely would, the code stated in some detail the procedure by which piece rates were to be determined (Articles 63, 115 ff.). The piece system also was the subject of controversy at the second trade union congress in January 1919. This congress, which projected a decidedly equalitarian wage scale, none the less resolved that

the basic principle of regulating wages in connection with the struggle for the restoration of the economic forces of the country must be the responsibility of each worker for the productivity of his labor before his union, and of the latter before the all-inclusive organizations of the proletariat. For this purpose the wage law must be posited on a system of remuneration of labor which incites the . . . workers . . . to increase productivity in the nationalized plants, that is on a piece and premium system, constructed on the basis of fixed norms of production . . .

In those branches of industry where it is impossible to determine norms of output, a time system of remuneration must be applied, but with the exact regulation of working time and with firmly established disciplinary rules.[2]

The early Soviet equalitarianism, then, was hardly utopian. The wage administrators clearly were motivated by a desire to

[1] See above, p. 155.
[2] *Vtoroi Vserossiiskoi S'ezd Professional'nykh Soiuzov, 16–25 Ianvaria 1919 goda, Stenog. Otchet* (Moscow, 1921), part I, pp. 153–154.

attain a more just distribution. But it is equally clear that their interest in justice was tempered by a concern for the maintenance of production. The reasons given for the temporary abandonment of the policy of leveling differentials in April 1920 only makes the realism of the policy formulators the more apparent. The fact that Lenin himself had a hand in determining early wage policy (Stalin's speech to the contrary) should all the more preclude a misconception on this account. Whether Lenin and the trade unionists departed from Marx in practice the reader must judge for himself. But, be it noted, Marx's analysis was a roomy one. The passage of Marx, quoted in Chapter II, on the conditions for full communism, is referred to approvingly and elaborated at length by Lenin in his "State and the Revolution." This work was completed in 1917.

The wage policy initiated by the third trade union congress in April 1920 remained in effect until December 1926, when the sixth congress assembled. The wage scales applied in this interval incorporated distinctly greater differentials than had been included in the scales projected by the second congress in January 1919.[3] At the same time the piece system was more widely applied, and it was freed of a restriction which encumbered its use.[4] In December 1924, in a joint circular, the Supreme Economic Council, the Commissar of Labor, and the Central Council of Trade Unions called for the introduction of the unlimited piece system (presumably one still subject to a lower limit of two-thirds of basic earnings) wherever norms of output could be established.[5]

Despite the equalitarian principles which it espoused, the seventh trade union congress, under the leadership of Tomsky as the earlier ones had been, acquiesced at least tacitly in the continued application of the unlimited piece system.[6] The re-

---

[3] See above, Chapter XIII, section 3. [4] Above, p. 160.

[5] Tsirkuliar VSNKH SSSR, NKT SSSR, i VTSSPS, December 30, 1924, *Isvestiia NKT SSSR*, 1925, no. 2–3, pp. 9 ff.

[6] See *Rezoliutsii VII Vsesoiuznogo S'ezda Professional'nykh Soiuzov, 6–18 Dekabria 1926 goda* (Moscow, 1928), pp. 42 ff.

formist zeal of its successor, which assembled in December 1928, was limited in this sphere to a vague declaration as to the expediency of a transition to a system of collective premiums where there was a "considerable mechanization of the processes of production." [7]

2

The information just presented contributes incidentally to the illumination of a much misunderstood period in Soviet history. Reference is to the years immediately following the revolution, when a near equality in the distribution of real income was achieved in association with the rationed distribution of goods.

It is a popularly held view that this equalization was a previously planned step in the direction of communism, a step which, once adopted, it was hoped to maintain. This interpretation must be contrasted with another, concisely stated by Trotsky in 1922, that the equalization of real income was the measure of a "besieged fortress," rather than the measure of a socialist economy.[8] The latter view has been advanced by other Soviet writers.[9] It is implicit in the name which has been adopted since to designate the period: *War Communism.*

That there were aspects of the period of "War Communism" which could not be explained in terms of the emergency confronting the Soviet state is not implausible. Nor is it unlikely that some revolutionaries sanguinely regarded events as a part of a communist honeymoon. But with respect to the equalization of real income there are convincing grounds for accepting Trotsky's interpretation. Under the strenuous conditions prevailing, the Soviet wage scales and the declarations of the gov-

[7] *Vos'moi S'ezd Professional'nykh Soiuzov SSSR, Stenog. Otchet* (Moscow, 1928), p. 522.

[8] L. Trotskii, *Sochineniia* (Moscow, 1925), XII, 309. In a prefatory note, dated December 1922, Trotsky indicates that the published materials were worked up from a report to the fourth congress of the communist international.

[9] Cf. A. G. Titov, *Itogi Bor'by s Uravnilovkoi v Oplate Truda Rabotnikov Sviazi* (Moscow, 1933), p. 36.

ernment and the party on the subject of relative wages surely are a better indication of Soviet long-run policy on distribution than the real-income distribution resulting from rationing. Yet, while the trade union wage scales involved a reduction of the pre-war differentials, they never approached equality. By 1920, when "War Communism" still prevailed, the scales already were moving in the opposite direction. The 1918 wage scale for government employees likewise greatly reduced inequality, but it did not result in equality. The provisions of the government labor code and the declarations of the party program of 1919 clearly indicate that no immediate approach to a communist distribution according to needs was envisaged.

There is additional evidence, however, in the rationed distribution itself. At the ninth congress of the Communist Party, March–April 1920, it was resolved that the system of food supply must be organized in such a manner as to give preference to the industrious worker.[10] The third trade union congress, which assembled a few days later, amplified this resolution. The congress acknowledged that the system of supply had led to a destruction of the wage scales. At the same time it was proposed that incentive premiums, strictly dependent on results, but in the form of goods, should be established.[11] At the fourth congress, May 1921, it was reported by Shmidt, for the Central Council, that an effort to arrange a system of premiums *in natura* had been made, but had failed. Among the reasons given for the failure was that local organs of supply were forced to distribute a fund, which was established for the payment of premiums, as ordinary rations instead.[12]

---

[10] *Vsesoiuznaia Kommunisticheskaia Partiia (b) v Rezoliutsiiakh ee S'ezdov i Konferentsii (1898–1926 gg.)*, third edition (Moscow, 1927), p. 269.

[11] *Tretii Vserossiiskii S'ezd Professional'nykh Soiuzov, 6–13 Aprelia 1920 goda, Stenog. Otchet* (1921), part I, pp. 112 ff.

[12] *Chetvertyi Vserossiiskii S'ezd Professional'nykh Soiuzov 17–25 Maia 1921 g., Stenog. Otchet* (Moscow, 1922), p. 29.

3

Granting that the Soviet equalitarians were not utopian equalitarians, it remains to consider a question of major interest: Why was their policy abandoned? Granting that the equalitarians were concerned to maintain production, did their ardor lead them in any case to appraise incorrectly the labor market, so that a shortage in the supply of skilled labor resulted from the leveling of differentials? Or did the equalitarians, as realistic equalitarians well might do, merely reduce differentials in accord with a favorable change in the skilled labor supply? The explanation of the abandonment of equalitarianism, in this case, would have to be sought elsewhere.

In considering these questions little will be lost if the first policy reversal of 1920 is passed by and attention focused on the circumstances attending the reversal in wage policy initiated by Stalin in June 1931. The evidence, it should be acknowledged at the outset, is inconclusive.

Stalin's attack on the equalitarian wage policy was delivered in the third year of the period of the first five-year plan. By that time great strides in industrial development already had been taken, and great ones still were projected. The number of wage earners and salaried workers employed in all branches of the Soviet economy increased from 11.6 million in 1928 to 19.0 million in 1931. By 1934 the number of employees was 23.7 million. In view of the limited size of the industrial population at the start of the five-year program, the vast increment in the labor force must have been extracted largely from the Soviet peasantry. The statement of Molotov, in reference to these new workers, that most of them "had no previous knowledge of equipment, instruments, and machines" [13] is hardly surprising. Under the circumstances a shortage in the supply of skilled labor and trained technical personnel was all but inevitable, and references to the subject in Soviet writings

[13] M. Krivitskii, editor, *Trud v Pervoi Piatiletke* (Moscow, 1934), p. 91.

leave no doubt that it existed.[14] But to attribute this shortage in total or in large part to the equalitarian wage policy then in effect is patently unwarranted.

The effect of the lower wage differentials on the supply of skilled labor becomes the more obscure when it is recalled that during the years 1929–31 an increasingly comprehensive system of rationing was applied. Particularly in this period the rationing system resulted in an equalization of real incomes much beyond that projected by the wage scales. If the incentives to acquire skill were inadequate, the cause must be sought in the rationing system of distribution no less than in the equalitarian wage policy.

In his address of June 1931 Stalin attributes a shortage of trained labor to the equalitarian wage policy only by implication. The evil charged explicitly to the equalitarians is the unusually high labor turnover which prevailed during the first years of the five-year plan. But the turbulent events of the period, here too, must have left no large role for the reduced differentials to play. The efforts of the Soviet worker "to seek his fortune" in another shop surely require no further explanation than the recentness of his departure from the country and the "hard times" that prevailed.[15]

4

The major share of whatever shortage in skilled labor existed prior to 1931, clearly, must be attributed to the demands of the five-year plan, rather than to the wage leveling. But the possibility that the equalitarian policy contributed in some measure to the shortage is not to be dismissed. Such an effect could only be exhibited in a long run, but equalitarianism of a more or less intense character prevailed for more than a decade after the revolution. On the average the quartile ratios

[14] Cf. *Report of the State Planning Commission, Summary of the Fulfillment of the First Five Year Plan* (Moscow, 1933), pp. 228 ff.; M. M. Kritvitskii, editor, *Ekonomika Truda*, second edition (Moscow, 1934), pp. 266 ff.; S. Kheiman *K Voprosu o Proizvoditel'nosti Truda v SSSR* (Moscow, 1933), pp. 64 ff.

[15] The Soviet labor turnover is discussed above in Chapter XI, section 3.

of the earnings frequency distributions studied in Table 3 (p. 69) increased from 47.2 to 55.7 per cent in the period 1914 to 1928.

The effect of this equalization of earnings on the supply of skilled labor, needless to say, is not readily susceptible to measurement. It is not altogether fruitless to examine the opposite side of the shield, however, and to consider whether the reduction in wage differentials could have been warranted by a concomitant change in the conditions affecting the skilled labor supply. On the whole the evidence as to the changes in the more tangible factors affecting the supply of skilled labor up to 1928 is not very impressive. It is difficult to find support for the reduction in differentials without resort to changes in intangible factors affecting the labor supply, that is, in the non-pecuniary incentives. Thus, the possibility that the reduction of wage differentials contributed in some measure to a shortage of skilled labor would seem to be a real one.

(1) *Trade unions.* It might be suggested, as the basis for a reduction in wage differentials in the Soviet Union, as compared with those in pre-war Russia, that with the revolution the superior bargaining position of skilled workers in union organizations was eliminated. The force of this suggestion, however, is greatly weakened by two considerations. First, the pre-war union movement was young and sporadic, and accordingly the bargaining power of the unions was weak. Not until after the revolution of 1905 was the right of workers to organize recognized by imperial decree.[16] Thereafter the union movement flourished for a brief period, but, to a great extent, in the years of reaction following the second Duma, the unions were suppressed.[17] A second period of development began only

---

[16] Prior to the 1905 revolution, such permanent labor organizations as existed largely operated underground in response to local police action (cf. S. P. Turin, *From Peter the Great to Lenin*, London, 1935; A. Lozovsky, *The Trade Unions in Soviet Russia*, Moscow, 1920, pp. 4, 5).

[17] Cf. S. P. Turin, *op. cit.*, p. 117; Lozovsky, *op. cit.*, p. 9. Turin, a former member of the Moscow trades council, which was organized in 1905, declares that by 1910 the Russian trade union movement had nearly ceased to exist.

shortly before the war. The second consideration which is pertinent to the bargaining position of the skilled workers is that the skilled craft organization was not a predominant one in Russia. In the printing trades where it might be expected particularly that the craft organization would prevail, the general form of organization, to the contrary, was along productive lines, and the craft union was the exception.[18] Among metal workers also both craft and industrial organizations existed, and here too the industrial rather than the craft union appears to have been more important. Both forms of unions were organized among the Baku oil workers.

(2) *Education.* The number of students in secondary vocational schools in the U.S.S.R. increased fivefold from 1915 to 1928, but the initial number was only 48 thousand.[19] In primary and secondary schools, other than vocational schools, the number of pupils increased from 7.8 to 12.1 million. So far as the supply of skilled wage earners is concerned, the latter expansion in some measure may have facilitated the acquisition of specialized crafts. This was not the primary purpose of the general schools, however.[20] The number of students in universities and higher technical institutes increased from 125 thousand in 1915 to 160 thousand in 1928.

(3) *Real income.* It might be argued that lower differentials might have been warranted in the Soviet Union by an overall change in the significance of money wage differentials, associated with a change in the level of real income. The manner in which a change in real income might be expected

---

See also Komissiia po Izucheniiu Istorii Professional'nogo Dvizheniia v SSSR, *Professional'nye Soiuzy SSSR* (Moscow, 1927), pp. 84, 112–114, 218.

[18] Komissiia po Izucheniiu . . . , *op. cit.*, p. 216; see also, on other unions, pp. 83–85, 87, 109–112.

[19] These and the immediately following data on education are from TSUNKHU, *Sotsialisticheskoe Stroitel'stvo v SSSR* (Moscow, 1936), pp. 557 ff.

[20] As a part of the Soviet emphasis on an understanding of the role of the worker in the economy (I believe this is a permissible interpretation of the so-called polytechnical curriculum), several hours' instruction a week in workshops was part of the educational program in the general schools. This program was not operative on a large scale, however, until after 1930.

to affect the significance of money wage differentials requires explanation. But it is not necessary to pursue the subject here.[21] For the change in real wages in Russia over the fourteen-year period 1914 to 1928 appears to have been small. Using Soviet statistics on money wages and prices, Professor Prokopovich has calculated that real *wages* in 1928 were 11.0 per cent greater than in 1913.[22] Colin Clark estimates that real *income* declined 7.5 per cent in this period.[23]

5

Its vast scale makes the Soviet experiment in equalitarianism historically unique. But the experiment cannot be regarded as conclusive. Contrary to a popular view, the abandonment of equalitarianism in the U.S.S.R. did not finally discredit it. In failing to adapt wage policy to the needs of the five-year plan, the wisdom of the equalitarians is surely questionable. But the shortage of skilled labor that existed must be attributed primarily to the imposing demands of the plan, rather than to the reduced wage differentials. A shortage of skilled labor apparently also prevailed in 1920, when Soviet equalitarianism met its first reversal. But in view of the prostrate and disorganized state of the Soviet economy at the time, the contribution of even the drastic wage leveling to the shortage cannot be disentangled. The possibilities of equalitarianism in a period less turbulent than the years 1918–31 in Russia are yet to be probed.

It is of great significance that Soviet equalitarianism was not of the utopian variety. That the worker requires a pecu-

---

[21] In reckoning what percentage of increment in money wages, and hence in real wages, is required to attract a worker into a new occupation at a given time it is necessary to consider not only (1) the worker's initial real wage, but (2) the utility derived from the increment of real wages. With a rising (or falling) real wage level, a given percentage increment in real wages would correspond to a larger (smaller) absolute increment in real wages. But the utility of this increment might be less than (greater than) that of a smaller (larger) absolute increment at a lower (higher) level of real wages.

[22] Cf. his *Biulleten'*, 1937, no. 138, "Ob Urovne Real'noi Zarabotnoi Platy."

[23] *A Critique of Russian Statistics* (London, 1939).

niary incentive to acquire skill, to accept responsibility, to perform more arduous labor, and to increase his productivity, was an accepted principle of Soviet wage policy even in the period of War Communism. The equalitarian's appreciation of the magnitude of the incentive required may have been dim, particularly before 1920. But at least a sanguine appraisal of the conditions of supply set a lower limit to the reduction in differentials. If we may recur to the subject which was broached at the outset of this study, Soviet equalitarianism represented not an abandonment of capitalist wage principles, but at most a distorted application of them.

It is significant too that, whatever its origin, a shortage of skilled labor prompted the reversal of wage policy in 1920. Despite the phraseology of Stalin's criticism, such a shortage also must have been the major factor in the abandonment of equalitarianism in 1931. The application of the principles of supply and demand to Soviet wages here requires no qualification.

In the years since 1931 capitalist principles of relative wages have been fastened more firmly on the Soviet economy as new forms of piece work have been applied, and the scope of the piece system has been extended. To judge from the data on wage variation for 1934, however, the increase in wage differentials that has been realized on Stalin's initiative is far less spectacular than the vigor of his attack on the equalitarians would suggest. A greater number of workers doubtless have been induced to enhance their qualifications, and to increase their productivity in other respects. On this score alone, Stalin's reversal of the equalitarian wage policy is a readily defended expedient. But if the shortage of skilled labor has been substantially relieved, this is probably due more largely to the fact that the rate of expansion of Soviet industry already has receded from the astounding tempos to which the first five-year plan geared it.

6

In Chapter V the approximate stability in the relative position of the quartile ratios in the U.S.S.R. and in pre-war Russia was regarded as specially significant for the application of the productivity theory of wages to the Soviet Union. In the light of the Soviet system of regulating wages, and in particular the construction of wage scales for all industries within the same range of basic rates, it might be suggested, however, that this uniformity has no special significance. The invariance, according to such a view, might be regarded as merely an expression of administrative convenience. A general and uniform reduction in differentials was simply an easier one to achieve, through the Soviet system, than one discriminating between industries.

The writer would be the first to agree that administrative convenience played a role in Soviet wage policy. Further, from the administrative technique used, there might be expected a greater uniformity in the relative position of the quartile ratios than otherwise would be the case. But the view expressed must be rejected. Much probably could be said against it on general grounds. Furthermore, it does scant justice to the intricacies of the Soviet wage system. The stability in the relative position of the quartile ratios was an expression of a uniform change in basic and supplementary earnings together. To ascribe this change to administrative convenience would be difficult indeed. But there is a more conclusive objection. When the three-industry comparison of wage variation, which was made in section 4 of the preceding chapter, is carried back to the first year for which statistics were gathered by the Central Bureau of Labor Statistics, 1924, the changes are erratic rather than uniform. For two of the industries the quartile ratios moved in opposite directions from 1924 to 1926, each changing about 5 per cent; for the third industry, the ratio remained the same. Whether these movements were due to fluctuations in supplementary earnings or not is uncertain. The changes suggest that in respect to the relative position of the ratios, as well as in their general level, there were departures from capitalist wage principles. But, the support that the final return to the 1914 relations gives the principles is in consequence all the more impressive.

CONCLUSION

THE MAIN CONCLUSIONS of this investigation may be stated briefly as follows:

(1) *Inequality of wages.* The inequality of earnings among Soviet industrial wage earners in 1928 was distinctly less than that among Russian wage earners in 1914. By 1934 the inequality of earnings in the U.S.S.R. had increased, but, it seems clear, it still was less than that which characterized the pre-revolutionary period. The highest-paid 20 per cent of the industrial wage earners investigated, for example, received 44.0 per cent of the average *daily* wage bill in June 1914, and 36.1 per cent of the wage bill in March 1928. Among the wage earners whose *monthly* earnings were studied, the upper 20 per cent received 35.6 per cent of the wage bill for the month of March 1928 and 37.3 per cent of the wage bill for the month of October 1934. In the same interval a parallel but more marked change occurred in the inequality of distribution among wage earners and salaried workers together.

Data on the variation of wages among workers in individual industries reveal a general change in the same direction as that exhibited by the overall earnings distributions. In an industry-by-industry comparison, also, the inequality of wages among the bulk of wage earners is nearly the same in the Soviet Union in 1928 and in the United States in 1904. Scattered statistics suggest that Soviet and American wage variations are proximate in more recent periods.

(2) *Money wages and real wages.* The significance of the inequality of Soviet money earnings in 1928 and in 1934 was affected only in small measure by the progressive income taxes and rental rates. The Soviet rationing system, however, equalized markedly the distribution of real income relative to that of money income in 1934. The wage adjustment for the derationing of bread, grits, and flour in January 1935 probably

reduced the inequality of money earnings nearly to the 1928 level. But this change in turn has been offset by recent wage-scale revisions and by the extension in the use of the progressive piece system, which was associated with the spread of Stakhonovism after the latter part of 1935.

(3) *The chart of inequality.* The change in the inequality of earnings among Soviet industrial workers in the intervals between the dates on which attention has been focused was not smooth. The effectiveness of the early post-revolutionary wage scales is open to question, but the first sets of scales at least *projected* a sharp reduction in wage differentials. An opposite course was initiated in 1920, and wage differentials were not again revised downward until after December 1926. The latter course in turn was reversed in 1931, and an upward trend has been maintained since. Soviet wage differentials, thus, exhibit two complete cycles of variation, rather than, as is commonly supposed, only one.

(4) *The wage principles; equalitarianism.* The wage statistics and other materials that have been presented offer strong support for the hypothesis suggested early in the course of the investigation: that the principles of relative wages in the Soviet Union are also capitalist principles. This conclusion is evidenced, first, by a striking invariance observed in the comparisons of wage variation in the Soviet and capitalist economies. Reference is to the stability exhibited by the relative values of the quartile ratios of the earnings frequency distributions for different industries.[1] Of significance, too, is the close

---

[1] It has been suggested, however, that the statistical invariance observed in the comparisons of wage variation might be only the expression of the "historical survival" in the socialist economy of capitalist wage differentials and capitalist allocations of the working force — or alternatively that the Soviet authorities simply copied the wage scales and allocations of labor used in a capitalist economy. Thus, it is argued, nothing may be said as to the continued operation of capitalist wage *principles* in the Soviet economy.

But for the fact that this suggestion comes from a respectable source, the writer would hesitate to dwell on it here. But taking it at its face value, the overwhelming objection must be raised that it still remains to be explained why capitalist wage scales, in contrast with a multitude of other capitalist institu-

proximity of the general level of wage variation in different industries in the U.S.S.R. in 1928 and in the United States in 1904. Though this remarkable result was not to be anticipated, it is hardly to be dismissed as a coincidence. Support for the application of capitalist principles to Soviet wages is to be found, finally, in the administrative techniques used in the Soviet Union to determine relative wages. From the widespread use of the piece system, in particular, it may be concluded that, at least among industrial workers employed at the same stage in production, differences in earnings in the Soviet Union approximate differences in productivity.

But it is not to be passed by that the inequality of earnings in the U.S.S.R. in 1928 was distinctly less than in capitalist Russia. This reduction in inequality, it seems clear, was prompted by an equalitarian motive. Though the necessity for a wage incentive was appreciated even by those responsible for the early Soviet wage policy, the incentives allowed may well have been inadequate. Whether there was a departure from capitalist wage principles on this score it is not possible to say. Certainly, in view of the pressure of the Soviet five-year programs for industrial expansion, the abandonment of equalitarianism in 1931 is not difficult to explain on other grounds. But whether there was a departure from capitalist principles or no, the upward movement in differentials *after* 1931 is hardly evidence of the application of a peculiarly socialist wage policy. It is rather the response to be expected of wage differentials when skilled labor is scarce and capitalist wage principles prevail.

tions, should have survived the revolution at all. Further, capitalist differentials were not maintained intact in the Soviet Union, but in the early years fluctuated violently. The relative inequality of earnings in different industries, too, shifted much in this tumultuous period.

APPENDIX A

NOTES ON RATIONING

Note 1. The Wage Adjustments for the Derationing of Bread and Other Grain Products. The region for which wage adjustments are given in the appended table is in the third, ranked according to height of commercial prices, of the eight price areas established at the time of derationing. Among the first five areas, which include almost all industrial workers (the last three areas are composed mainly of far eastern and northern regions), the wage adjustments in it were at an approximately middle position.

AVERAGE EARNINGS IN OCTOBER 1934, RATION CLASSIFICATION, AND WAGE IN-
CREASES ORDERED TO ACCOMPANY THE DERATIONING OF BREAD, FLOUR, AND GRITS
FOR WAGE EARNERS IN SPECIFIED BRANCHES OF LARGE-SCALE INDUSTRY
IN THE MOSCOW OBLAST *

	(1) Average Earnings, Oct. 1934 (rubles)	(2) Ration List	(3) Wage Increase (rubles)
Basic chemical products	197		
War supplies		Special	22.0,23.7 †
Other branches		I	16.2,18.2 †
Ferrous metallurgy	193	I	16.2,18.2 †
Woolen textiles	144		
The most important establishments		I	21.0
Other establishments		II	17.5
Cotton textiles	133		
The most important establishments		I	21.0
Other establishments		II	17.5

* Sources: Col. 1 from TSUNKHU, *Zarabotnaia Plata Rabochikh Krupnoi Promyshlennosti v Oktrabre 1934 g.* (Moscow, 1935), pp. 288 ff.; Col. 2 from Zberzhkovskii, "Proidennyi Etap," *Sovetskaia Torgovlia*, November–December 1934, pp. 17, 18; Col. 3 from *B.F.Kh.Z.*, 1935, no. 1, pp. 36–39.
† The second figure in each pair in Col. 3 is the special adjustments for workers doing hot or injurious work. Zberzhkovskii does not indicate the precise nature of the "most important establishments" category of woolen and cotton textile establishments.

Note 2. Shortages and the Introduction of Rationing in 1928 and After. It is not possible to review all the circumstances that may have been relevant to the introduction of rationing; only the more important developments are indicated. The total grain harvest in the

U.S.S.R., after a recovery which by 1926 approached pre-war level, declined steadily thereafter — with one important respite in 1930 — through 1932, when it was 90 per cent of the 1926 level.[1] To a large extent this otherwise hardly serious drop in the harvest was made critical by the fact that during the same period the state was attempting an enormous expansion of the industrial machine. During the six-year period following 1926 the urban population of the U.S.S.R. increased over 50 per cent, and the total number of wage earners and salaried workers more than doubled. There were other aggravating factors. Since the reduced harvest was unaccompanied by a reduction in the agricultural population, it should be expected in any case that the excess of produce over the peasantry's own consumption would decline more sharply. But to this fact must be added a growing peasant hostility to the terms the government was offering in return for the surplus.[2] In response to these combined circumstances the state's grain collections (not the entire surplus) declined 5 per cent in the agricultural year following 1926/27, and then another 30 per cent in 1928/29.[3] In these years and in the ensuing ones the hostility of the peasantry increased as the government measures to solve the grain problem took on extraordinary forms culminating after the fall of 1929 with the expropriation of the kulaks and an intensive pressure for collectivization. Concise expression of the critical situation in the rural regions, and at the same time a further indication of the shortage of agricultural produce, is found in the livestock statistics. The total food and raw material producing livestock in the U.S.S.R. in 1928 was slightly above the 1913 levels. It declined thereafter through July 1933, when for different sorts the number was between 45 and 55 per cent of that of 1928.[4]

[1] TSUNKHU, *Sotsialisticheskoe Stroitel'stvo* (Moscow, 1936, pp. xxiv, xxv, 280, 336.

[2] V. Timoshenko, *Agricultural Russia and the Wheat Problem* (Stanford, 1932), pp. 451 ff.

[3] *Ibid.*, pp. 453, 454, 463. The grain collection statistics exclude a small amount of unplanned collections by state agencies.

[4] TSUNKHU, *op. cit.*, pp. xxiv, 354.

CERTAIN STATISTICAL CATEGORIES REFERRED TO, AND THEIR RUSSIAN EQUIVALENTS

1. The Classification of Workers

The category or categories in Russian and Soviet wage statistics which correspond to the two classes "wage earner" and "salaried worker" studied in the present investigation may be tabulated as follows:

	Russian Factory-Inspection Data June 1914	Central Bureau of Labor Stat. Data, March 1928	TSUNKHU Data, October 1934
1. Wage earners	1a. Rabochie	1a. Rabochie	1a. Rabochie
		b. Ucheniki	b. Ucheniki
		c. Mladshii Obsluzhiv-aiushchii Personal	c. Mladshii Obsluzhiv-aiushchii Personal
2. Salaried workers	......	2a. Sluzhashchie	2a. Sluzhashchie
			b. Inzhenerno-Technicheskie Rabotniki

A multiplication in the number of Soviet statistical categories in 1928 and again in 1934 is apparent. In the pre-war Russian statistics, the statistical category *rabochii* corresponds to the category "wage earner" in the present study. This usage of the word *rabochii* is still common in the Soviet Union, but in statistical practice two classes of wage earners have been segregated and data on these classes are presented separately in the March 1928 and October 1934 investigations. These classes are first, *ucheniki*, or apprentices, and second, the so-called MOP, which is comprised of janitors, watchmen, scrub-women, messengers, etc.

The Soviet statistical category corresponding to the category "salaried worker" in the March 1928 investigation is *sluzhashchii*. In the 1934 investigation this usage, too, was altered, and the salaried workers were classified in two groups. One is *inzhenerno-techni-*

cheskie rabotniki, which consists of engineers and various types of technical personnel, and supervisory and administrative workers in charge of productive operations. The other category goes by the same name as the two categories together in the 1928 investigation. Included in it in 1934 are the administrative and supervisory personnel in charge of supply, finance, personnel, accounting, as well as office clerks, bookkeepers and accountants, economists (certain of these are included in the first category of salaried workers), lawyers, *et al.*

The dividing line between the "wage earners" and "salaried workers," or the groups of workers corresponding to them in the Russian and Soviet statistics, is consistently at the level of "foremen." Foremen, except apparently for those whose supervisory function was a minor one, are classified in the category "salaried worker," or its equivalent.

In the 1928 and 1934 statistical investigation the equivalent or equivalents of the category "salaried worker" extend to and include the highest administrative personnel of the industrial establishment. The director of the factory, in 1934, was classified with engineers and technical personnel.

2. The Classification of Industrial Establishments

a. Factory-inspection establishments

The pre-war Russian factory inspectors collected wage statistics only incidentally to the performance of their especial task of supervising the application of the imperial factory law. The scope of the statistics corresponded to the scope of the factory inspection, and whether a particular establishment was covered by the statistics or not depended on whether or not the particular establishment was required to conform to the factory law.

The organic law itself established only very general principles for the guidance of those charged with its administration. The scale of the plant and the use of machinery were mentioned as the factors to be considered in determining whether a given shop was subject to the factory law and, hence, to the factory inspection. A more definite criterion was established in 1895, by the Minister of Finance in a circular to the organs of factory inspection. The employment of fifteen or more wage earners, or the use of steam engines or power machinery was declared a sufficient condition for the extension of the factory regulations to a particular establishment.[1] A former factory

[1] V. E. Den i B. I. Karpenko, editors, *Khoziaistvennaia Statistika SSSR* (1930), pp. 141–142.

inspector, Col. A. M. Platoff of Washington, D. C., however, informs me that these conditions were not final. The organs of factory inspection, and, subject to appeal, even the factory inspectors themselves, might exercise discretion in applying the factory law to particular establishments.

b. *Large-scale industry* (Krupnaia promyshlennost')

This category of Soviet statistics has been defined as follows:

"In large-scale industry are included all industrial establishments employing more than sixteen wage earners and using mechanical power, or employing more than thirty wage earners without mechanical power. The following are included in any case:

(1) Electric stations having a capacity of more than 15 kilowatts
(2) All brick factories having continuously active furnaces
(3) All glass factories with generator furnaces
(4) All printing shops employing more than 15 wage earners . . .
(5) All tanning shops having more than ten vats or three drumheads
(6) All grain mills with five or more milling units and all hulling mills with three or more units
(7) All establishments engaged in the production of liquor and spirits . . ." [2]

The general criteria used to distinguish large-scale industry were used prior to 1932 to delimit Soviet census industry. To this extent the two terms may be used interchangeably in the earlier period. However, the special criteria for particular industries listed above were established only in the course of time, and as late as 1932 the census establishments of the milling industry were distinguished by the employment of more than fifteen milling units rather than by the criteria that have been listed. [3]

[2] TSUNKHU, *Sotsialisticheskoe Stroitel'stvo v SSSR* (Moscow, 1936), p. 703.
[3] Cf. A. I. Rotshtein, *Problemy Promyshlennoi Statistiki* (Leningrad, 1936), pp. 69 ff.

APPENDIX C

ADDITIONAL NOTES TO TABLES IN THE TEXT

NOTES TO TABLES 3, 4, 5

1. Sources of the 1914 wage data and data on the numbers of male and female wage earners. TSU, *Trudy*, vol. VII, part 1, *Statisticheskii Sbornik za 1913–1917 gg.* (Moscow, 1921), pp. 124 ff.; the wage data in this source are taken from I. M. Koz'minykh-Lanin, *Zarabotki Fabrichno-Zavodskikh Rabochikh Rossii (Iiun' 1914 g. i Iiun' 1916 g.),* part 1, po. materialam obrabotannym v. B. M-ve Torg. i Prom. i v B. M-ve Truda, Izd. Moskovskogo Obl. Prodov. K- ta (Moscow, 1918).

A. Rashin, *Zarabotnaia Plata za Vosstanovitel'nyi Period Khoziaistva SSSR, 1922/23–1926/27 gg.* (Moscow, 1928); this is the source of the data on average earnings of male and female wage earners in June 1914.

2. Sources of the 1928 wage data and data on the numbers of male and female wage earners. Tsentral'nce Biuro Statistiki Truda, *Differentsiatsiia Zarabotnoi Platy v Fabrichno-Zavodskoi Promyshlennosti Soiuza SSSR za 1927 i 1928 gg.* (Moscow, 1929).

3. Supplementary information on the wage data. Ministerstvo Torgovli i Promyshlennosti, *Svod Otchetov Fabrichnykh Inspektorov za 1914 god* (Petrograd, 1915); A. Rashin, *op. cit.*

4. Estimates used. The all-under class (earnings of less than 50 kopeks) of the frequency distribution of wage earners in the woolen and worsted goods industry in June 1914 contains 36.2 per cent of the wage earners in the industry. To determine the position of the first quartile the tail end of the same distribution for June 1916 was used as a guide for interpolation within the all-under class. The same procedure was followed in the case of the linen goods industry, where 35.5 per cent of the wage earners fell in the all-under class. The interpolation procedure used was supported in both cases by the fact that the overall cumulative frequency distribution in each industry had the same shape (when plotted on a semi-log scale) in June 1916 as in June 1914.

In the case of certain of the June 1914 frequency distribution of wage earners in the metal products group the third quartile fell within class limits which differed by 100 kopeks, a relatively large interval.

A graphic interpolation was made in this case to check the results obtained by use of the usual interpolation formula. The check indicates that the 1914 quartile ration may be as much as 1.6 per cent greater than that calculated from the usual interpolation formula. In several other industries the third quartile was interpolated within 50 kopek earnings class. Here the quartile ratios are probably understated by less than 1 per cent.

In the case of a small group of workers, the so-called MOP, composed of janitors, watchmen, etc., monthly earnings distributions had to be used to estimate daily earnings distributions for March 1928. The crude procedure was used of dividing the class limits of the monthly earnings distributions by 25.5, and deducting an additional 5.5 per cent for items in the monthly earnings fund not included in the daily earnings fund.

5. *Weighting.* In combining the wage frequency distributions of different industries for 1928 to obtain distributions for industry groups comparable to those appearing in the 1914 statistics, the various frequency distributions were weighted according to the number of wage earners engaged in all large-scale establishments in the respective industries on March 1, 1928.

Notes to Table 6

1. Soviet 1928 wage data. These are from the same source as the data used in Tables 3, 4, 5.

2. Source of American wage data. Bureau of Census, *Special Reports of the Census Office, Manufactures 1905*, part iv (Washington, 1908).

3. Estimates. For certain of the Soviet apprentices, all of whom are included with wage earners in the present study, it was necessary to estimate monthly wage frequency distributions from average daily wage frequency distributions.

Notes to Table 7

1. 1928 data. These are from the same source as that used in Tables 3, 4, 5.

2. 1934 data. TSUNKHU, *Zarabotnaia Plata Rabochikh Krupnoi Promyshlennosti v Oktiabre 1934 g.* (Moscow, 1935); TSUNKHU, *Zarabotnaia Plata Inzhenerno-Tekhnicheskikh Rabotnikov, Sluzhashchikh i Uchenikov v Sentiabre-Oktiabre 1934 g.* (Moscow, 1936).

3. Estimates used. See Appendix C, note 3 to Table 6.

Notes to Table 8

1. The 1904 data. These are from the same source as was used in Table 6.

2. Other data. U. S. Bureau of Labor Statistics, Bulletins 533, 551, 539, 567.

62nd Congress, First Session, Senate Document 110, *Report on Conditions of Employment in the Iron and Steel Industry*, vol. I (Washington, 1911).

62nd Congress, Second Session, House of Representatives Document 643, *Report of the Tariff Board on Schedule I of the Tariff Law, Cotton Manufactures*, vol. II (Washington, 1912).

62nd Congress, Second Session, House of Representatives Document 342, *Report of the Tariff Board on Schedule K of the Tariff Law*, vol. II (Washington, 1912).

Note to Table 11

1. Calculation of the earnings distributions from the aggregate frequency distributions; estimates used. In general, in computing the earnings distributions from aggregate frequency distributions the usual procedure was followed of centering the frequency of each earnings class at the mid-point of the earnings class. The proportion of the earnings bill accruing to the workers in each earning class was computed on this assumption. This procedure could not be followed, however, in the case of all-over and all-under earnings classes (See Tables 7–10, Appendix D), and certain other departures from the customary procedure were made where it seemed reasonable to do so.

In all cases frequencies in all-under and all-over earnings classes were centered on the bases of a consideration of the entire shape of the earnings distribution. Since the March 1928 and October 1934 earnings data include data on average earnings, and thus on the total earnings bill in each period, it was necessary to estimate for these periods only the proportion of the earnings bill accruing to the workers in one extreme class, the proportion received by workers in the other extreme class being a residual.

In the case of each of the all-under classes it was possible also to establish a plausible range within which it appeared highly probable that the centering point of the frequency in the class would fall. On this basis likely limits for the error in each estimate were calculated. For example, in the case of the distribution of the wage bill for the month of March 1928, the calculated proportion of earnings accruing to the less than 30 rubles class was 1.64 per cent and the centering point used for this class in the calculation was 20 rubles. The limits within which it appeared that the centering point would in any case fall were 15 rubles and 25 rubles. If either one of these limits were the correct figure, the proportion of earnings accruing to workers in the all-under class would be altered by not more than .4 per cent. A likely limit of error was computed similarly for the estimated proportion of earnings accruing to the all-under class in each of the other earnings distributions for 1928 and 1934. The limit in each case was found to be less than .4 per cent, except for the 1928 daily wage distribution, where the error may have been as much as .8 per cent.

The frequency distribution used to compute the distribution of the daily wage bill in June 1914 consists of but eight earnings classes. Rather than center the frequencies at the mid-points of these large class intervals, a graphic interpolation from an ogive curve was used first to break down the frequency distribution into a larger number of classes.

In the case of the two 1928 monthly earnings distributions it was deemed wise to treat the earnings accruing to the workers in the two extreme 50-ruble classes (see Table 9, Appendix D) together with the earnings accruing to workers in the all-over class as a residual. This residual was then distributed among the workers in the three classes. The number of workers in all three classes together is less than 10 per cent of the total number of workers in each of the 1928 frequency distributions. On this score the manner in which the residual earnings are distributed among the three extreme earnings classes is a matter of indifference so far as the data in Table 11 are concerned.

It was found when such a distribution was attempted, however, that the adoption of even very low centering points, among those which were plausible, left the calculated March 1928 wage bill 3.1 per cent greater than it should have been; and the calculated March 1928 wage and salary bill, 1.9 per cent larger than it should have been. This discrepancy could not have been accounted for by a too high centering of the workers in the all-under earnings class. It indicates, accordingly, that some or all of the centering points used for calculating the earnings accruing to workers in the non-extreme earnings classes were too high. The discrepancy was rectified by a proportional adjustment in earnings accruing to the workers in all earnings classes. The adjustment, with some reason, could have been confined to classes above the mode of the frequency distribution. In this case the calculated inequality of distribution would have been less.

APPENDIX D

SUPPLEMENTARY TABLES

TABLE 1

COVERAGE OF THE INVESTIGATIONS OF DAILY WAGES USED IN CHAPTER V,
TABLE 3, BY SPECIFIED INDUSTRIES

(1) Industry	(2) MINISTRY OF TRADE STUDY, RUSSIA, JUNE 1914		(3) CENTRAL BUREAU OF LABOR STAT. STUDY, U.S.S.R., MARCH 1928	
	(a) Number of Wage Earners Studied, in Thousands	(b) In Per Cent of Number in Factory-Inspection Industry	(a) Number of Wage Earners Studied, in Thousands	(b) In Per Cent of Number in Large-Scale Industry
1. Cotton goods	425.9	87.7	159.1	30.3
2. Linen goods, hemp products	80.4	83.0	47.7	40.2
3. Saw mills, plywood, furniture and other wood products	39.4	37.0	20.8	19.8
4. Woolen and worsted goods	72.3	77.1	26.9	37.5
5. Metal products, machinery and equipment ..	190.0	54.8	245.1	35.4
6. Paper, printing	32.8	35.6	29.4	29.3
7. Leather, shoe	22.2	44.0	28.3	34.5
8. Rubber products, oil extraction and refining, chemical products, matches	61.1	53.1	84.6	65.5
All industries	924.1	66.6	641.9	35.2

Source of data on the number of wage earners in factory-inspection industry: Ministerstvo Torgovli i Promyshlennosti, *Svod Otchetov Fabrichnykh Inspektorov za 1914 god* (Petrograd, 1915).

Source of data on the number of wage earners in large-scale industry: "Sostav Fabrichno-Zavodskogo Personala . . . na 1-e Ianvaria 1928 g. po SSSR," *Statistika Truda*, 1928, no. 8, pp. 12 ff.; V. Sats, "Chislennost' i Sostav Rabochikh i Sluzhashhikh v Promyshlennosti SSSR na 1-e Ianvaria 1929 g.," *Statistika Truda*, 1929, no. 5–6, pp. 1 ff.

The data on the number of wage earners in factory-inspection industry used are the average number employed during the year in establishments subject to the inspection at the end of 1914. The data on the number of wage earners in large-scale industry used are, with minor qualifications, estimates as of March 1, 1928, these data being estimated from the data in the source referred to above.

Data on the number of wage earners in large-scale establishments in the different industries and industry groups include wage earners in a number of minor allied industries which were probably not covered by the 1928 wage study. This was done to make the coverage data more nearly comparable with that for 1914. These allied industries are included with the major branches in the industry classes studied in the 1914 wage investigation and in the factory inspection reports.

The metal products, etc., industry group in 1928 includes wage earners engaged in converting metals, and the finishing departments attached to them.

TABLE 2

AVERAGE DAILY WAGE OF WAGE EARNERS STUDIED IN THE MARCH 1928 WAGE
INVESTIGATION, AND OF WAGE EARNERS STUDIED IN THE MONTHLY REPORTS FOR
MARCH 1928, BY SPECIFIED INDUSTRIES (REFERRED TO IN CHAPTER V, P. 65)

(1) Industry	(2) Average Daily Wage, Central Bureau of Labor Stat. Study, March 1928 (*kopeks*)	(3) Average Daily Wage, Monthly Reports, March 1928 (*kopeks*)	(4) (2) as Per Cent of (3)
1. Cotton goods	245.9	240.3	102.3
2. Linen goods, hemp products	188.3	186.9	100.7
3. Saw mills, plywood, furniture and other wood products	249.7	258.3	96.7
4. Woolen and worsted goods	255.5	251.5	101.6
5. Metal products, machinery and equipment	358.1	332.6	107.7
6. Paper, printing	324.4	310.4	104.5
7. Leather, shoe	384.6	366.9	104.8
8. Rubber products, oil extraction and refining, chemical products, matches	305.3	321.9	94.8

Source of data in Col. 3: A. Rashin, "Zarabotnaia Plata v Krupnoi Promyshlennosti v I-m Polugodii 1927/28 g.," *Statistika Truda*, 1928, no. 5–6, pp. 9 ff., Table, pp. 14–15.
The wage earners for whom average wages are presented in the table do not include the so-called MOP group of wage earners, that is, janitors, watchmen, etc.
As distinct from the wage frequency distributions from which the quartile ratios in Table 3 were computed, the daily wages studied in Col. 2 include payments for overtime work as well as any payments made to cover the workers' rent, and certain other payments. Such payments, it is believed, are also included in the daily wages studied in Col. 3.
The monthly reports relate only to establishments employing 250 or more workers.

TABLE 3

COVERAGE OF THE WAGE INVESTIGATIONS USED IN CHAPTER VI, TABLE 6,
BY SPECIFIED INDUSTRIES

(1) Industry	(2) CENTRAL BUREAU OF LABOR STAT. STUDY, U.S.S.R., MONTHLY WAGES, MARCH 1928		(3) CENSUS OFFICE STUDY U.S., WEEKLY WAGES, ONE WEEK, 1904	
	(a) No. of Wage Earners Studied (*thousands*)	(b) In Per Cent of No. in Large-Scale Industry	(a) No. of Wage Earners Studied (*thousands*)	(b) In Per Cent of No. in Census Industry
1. Cotton goods	159.5	30.7	202.2	57.5
2. Matches	9.5	56.9	1.3	36.1
3. Woolen and worsted goods	26.8	37.7	89.7	55.9
4. Linen goods	42.5	44.7	1.7	42.5
5. Ferrous metallurgy	78.0	40.0	142.9	47.1
6. Electrical machinery, apparatus	16.0	53.3	36.9	47.1
7. Shoes	13.2	44.5	92.0	52.6
8. Rubber products	17.8	87.0	35.0	70.4
9. Glass	18.9	28.2	36.4	41.6
10. Brewing	4.1	33.4	28.4	65.3
11. Paper	11.3	35.4	38.3	50.7
12. Leather	15.1	44.8	40.3	58.8
All industries	412.9	36.8	745.1	53.2

Source of data on the number of wage earners in Soviet large-scale industry: *Statistika Truda*, 1928, no. 8, pp. 12 ff.; Sats, *Statistika Truda*, 1929, no. 5–6, pp. 1 ff.

Source of data on the number of wage earners in American census industry: Bureau of Census, *Special Reports of the Census Office, Manufacturers 1905*, part iv (Washington, 1908).

The data on the number of wage earners in Soviet large-scale industry used are estimates as of March 1, 1928, these data being estimated from the data in the source referred to above. The number of wage earners in American census industry is the sum for each industry of the greatest number employed in each establishment during the year.

The minor allied industries which were grouped with major branches of the Soviet industries studied in Appendix D, Table 1 are not included in the Soviet industries studied in the present table.

In Col. 2, data for ferrous metallurgy relate to the whole Soviet Union. Coarse woolen cloth production is included in the woolen and worsted goods group. Data for the American cotton goods industry in Col. 3 relate to the whole United States. In both Col. 2 and Col. 3 the glass industry includes sheet glass production as well as the production of glass ware.

TABLE 4

COVERAGE OF THE INVESTIGATIONS OF MONTHLY WAGES USED IN CHAPTER VII,
TABLE 7, BY SPECIFIED INDUSTRIES

(1) Industry	(2) CENTRAL BUREAU OF LABOR STAT. STUDY MARCH 1928		(3) TSUNKHU STUDY, OCTOBER 1934	
	(a) No. of Wage Earners Studied (*thousands*)	(b) In Per Cent of No. in Large-Scale Industry	(a) No. of Wage Earners Studied (*thousands*)	(b) In Per Cent of No. in Census Industry
1. Rubber products	17.8	87.0	16.6	31.0
2. Tobacco	18.1	69.5	8.5	57.8
3. Cotton goods	159.5	30.7	140.2	27.4
4. Matches	9.5	56.9	4.8	25.6
5. Linen goods	42.5	44.7	25.4	27.5
6. Liquor	4.3	27.9	1.8	8.2
7. Confectionery	10.3	54.2	11.1	19.9
8. China, porcelainware	10.9	46.7	8.1	27.6
9. Saw mills, plywood	15.1	18.8	23.3	12.1
10. Electric power	3.8	18.8	18.3	27.7
11. Basic chemical products ..	5.7	36.9	21.0	30.5
12. Woolen and worsted goods	26.8	37.7	20.5	25.6
13. Paper	11.3	35.4	15.3	32.0
14. Leather	15.1	44.8	14.0	22.5
15. Non-ferrous metallurgy ..	9.6	40.5	19.3	41.2
16. Metal products, machinery, and equipment	123.3	26.6	392.4	28.1
17. Ferrous metallurgy	78.0	40.0	199.6	56.8
18. Shoe	13.2	44.5	22.4	31.5
19. Printing	18.1	29.9	17.8	22.2
20. Coal	54.0	20.6	95.0	20.8
21. Oil extraction, refining ...	34.6	77.8	22.7	34.0
22. Milling	5.9	18.8	9.1	16.6
23. Furniture	2.5	10.9	2.4	11.5
24. Clothing	19.7	39.4	66.4	31.5
25. Baking	4.9	22.8	11.7	17.5
26. Glass	18.9	28.2	11.6	14.9
All industries	733.4	32.4	1199.3	28.5

Data on the number of wage earners in Soviet large-scale establishments on March 1, 1928 were estimated from (1) data on the number of ordinary laborers (*rabochie*) and apprentices employed in these establishments, *Statistika Truda*, 1928 no. 8, pp. 12 ff.; Sats, *Statistika Truda*, 1929, no. 5–6, pp. 1 ff., and (2) data on the proportion of these workers to all the wage earners in the establishments covered by the March 1928 wage investigation. The data in Col. 3b are the ratios of ordinary laborers in the establishments covered by the wage investigation to the number of ordinary laborers in all large-scale establishments. These data were obtained directly from TSUNKHU, *Zarabotnaia Plata Rabochikh Krupnoi Promyshlennosti v Oktiabre 1934* (Moscow, 1935), p. 313.

Unlike the data used in Appendix D, Table 1, the data used here on the number of wage earners in large-scale establishments do not include the wage earners in several minor branches of the different industries studied.

TABLE 5

Industry	Number of Wage Earners (*In Per Cent*)	
	1914	1928
1. Cotton goods	35.00	30.57
2. Metal products, machinery and equipment ..	25.00	36.13
3. Rubber products, oil extraction and refining, chemical products, and matches	8.30	6.73
4. Saw mills, plywood, furniture and other wood products	7.66	6.21
5. Linen goods, hemp products	6.98	6.97
6. Woolen and worsted goods	6.77	4.20
7. Paper, printing	6.65	5.45
8. Leather, shoe	3.64	3.74
All industries	100.00	100.00

Sources: Data on the number of wage earners in factory-inspection establishments in Russia in 1914 are from Ministerstvo Torgovli i Promyshlennosti, *Svod Otchetov Fabrichnykh Inspektorov za 1914 g.* (Petrograd, 1915). Data on the number of wage earners in large-scale establishments on March 1, 1928, are estimates based on (1) the number of ordinary laborers (*rabochie*) and apprentices employed in these establishments, from *Statistika Truda*, 1928 no. 8, pp. 12 ff., Sats, *Statistika Truda*, 1929, no. 5–6, pp. 1 ff., and (2) data on the proportion of these workers to all wage earners in the establishments covered by the March 1928 wage investigation.

The Russian data on the number of wage earners in factory-inspection industry are the average number employed during the year in establishments subject to the factory inspection at the end of 1914.

The minor allied industries which were grouped with their corresponding major branches for purposes of computing the 1928 coverage data in Appendix D, Table 1, have not been so grouped in computing the weight assigned a particular industry in the present table.

TABLE 6

NUMBER OF WORKERS EMPLOYED IN LARGE-SCALE ESTABLISHMENTS IN EACH OF TWENTY-SIX INDUSTRIES STUDIED IN RELATION TO THE NUMBER EMPLOYED IN LARGE-SCALE ESTABLISHMENTS IN ALL TWENTY-SIX INDUSTRIES, U.S.S.R., MARCH 1, 1928, AND NOVEMBER 1, 1934. (WEIGHTS USED IN COMPUTING DATA IN CHAPTER X, TABLE 11)

| Industry | MARCH 1928 | | OCTOBER 1934 | |
	Number of Wage Earners (In Per Cent)	Number of Wage Earners & Salaried Workers (In Per Cent)	Number of Wage Earners (In Per Cent)	Number of Wage Earners & Salaried Workers (In Per Cent)
1. Cotton goods	22.87	21.72	12.14	11.27
2. Metal products, machinery, and equipment ..	20.51	21.77	33.24	35.13
3. Coal	11.55	11.31	10.71	10.07
4 Ferrous metallurgy	8.60	8.62	8.36	8.16
5. Linen goods	4.21	3.96	2.19	2.02
6. Saw mills, plywood	3.64	3.60	4.58	4.50
7. Woolen and worsted goods	3.14	3.08	1.90	1.80
8. Glass	2.96	2.87	1.85	1.74
9. Printing	2.67	2.74	1.90	1.88
10. Clothing	2.21	2.18	5.00	4.87
11. Oil	1.96	2.14	1.59	1.66
12. Leather	1.65	1.68	1.48	1.53
13. Paper	1.41	1.40	1.14	1.10
14. Milling	1.39	1.47	1.30	1.38
15. Shoe	1.31	1.31	1.69	1.67
16. Tobacco	1.15	1.13	.35	.33
17. Non-ferrous metallurgy	1.05	1.08	1.11	1.16
18. China, porcelainware ..	1.03	1.00	.70	.69
19. Furniture	1.01	1.04	.49	.48
20. Baking	.95	.97	1.59	1.69
21. Rubber	.90	.89	1.27	1.24
22. Electric power	.89	1.02	1.49	1.54
23. Confectionery	.84	.83	1.33	1.37
24. Match	.74	.71	.44	.42
25. Liquor	.68	.79	.52	.55
26. Basic chemical products	.68	.69	1.64	1.75
All industries	100.00	100.00	100.00	100.00

Sources: Data on the number of ordinary laborers (*rabochie*) and apprentices in large-scale establishments on March 1, 1928, and data on the number of ordinary laborers in large-scale establishments on November 1, 1934, were obtained from the sources cited in Appendix D, Table 4. Data on the total number of wage earners and salaried workers employed in large-scale establishments in the different industries studied were estimated from the data just referred to and from information on the proportion of ordinary laborers and apprentices to the total number of employees in the large-scale establishments covered by the wage studies.

As to the particular industries in the table, the following should be noted: Tobacco: this includes *makhorka* in 1928, but does not include it in 1934; Leather: workers in the fur industry are included.

TABLE 7

WAGE EARNERS IN RUSSIAN INDUSTRY CLASSIFIED ACCORDING TO THEIR AVERAGE
DAILY WAGES IN JUNE 1914

Earnings in Kopeks	Per Cent of Wage Earners
Less than 51	14.6
51 to 76	23.7
76 to 101	18.8
101 to 151	20.4
151 to 201	9.6
201 to 301	8.9
301 to 401	2.6
More than 401	1.4
Total	100.0

These data relate to the wage earners in the eight industries and industry groups listed in Chapter V, Table 3. The source of the data and other information on them are presented in the notes to the latter table. In combining the daily wage frequency distribution for the eight industries, each industry was given a weight proportional to the number of wage earners subject to factory inspection in that industry. The weights used are listed in Appendix D, Table 5.

TABLE 8

WAGE EARNERS IN SOVIET INDUSTRY CLASSIFIED ACCORDING TO THEIR AVERAGE
DAILY WAGES IN MARCH 1928

Earnings in Kopeks	Per Cent of Wage Earners
Less than 140.1	10.8
140.1 to 180.0	13.5
180.1 to 220.0	15.7
220.1 to 260.0	14.6
260.1 to 300.0	11.4
300.1 to 340.0	8.1
340.1 to 380.0	6.1
380.1 to 420.0	5.0
420.1 to 460.0	3.8
460.1 to 500.0	3.0
500.1 to 540.0	2.3
540.1 to 580.0	1.6
More than 580.0	4.1
Total	100.0

These data relate to the wage earners in the eight industries and industry groups listed in Chapter V, Table 3. The source of the data and other information on them are presented in the notes to the latter table. In combining the daily wage frequency distributions for the eight industries, each industry was given a weight proportional to the number of wage earners in large-scale establishments in that industry. The weights used are listed in Appendix D, Table 5.

TABLE 9

WAGE EARNERS AND SALARIED WORKERS IN SOVIET INDUSTRY CLASSIFIED ACCORD-
ING TO THEIR EARNINGS IN MARCH 1928

Earnings in Rubles	Per Cent of Wage Earners	Per Cent of Wage Earners & Salaried Workers
Less than 30.01	6.0	5.6
30.01 to 40.00	9.4	8.7
40.01 to 50.00	12.7	11.8
50.01 to 60.00	13.7	12.9
60.01 to 70.00	13.0	12.6
70.01 to 80.00	10.5	10.5
80.01 to 90.00	8.1	8.3
90.01 to 100.00	6.2	6.4
100.01 to 110.00	5.1	5.2
110.01 to 120.00	3.8	4.0
120.01 to 130.00	2.9	3.1
130.01 to 140.00	2.3	2.5
140.01 to 150.00	1.7	1.9
150.01 to 200.00	3.7	4.6
200.01 to 250.00	.7	1.3
More than 250.00	.2	.6
Total	100.0	100.0

The data relate to workers in the twenty-six industries listed in Chapter VII, Table 7. The
sources of the data and other information on them are presented in the notes to that table. In
combining the wage and salary frequency distributions for the different industries to obtain
a single frequency distribution for all industries, each industry was given a weight proportional
to the number of workers in large-scale establishments in that industry. The weights used are
listed in Appendix D, Table 6.

TABLE 10

WAGE EARNERS AND SALARIED WORKERS IN SOVIET INDUSTRY CLASSIFIED ACCORDING TO THEIR EARNINGS IN OCTOBER 1934

Earnings in Rubles		Per Cent of Wage Earners	Per Cent of Wage Earners and Salaried Workers
Less than 50.01		3.6	3.1
50.1 to	60.0	1.8	1.6
60.1 to	80.0	7.1	6.2
80.1 to	100.0	11.6	10.2
100.1 to	120.0	13.3	12.0
120.1 to	140.0	12.8	11.9
140.1 to	160.0	10.7	10.3
160.1 to	180.0	8.5	8.3
180.1 to	200.0	6.7	6.7
200.1 to	220.0	5.1	4.9
220.1 to	240.0	4.1	4.2
240.1 to	260.0	3.2	3.6
260.1 to	300.0	4.6	5.4
300.1 to	340.0	2.6	3.1
340.1 to	380.0	1.6	2.5
380.1 to	420.0	1.0	1.7
420.1 to	500.0	1.7*	2.1
500.1 to	580.0	..	.9
580.1 to	660.0	..	.5
660.1 to	780.0	..	.4
780.1 to	940.0	..	.2
940.1 to	1100.0	..	.1
1100.1 to	1260.0	..	†
1260.1 to	1420.0	..	†
More than 1420.0		..	†
Total		100.0	100.0

* Over 420.1.
† Before rounding off decimals, these frequencies were .03, .03, and .02.
The data relate to workers in the twenty-six industries listed in Chapter VII, Table 7. The sources of the data and other information on them are presented in the notes to that table. In combining the wage and salary frequency distributions for the different industries to obtain a single frequency distribution for all industries, each industry was given a weight proportional to the number of workers in large-scale establishments in that industry. The weights used are listed in Appendix D, Table 6.

APPENDIX E

DATA USED TO CONSTRUCT CHARTS

TABLE 1

WAGE EARNERS IN THE SOVIET METAL PRODUCTS, MACHINERY AND EQUIPMENT
INDUSTRY CLASSIFIED ACCORDING TO AVERAGE DAILY WAGES, MARCH 1928
(DATA FOR *CHART* 1, p. 53)

Earnings in Kopeks	Per Cent of Wage Earners
Less than 140.1	6.8
140.1 to 180.0	7.7
180.1 to 220.0	9.4
220.1 to 260.0	11.2
260.1 to 300.0	10.9
300.1 to 340.0	10.0
340.1 to 380.0	9.0
380.1 to 420.0	7.8
420.1 to 460.0	6.5
460.1 to 500.0	5.1
500.1 to 540.0	4.1
540.1 to 580.0	3.0
More than 580.0	8.5
All wage earners	100.0

See the notes to Table 3 in Chapter V.

TABLE 2A

CUMULATIVE FREQUENCY DISTRIBUTIONS OF WAGE EARNERS CLASSIFIED ACCORDING TO AVERAGE DAILY WAGES: SPECIFIED INDUSTRIES, RUSSIA, JUNE 1914 (DATA FOR CHART 2, pp. 71-72)

COTTON GOODS		LINEN GOODS, HEMP PRODUCTS		SAW MILLS, PLYWOOD FURNITURE AND OTHER WOOD PRODUCTS		WOOLEN AND WORSTED GOODS	
Earnings (Per Cent of Median)	Cumulative Per Cent of Wage Earners	Earnings (Per Cent of Median)	Cumulative Per Cent of Wage Earners	Earnings (Per Cent of Median)	Cumulative Per Cent of Wage Earners	Earnings (Per Cent of Median)	Cumulative Per Cent of Wage Earners
Less than 67.0	14.4	Less than 66.3	21.5	Less than 43.7	7.4	Less than 50.3	15.1
" " 100.4	50.5	" " 82.9	35.5	" " 65.5	22.9	" " 78.6	36.2
" " 133.9	76.7	" " 124.3	70.6	" " 87.3	41.5	" " 117.9	61.6
" " 200.9	95.0	" " 165.8	87.9	" " 131.0	70.7	" " 157.2	80.7
" " 267.8	98.3	" " 248.7	97.5	" " 176.4	87.0	" " 235.8	96.0
" " 401.7	99.7	" " 331.6	99.5	" " 262.0	97.7	" " 314.5	98.9
" " 535.6	99.9	" " 497.3	99.9	" " 349.3	99.3	" " 471.7	99.8
All	100.0	" " 663.1	100.0	All	100.0	" " 628.9	99.9
		All*	100.0			All	100.0

TABLE 2A (continued)

METAL PRODUCTS, MACHINERY AND EQUIPMENT		PAPER, PRINTING		LEATHER, SHOE		RUBBER PRODUCTS, OIL EXTRACTION AND REFINING, CHEMICAL PRODUCTS, MATCHES	
Earnings (Per Cent of Median)	Cumulative Per Cent of Wage Earners	Earnings (Per Cent of Median)	Per Cent of Wage Earners	Cumulative Earnings (Per Cent of Median)	Cumulative Per Cent of Wage Earners	Earnings (Per Cent of Median)	Cumulative Per Cent of Wage Earners
Less than 30.7	4.6	Less than 57.5	18.7	Less than 48.9	15.0	Less than 49.5	9.9
" " 46.0	12.8	" " 86.3	41.6	" " 73.3	32.2	" " 74.3	23.2
" " 61.4	22.5	" " 115.1	59.3	" " 97.8	49.0	" " 99.0	49.4
" " 92.1	45.1	" " 172.6	77.3	" " 146.6	70.2	" " 148.6	79.6
" " 122.8	64.3	" " 230.2	88.1	" " 195.5	82.6	" " 198.2	89.4
" " 184.2	87.4	" " 345.2	96.6	" " 293.3	95.9	" " 297.3	97.0
" " 245.5	95.3	" " 460.3	98.9	" " 391.0	99.1	" " 396.4	99.1
All	100.0	All	100.0	All	100.0	All	100.0

* Frequency above 663.1, before rounding, .01.
See the notes to Table 3 in Chapter V.
The frequencies below the first earnings class in the linen goods, hemp products, and the woolen and worsted goods earnings distributions were extrapolated.

TABLE 2B

CUMULATIVE FREQUENCY DISTRIBUTIONS OF WAGE EARNERS CLASSIFIED ACCORDING TO AVERAGE DAILY WAGES: SPECIFIED INDUSTRIES, U.S.S.R., MARCH 1928 (DATA FOR CHART 2, pp. 71-72)

COTTON GOODS		LINEN GOODS, HEMP PRODUCTS		SAW MILLS, PLYWOOD FURNITURE AND OTHER WOOD PRODUCTS		WOOLEN AND WORSTED GOODS	
Earnings (Per Cent of Median)	Cumulative Per Cent of Wage Earners	Earnings (Per Cent of Median)	Cumulative Per Cent of Wages Earners	Earnings (Per Cent of Median)	Cumulative Per Cent of Wage Earners	Earnings (Per Cent of Median)	Cumulative Per Cent of Wage Earners
Less than 64.0	10.8	Less than 59.9	5.9	Less than 63.8	16.0	Less than 63.6	14.9
" " 82.3	28.0	" " 83.9	30.7	" " 82.1	33.0	" " 81.7	32.1
" " 100.6	50.8	" " 107.8	59.4	" " 100.3	50.3	" " 99.9	49.9
" " 118.9	71.1	" " 131.8	77.9	" " 118.5	67.2	" " 118.1	66.0
" " 137.2	84.4	" " 155.8	87.2	" " 136.8	79.4	" " 136.2	76.5
" " 155.5	90.7	" " 179.7	92.5	" " 155.0	86.2	" " 154.4	84.6
" " 173.8	93.8	" " 203.7	95.8	" " 173.2	91.0	" " 172.6	90.9
" " 192.0	96.1	" " 227.7	97.7	" " 191.5	93.9	" " 190.7	94.4
" " 210.3	97.5	" " 251.6	98.8	" " 209.7	96.1	" " 208.9	96.3
" " 228.6	98.5	" " 275.6	99.4	" " 227.9	97.5	" " 227.1	97.7
" " 246.9	99.2	" " 299.6	99.6	" " 246.2	98.2	" " 245.2	98.6
" " 265.2	99.5	" " 323.5	99.8	" " 264.4	98.9	" " 263.4	99.1
All	100.0	" " 347.5	99.9	All	100.0	All	100.0
		All	100.0				

TABLE 2B (continued)

| Metal Products, Machinery and Equipment | | Paper, Printing | | Leather, Shoe | | Rubber Products, Oil Extraction and Refining, Chemical Products, Matches | |
Earnings (Per cent of Median)	Cumulative Per Cent of Wage Earners	Earnings (Per Cent of Median)	Cumulative Per Cent of Wage Earners	Earnings (Per Cent of Median)	Cumulative Per Cent of Wage Earners	Earnings (Per Cent of Median)	Cumulative Per Cent of Wage Earners
Less than 44.3	6.8	Less than 52.4	9.4	Less than 53.1	10.2	Less than 54.7	9.3
" " 56.9	14.5	" " 67.3	19.7	" " 64.9	18.8	" " 70.3	22.3
" " 69.6	23.9	" " 82.3	35.0	" " 76.7	28.9	" " 86.0	38.3
" " 82.3	35.1	" " 97.2	48.1	" " 88.5	39.5	" " 101.6	51.3
" " 94.9	46.0	" " 112.2	58.4	" " 100.3	50.3	" " 117.2	63.2
" " 107.6	56.0	" " 127.2	68.0	" " 112.1	60.0	" " 132.9	72.4
" " 120.2	65.1	" " 142.1	74.9	" " 123.9	68.6	" " 148.5	79.5
" " 132.9	72.9	" " 157.1	81.0	" " 135.7	75.8	" " 164.1	86.3
" " 145.5	79.4	" " 172.0	85.8	" " 147.5	81.9	" " 179.8	90.4
" " 158.2	84.4	" " 187.0	90.0	" " 159.3	86.7	" " 195.3	93.2
" " 170.8	88.5	" " 201.9	93.4	" " 171.1	90.5	" " 211.0	96.2
" " 183.5	91.5	" " 216.9	95.6	All	100.0	" " 226.7	97.3
All	100.0	All	100.0			All	100.0

See the notes to Table 3 in Chapter V.

APPENDIX F

CERTAIN LAWS ON EDUCATION AND LABOR RECENTLY ENACTED IN THE U.S.S.R.

I. *Decree of the Council of Commissars of the U.S.S.R. of October 2, 1940: On the Establishment of Fees for Instruction in the Senior Classes of Secondary Schools and in Higher Educational Institutions in the U.S.S.R. and on the Change in the System of Awarding Stipends.*[1]

Taking into account the rise in the living standards of the working people and the substantial expenditures borne by the Soviet State for the construction, equipment and maintenance of the ever-increasing number of secondary and higher educational schools, the Council of People's Commissars of the U.S.S.R. considers it necessary that part of the expenses of tuition in secondary schools and higher educational establishments be borne by the working people themselves, and in this connection has decided:

1. To introduce as of September 1, 1940, tuition fees for the 8th, 9th, and 10th classes of secondary schools and in higher educational establishments.

2. To set the following tuition fees for the 8th to 10th classes of secondary schools:

   a. 200 rubles a year for the schools of Moscow and Leningrad, and also for the schools in the capitals of the Union Republics;

   b. 150 rubles a year for the schools of all other cities, as well as villages.

   Note: The tuition fees for the 8th to 10th classes of secondary schools apply to students of technikums, pedagogical, agricultural and medical schools and other special secondary schools.

3. To set the following tuition fees for higher educational establishments of the U.S.S.R.:

[1] *S.P.R. SSSR*, 1940, no. 27, section 637, pp. 910 ff. With minor revisions and additions, the translation of this decree, and the translations of the edicts of October 2 and October 19 inserted in the following pages, are taken from the *American Review of the Soviet Union*, with the permission of the publishers. The translation of the Edict of June 26, below, is my own.

a. 400 rubles a year for higher educational establishments in Moscow, Leningrad, and the capital of the Union Republics;

b. 300 rubles a year for higher educational establishments in other cities;

c. 500 rubles a year for higher educational establishments giving instruction in art, the theater, and music.

4. Tuition fees are to be paid to the corresponding educational institutions in equal sums, twice a year: on September 1 and February 1.

> Note: Payment for the first half of the 1940–41 term to be made not later than November 1, 1940.

5. Payment for correspondence courses in secondary and higher educational establishments is to be fixed at half the regular tuition fee.

6. Beginning November 1, 1940, stipends are to be granted only to those students of higher educational establishments as well as pupils of technical schools who excel in their studies.

II. *Edict* (Ukaz) *of the Supreme Soviet of the U.S.S.R., June 26, 1940: On the Change to an Eight-Hour Working Day, a Seven-Day Working Week and on the Suppression of the Voluntary Departure of Wage Earners* (Rabochikh) *and Salaried Workers* (Sluzhashchikh) *from Enterprises and Institutions.*[2]

In accord with the proposal of the all-union Central Congress of Trade Unions, the Presidium of the Supreme Soviet of the U.S.S.R. decrees:

3. To suppress the voluntary departure of wage earners and salaried workers from state, coöperative, and communal enterprises and institutions, and also voluntary transfer from one enterprise to another or from one institution to another.

Only the director of an enterprise or the chief of an institution may permit departure from an enterprise or institution, or transfer from one enterprise to another, or from one institution to another.

4. To establish that the director of an enterprise or the chief of an institution has the right and is obligated to permit the departure of a wage earner or salaried worker from an enterprise or institution in the following cases:

a. When the wage earner or salaried worker, according to the finding of the medical-labor expert commission, cannot fulfill his previous work in consequence of illness or invalidism, and the administration cannot offer him other suitable work in

---

[2] *Izvestiia TSIK*, June 27, 1940. Articles 1 and 2, which are not quoted here, relate to the change in working hours.

the same enterprise or institution, or when a pensioner, to whom an old age pension has been granted, wishes to leave work;

b. When the wage earner or salaried worker must stop work in connection with his admission into a higher or secondary educational institution.

5. To establish that wage earners and salaried workers voluntarily leaving a state coöperative, or communal enterprise or institution are brought to trial and on sentence of the people's court are subject to imprisonment for a period of two to four months.

To establish that for absence from work without important reason wage earners and salaried workers of state, coöperative, and communal enterprises and institutions are brought to trial and by sentence of the people's court are punished by correctional labor at their place of work for up to six months with reduction in wages of up to 25 per cent.

In connection with this, to abolish [the requirement of] obligatory dismissal for absence without important reason.

To propose to the people's courts that all cases indicated in the present article should be examined in not more than 5 days and that sentences should be carried out immediately.

6. To establish that a director of an enterprise or a chief of an institution who fails to bring to trial individuals, guilty of voluntarily departing from an enterprise or institution, and individuals, guilty of absenteeism — are to be brought to trial.

To establish also that the director of an enterprise or a chief of an institution employing fugitives, who have voluntarily left an enterprise or institution, are to be brought to trial.

7. The present edict is effective as of June 27, 1940.

III. *Edict of the Presidium of the Supreme Soviet of the U.S.S.R., October 2, 1940: On State Labor Reserves in the U.S.S.R.*[3]

The task of further developing our industry requires a continual flow of new labor into the pits, mines, transport, and factories. Without the uninterrupted replenishment of the labor force the successful growth of our industry is impossible.

In our country unemployment is fully liquidated, poverty and waste are forever ended in the country and the city. Accordingly, there are here no people who are forced to plead for work in the factories, automatically forming, in this way, a constant reserve labor force for industry.

---

[3] *Izvestiia TSIK*, October 3, 1940.

In these circumstances the government is confronted with the task of organizing the preparation of new workers from the urban and farm youth and of creating the necessary labor reserves for industry.

With the object of creating state labor reserves for industry, the Presidium of the Supreme Soviet of the U.S.S.R. resolves:

1. To recognize as essential the annual training for industry of state labor reserves of from 800,000 to 1,000,000 persons by teaching the urban and collective farm youths definite industrial professions in Trade Schools, Railway Schools and Industrial Training Schools.

2. To organize Trade Schools with a two-year course of study in cities for training skilled metal workers, metallurgists, chemists, miners, oil workers and workers of other skilled professions, as well as qualified workers for marine transport, river transport and communications.

3. To organize Railway Schools with a two-year course of study for the training of skilled railway workers, assistant locomotive engineers, locomotive and car repair men, boiler makers, crew leaders for track repairs and other skilled workers.

4. To organize Industrial Training Schools with a six months' course of study for training workers of the more widely applied professions, in the first place for the coal, mining, metallurgical and oil industries, and building trades.

5. To establish that instruction in Trade Schools, Railway Schools and Industrial Training Schools is to be free of charge, and that pupils are to be maintained by the state during the period of their studies.

6. To establish that the State reserves of labor power are to be under the direct jurisdiction of the Council of People's Commissars of the U.S.S.R. and are not to be utilized by people's commissariats and enterprises without permission of the Government.

7. To empower the Council of People's Commissars of the U.S.S.R. annually to draft (mobilize) from 800,000 and 1,000,000 persons of the urban and collective farm youths (male) of 14 and 15 years of age, for training in Trade and Railway Schools, and of 16 and 17 years of age, for Industrial Training Schools.

8. To obligate chairmen of collective farms to designate by drafting (mobilizing) annually two youths (male) of 14 and 15 years of age for Trade and Railway Schools and of 16 and 17 years of age for Industrial Training Schools per each 100 members of the collective farm, counting men and women between the ages of 14 and 55.

9. To obligate City Soviets of Working People's Deputies annually to designate by drafting (mobilizing) youths (male) of 14 and 15

years of age for Trade and Railway Schools and of 16 and 17 years of age for Industrial Training Schools, the number being fixed annually by the Council of People's Commissars of the U.S.S.R.

10. To establish that all those who graduate from the Trade Schools, Railway Schools and Industrial Training Schools are to be considered as mobilized and are obliged to work four years continuously in state enterprises, as directed by the Central Labor Reserves Administration under the Council of People's Commissars of the U.S.S.R., securing them wages at the place of work in accordance with general rates.

11. To establish that all persons graduating from Trade Schools, Railway Schools and Industrial Training Schools are to be temporarily exempted from being drafted into the Red Army and Navy until the period of obligatory work in state enterprises, in accordance with Article 10 of the present edict, expires.

IV. *Edict of the Presidium of the Supreme Soviet of the U.S.S.R., October 20, 1940: On the Procedure for the Obligatory Transfer of Engineers, Technicians, Foremen, Office Workers* (Sluzash-chikh), *and Skilled Workers from One Enterprise to Another.*[4]

The problem of securing skilled forces for new plants, factories, mines, construction jobs and transport services, as well as for enterprises undertaking the production of new lines, demands the correct distribution of engineers, technicians, foremen, employees and skilled workers among the different enterprises and the transfer of industrial personnel from enterprises possessing skilled forces to enterprises experiencing a shortage of them.

The existing situation, under which the People's Commissariats do not have the right of obligatory transfer of engineers, employees and skilled workers from one enterprise to another, is an obstacle to the development of the national economy.

The Presidium of the Supreme Soviet of the U.S.S.R. decrees:

1. To invest the People's Commissars of the U.S.S.R. with the right of obligatory transfer of engineers, designers, technicians, foremen, draftsmen, bookkeepers, economists, accountants and planning personnel, as well as skilled workers of the sixth category and up, from one enterprise or institution to another, regardless of the territorial location of the institutions or enterprises.

2. The transfer of engineers, employees and skilled workers, in accordance with this Edict, to employment in other localities must in no way lead to any material loss to the person transferred. To estab-

---

[4] *Izvestiia TSIK*, October 20, 1940.

lish in this connection that the People's Commissariat is obligated to pay the person transferred: (a) the traveling expenses for himself and members of his family to the new place of employment; (b) the cost of transporting his effects; (c) a daily allowance while en route; (d) wages while en route, plus an additional six days; (e) lump sum assistance for setting up home in the new place to the amount of three or four months' wages (depending upon the district) at the former place of work for the person transferred and one-quarter of his monthly earnings for each member of his family who moves to his new place of employment.

3. To establish that engineers, employees and skilled workers transferred from one enterprise to another in the same locality are to preserve their record of continuous service (*stazh*) and those transferred to other localities are to have one year added to their record.

4. To establish that directors of enterprises and heads of institutions are obligated to release from their enterprise or institution wives of engineers, employees and skilled workers transferred to other localities in accordance with the present Edict.

5. Persons failing to carry out the instructions of the People's Commissar on their obligatory transfer to another enterprise or institution are to be regarded as having left the enterprise or institution without permission and are committed for trial in accordance with Article 5 of the Edict of the Presidium of the Supreme Soviet of the U.S.S.R. of June 26, 1940, prohibiting workers and employees from leaving enterprises or institutions without permission.

6. To cancel, as of October 20, 1940, contracts concluded for a specified time by People's Commissariats and enterprises with the engineers, employees and skilled workers enumerated in Article I of the present Edict, and to permit the People's Commissars of the U.S.S.R. to retain these engineers, employees and skilled workers at the enterprise where they are at present employed on contract.

V. *Decree of the Council of Commissars of the U.S.S.R. of November 1, 1937: On Increasing the Wages of Low-Paid Wage Earners* (Rabochikh) *and Salaried Workers* (Sluzhashchikh) *of Industry and Transport.*[5]

The Council of Commissars of the U.S.S.R. decrees:

1. That from November 1, 1937, the wages of low paid wage earn-

---

[5] *S.Z.R. SSSR*, 1937, part I, no. 71, section 340, p. 734. The decree contains two sections, 4 and 5, not quoted here, which deal with the manner in which the increase in wages is to be treated in calculating piece rates (the increase is excluded), pensions (the increase is taken into account), etc.

ers and salaried workers of industrial establishments in all commissariats and departments of the U.S.S.R. and also of wage earners and salaried workers in railway and water transport be increased.

2. That in increasing wages . . . the following conditions be observed:

    a. For time workers, the increase in wages is to be such that the basic wage rate (tarifnaia stavka) together with the increase should not be less than 115 rubles a month, not counting premiums and other extras.

    b. That for wage earners and salaried workers engaged in piece work, the increase be such that their basic accounting wage (raschetnaia stavka) together with the increase should not be less than 110 rubles a month, not considering premiums and other extras.

3. That in correspondence with this it be provided in the plan for 1938 that the wage fund be increased by 600 million rubles, and for November and December 1937, by 100 million rubles.

RUSSIAN STUDIES CITED
WITH TRANSLATIONS OF TITLES [1]

THE FOLLOWING transliteration of the Russian alphabet in the new orthography is used in the present study. Russian letters in the old orthography are represented by the same English letters as are the equivalent Russian letters in the new orthography.

А	а	A		Р	р	R
Б	б	B		С	с	S
В	в	V		Т	т	T
Г	г	G		У	у	U
Д	д	D		Ф	ф	F
Е	е	E		Х	х	KH
Ж	ж	ZH		Ц	ц	TS
З	з	Z		Ч	ч	CH
И	и	I		Ш	ш	SH
Й	й	I		Щ	щ	SHCH
К	к	K		Ъ	ъ	'[2]
Л	л	L		Ы	ы	Y
М	м	M		Ь	ь	'
Н	н	N		Э	э	E
О	о	O		Ю	ю	IU
П	п	P		Я	я	IA

[1] The bibliography includes a number of titles reference to which was sacrificed in the course of one or another of the various revisions which the present study has undergone.

[2] Omitted at the end of a word.

GOVERNMENT AND PARTY PUBLICATIONS (EXCEPT JOURNALS)

LAWS, DECREES, RESOLUTIONS:

Biulleten' Financogo i Khoziaistvennogo Zakonodatel'stva, abbr. as *B.F.Kh.Z.* [Bulletin of Financial and Economic Law].

Biulleten' Narodnogo Komissariata Prosveshchenia RSFSR, abbr. as *Biulleten' NKProsa RSFSR* [Bulletin of the Peoples' Commissariat of Education of the RSFSR].

Izvestiia Narodnogo Komissariata Truda SSSR, abbr. as *Izvestiia NKT SSSR* [News of the Peoples' Commissariat of Labor of the U.S.S.R.].

Khronologicheskii Perechen' Zakonov RSFSR deistvuiushchikh na . . . [Chronologic List of Laws of the R.S.F.S.R. operative on . . .].

Polnoe Sobranie Zakonov Rossiiskoi Imperii, Sobranie Tretie . . . [Complete Collection of Laws of the Russian Empire, Third Collection, . . .].

Sobranie Uzakonenii i Rasporiazhenii Rabochago i Krest'ianskago Pravitel'stva, abbr. as *S.U.R.* [Collected Laws and Decrees of the Workers' and Peasants' Government].

Sobranie Uzakonenii i Rasporiazhenii Raboche-Krest'ianskogo Pravitel'stva RSFSR, abbr. as *S.U.R. RSFSR* [Collected Laws and Decrees of the Workers' and Peasants' Government of RSFSR].

Sobranie Zakonov i Rasporiazhenii Raboche-Krest'ianskogo Pravitel'stva SSSR, abbr. as *S.Z.R. SSSR* [Collected Laws and Decrees of the Workers' and Peasants' Government of the U.S.S.R.].

Zakonodatel'stvo i Rasporiazheniia po Torgovle SSSR [Laws and Decrees on Trade of the U.S.S.R.].

Vsesoiuznaia Kommunisticheskaia Partiia (b) v Rezoliutsiiakh ee S'ezdov i Konferentsii (1898–1926 gg.) [All-Union Communist Party in Resolutions of Its Congresses and Conferences, 1898–1926]. Moscow, 1927. Also cited, fifth edition, Moscow, 1936.

Zhilishchnoe Upravlenie Mossoveta [Housing Administration of the Moscow Soviet], *Zhilishchnyi Spavochnik* [Housing Handbook]. Moscow, 1936.

STATISTICS, OTHER PUBLICATIONS:

Gosudarstvennaia Planovaia Komissiia, abbr. as Gosplan [State Planning Commission], *Energeticheskoe Khoziaistvo SSSR* [Power Economy of the U.S.S.R.], vol. II. Moscow, 1932.

——, *Kontrol'nye Tsifry Narodnogo Khoziaistva SSSR na 1927/*

1928 god [Control Figures of the Social Economy of the U.S.S.R. for 1927/1928]. Moscow, 1928.

——, *Kontrol'nye Tsifry Narodnogo Khoziaistva SSSR na 1928/ 1929 god* [Control Figures of the Social Economy of the U.S.S.R. for 1928/1929]. Moscow, 1929.

——, *Narodno-Khoziaistvennyi Plan na 1935 god* [Social-Economic Plan for 1935]. First and second editions, Moscow, 1935.

——, *Piatiletnii Plan Narodno-Khoziaistvennogo Stroitel'stva SSSR* [Five Year Plan of the Social-Economic Construction of the U.S.S.R.], vol. II, part 1. Moscow, 1929.

Materialy Osobogo Soveshchaniia . . . pri Presidiume VSNKH SSSR, Seriia I, Piatiletnie Gipotezy po Otracliam Promyshlennosti, Kniga 22, Kozhevenno-Obuvnaia Promyshlennost'; Kniga 27, Khlopchato-Bumazhnaia Promyshlennost' [Materials of the Special Conference . . . under the Presidium of VSNKH U.S.S.R., Series I, Five Year Plan Hypotheses by Branches of Industry, Book 22, Leather, Shoe; Book 27, Cotton Textile]. Moscow, 1926.

Ministerstvo Torgovli i Promyshlennosti [Ministry of Trade and Industry], *Dannye o Prodolzhitel'nosti . . . Rabochego Vremeni . . . za 1913 god* [Statistics on the Length of the Working Day . . . in 1913]. St. Petersburg, 1914.

——, *Svod Otchetov Fabrichnykh Inspektorov za 1914 god* [Summary of the Reports of the Factory Inspectors for 1914]. Petrograd, 1915.

Narodnyi Komissariat Zdravookhraneniia RSFSR, abbr. as NKZdrav RSFSR [Peoples' Commissariat for Health of the R.S.F.S.R.], *Statisticheskie Materialy . . . za 1913–1923* [Statistical Materials . . . for 1913–1923]. Moscow, 1926.

Tsentral'noe Biuro Statistiki Truda [Central Bureau of Labor Statistics], *Differentsiatsiia Zarabotnoi Platy v Fabrichno-Zavodskoi Promyshlennosti Soiuza SSR za 1927 i 1928 gg.* [Differentiation of Wages in Factory Industry of the U.S.S.R. in 1927 and 1928]. Moscow, 1929.

Tsentral'noe Statisticheskoe Upravlenie, abbr. as TSU [Central Statistical Administration], *Narodnoe Prosveshchenie v SSSR, 1926–1927* [Social Education in the U.S.S.R., 1926–1927]. Moscow, 1929.

——, *Rabochii Den' v Fabrichno-Zavodskoi Promyshlennosti v 1928 g.* [The Working Day in Factory Industry in 1928]. Moscow, 1929.

——, *Trudy*, vol. VII, part 1, *Statisticheskii Sbornik za 1913–*

1917 gg. [Works, vol. VII, part 1, Statistical Materials for 1913–1917]. Moscow, 1921.

——, *Trudy*, vol. XXVI, parts 1, 2, *Fabrichno-Zavodskaia Promyshlennost' v Period 1913–1918 gg.* [Works, vol. XXVI, parts 1, 2, Factory Industry in the Years 1913–1918]. Moscow, 1926.

——, Tsentral'naia Bukhalteriia [Central Accounting Office], *Zakony i Rasporiazhenia po Bukhalterii* [Laws and Decrees on Accounting]. Moscow, 1929.

Tsentral'noe Upravlenie Narodno-Khoziaistvennogo Ucheta, abbr. as TSUNKHU [Central Administration of Social-Economic Accounting], *Kulturnoe Stroitel'stvo SSSR 1930–1934* [Cultural Construction in the U.S.S.R., 1930–1934]. Moscow, 1935.

——, *Melkaia Promyshlennost' SSSR* [Small Scale Industry of the U.S.S.R.]. Moscow, 1933.

——, *Narodnoe Khoziaistvo SSSR, 1932* [Social Economy of the U.S.S.R., 1932]. Moscow, 1932.

——, *Sotsialisticheskoe Stroitel'stvo v SSSR* [Socialist Construction in the U.S.S.R.]. Moscow, 1936.

——, *Trud v SSSR* [Labor in the U.S.S.R.]. Moscow, 1932; Moscow, 1936.

——, *Zarabotnaia Plata Inzhenerno-Technicheskikh Rabotnikov, Sluzhashchikh i Uchenikov v Sentiabre-Oktiabre 1934 g.* [Wages of Engineers and Technical Workers, Office Workers, and Apprentices in September and October 1934]. Moscow, 1936.

——, *Zarabotnaia Plata Rabochikh Krupnoi Promyshlennosti v Oktiabre 1934 g.* [Wages of Workers of Large Scale Industry in October 1934]. Moscow, 1935.

——, *Zdorov'e i Zdravookhranenie Trudiashchikhsia SSSR* [Health and Health Care of the Workers of the U.S.S.R.]. Moscow, 1936.

Upravlenie Glavnago Vrachebnago Inspektora M.V.D. [Department of the Chief Medical Inspector M.V.D.], *Otchet o Sostoianii Narodnago Zdraviia za 1907 god* [Report on the Condition of Public Health for 1907]. St. Petersburg, 1909.

Vysshii Sovet Narodnogo Khoziaistva, abbr. as VSNKH [Supreme Council of the Social Economy], *Chastnyi Kapital v Narodnom Khoziaistve* [Private Capital in the Social Economy]. Moscow, 1927.

——, *Promyshlennost' SSSR v 1927/28 godu.* [Industry of the U.S.S.R. in 1927/28]. Moscow, 1930.

Trade Union Publications

Vtoroi Vserossiiskii S'ezd Professional'nykh Soiuzov, 16–25 Ianvaria 1919 goda, Stenog. Otchet [Second All-Russian Congress of Trade Unions, January 16 to 25, 1919, Stenographic Account]. Moscow, 1921.

Tretii Vserossiiskii S'ezd Professional'nykh Soiuzov, 6–13 Aprelia 1920 goda, Stenog. Otchet [Third All-Russian Congress of Trade Unions, April 6 to 13, 1920, Stenographic Account]. Moscow, 1921.

Chetvertyi Vserossiiskii S'ezd Professional'nykh Soiuzov 17–25 Maia 1921 g., Stenog. Otchet [Fourth All-Russian Congress of Trade Unions, May 17 to 25, 1921, Stenographic Account]. Moscow, 1922.

Otchet Vserossiiskogo Tsentral'nogo Soveta Professional'nykh Soiuzov, 5 Maia 1921 g. po Aprel' 1922 g. [Report of the All-Russian Central Council of Trade Unions, May 5, 1921 to April 1922]. Petrograd, 1922.

Professional'nye Soiuzy SSSR, 1924–1926, Otchet VTSSPS k VII S'ezdu Professional'nykh Soiuzov [Trade Unions of the U.S.S.R., 1924–1926, Report of the Central Council to the Seventh Congress of Trade Unions]. Moscow, 1926.

Sed'moi S'ezd Professional'nykh Soiuzov SSSR, 6–18 Dek. 1926 g., Stenog. Otchet [Seventh Congress of Trade Unions of the U.S.S.R., December 6 to 18, 1926, Stenographic Account]. Moscow, 1927.

Professional'nye Soiuzy SSSR, 1926–1928, Otchet VTSSPS k VIII S'ezdu Professional'nykh Soiuzov [Trade Unions of the U.S.S.R., 1926–1928, Report of the All-Union Central Council of Trade Unions to the VIII Congress of Trade Unions]. Moscow, 1928.

Vos'moi S'ezd Professional'nykh Soiuzov SSSR, 10–24 Dek. 1928. Stenog. Otchet [Eighth Congress of Trade Unions of the U.S.S.R., December 10 to 24, 1928, Stenographic Account]. Moscow, 1929.

Deviatyi Vsesoiuznyi S'ezd Professional'nykh Soiuzov SSSR, Stenog. Otchet [Ninth Congress of Trade Unions of the U.S.S.R., Stenographic Account]. Moscow, 1933.

References to Journals, Bulletins, Newspapers

Ekonomicheskoe Obozrenie [Economic Review]:

A. Kaktyn', "Rost Planovosti v Narodnom Khoziaistve SSSR" [Growth of Planning in the Social Economy of the U.S.S.R.]. January 1927.

IU. Larin, "Chastnyi Kapital v Promyshlennosti." June 1927.

VSNKH, Tsentral'nyi Otdel Statistiki, *Ezhemesiachnyi Statisticheskii Biulleten'* [VSNKH, Central Bureau of Statistics, Monthly Statistical Bulletin]. March–April 1928.

Izvestiia TSIK [News of the Central Executive Committee].

Planovoe Khoziaistvo [Planned Economy]:

Z. Bolotin, "Edinaia Tsena i Ocherednye Zadachi Tovarooborota" [The Single Price and the Coming Problems of the Turnover]. 1935, no. 8.

"Dokladnaia Zapiska Gosplana SSSR Sovetu Truda i Oborony, Peresmotr Kontrol'nykh Tsifrov Narodnogo Khoziaistva na 1925/26 g." [Memorandum of the State Planning Commission of the U.S.S.R. to the Council of Labor and Defense, Review of the Control Figures for the Economy for 1925/26]. 1926, no. 2.

S. G. Strumilin, "Na Planovom Fronte" [On the Planning Front]. 1926, no. 1.

Pravda [Truth].

Sovetskaia Torgovlia [Soviet Trade]:

"Sovetskaia Torgovlia v Tsifrakh" [Soviet Trade in Figures]. May 1935.

G. Zberzhkovskii, "Itogi Tovarooborota v I Kvartale 1935 g." [Sums of the Turnover in the First Quarter 1935]. April 1935.

——, "Proidennyi Etap" [A Completed Stage]. November–December 1934.

Statistika Truda [Statistics of Labor]:

A. Rashin, "Zarabotnaia Plata v Krupnoi Promyshlennosti v I-m Polugodii 1927/28 g." [Wages in Large-Scale Industry in the First Half of 1927/28]. 1928, no. 5–6.

V. Sats, "Chislennost' i Sostav Rabochikh i Sluzhashchikh v Promyshlennosti SSSR na 1-e Ianvaria 1929 g." [Number and Composition of Wage Earners and Salaried Workers in Industry of the U.S.S.R. on January 1, 1929]. 1929, no. 5–6.

N. Shesterkina, "Kvartirnoe Dovol'stvie i Uderzhanie iz Zarabotka. . . ." [Apartment Bonuses and Deductions from Wages]. 1927, no. 7.

"Sostav Fabrichno-Zavodskogo Personala . . . na 1-e Ianvaria 1928 g. po SSSR" [Composition of the Personnel of Factory Industry of the U.S.S.R. . . . on January 1, 1928]. 1928, no. 8.

Vestnik Truda [Labor Messenger]:

A. Andreev, "Ocherednye Zadachi Soiuzov" [Next Tasks of the Unions]. October 1920.

——, "Profsoiuzy za 4 Goda Proletarskoi Revoliutsii" [Trade Unions During Four Years of the Revolution]. October–November 1921.

A. Goltsman, "Tarifnaia Rabota" [Work on the Wage Scales]. October 1920.

A. Gurevich, "Chto Skazal VII S'ezd Profsoiuzov o Regulirovanii Zarabotnoi Platy na Predpriiatii" [What Was Said by the Seventh Congress of Trade Unions on the Regulation of Wages in the Establishment]. January 1927.

P. Revzin, "K Probleme Regulirovaniia Zarplaty" [On the Problem of Regulating Wages]. May 1926.

V. Verzhbitskii, "Promyshlennost' i Tarify" [Industry and the Wage Rates]. October 1920.

Za Industrializatziiu [For Industrialization].

OTHER REFERENCES

D. Antoskin, *Professional'noe Dvizhenie Sluzhashchikh, 1917–1924 gg.* [The Trade Union Movement among White Collar Workers, 1917–1924]. Moscow, 1927.

Z. Bolotin, *Voprosy Snabzheniia* [Problems of Supply]. Moscow, 1934.

Bol'shaia Sovetskaia Entsiklopediia [The Great Soviet Encyclopedia].

N. Bronshtein, *Zhilishchnye Zakony* [Housing Laws]. Moscow, 1935.

——, *Oplata Zhilykh Pomeshchenii* [Payment for Living Quarters]. Moscow, 1928.

E. N. Danilova, *Deistvuiushchee Zakonodatel'stvo o Trude* [Effective Law on Labor], vols. I and II. Second edition, Moscow, 1927.

V. E. Den, *Kurs Ekonomicheskoi Geografii* [Course in Economic Geography]. Third edition, Moscow, 1928.

Z. Grishin, *Sovetskoe Trudovoe Pravo* [Soviet Labor Law]. Moscow, 1936.

E. L. Granovskii i B. L. Markus, editors, *Ekonomika Sotsialisticheskoi Promyshlennosti* [Economics of Socialist Industry]. Moscow, 1940.

R. Kats i N. Sorokin, *Sotsial'noe Strakhovanie* [Social Insurance]. Second edition, Moscow, 1936.

S. Kheiman, *K Voprosu o Proizvoditel'nosti Truda v SSSR* [On the Problem of the Productivity of Labor in the U.S.S.R.]. Moscow, 1933.

IA. Kiselev, *Spravochnik po Trudovomu Zakonodatel'stvu* [Handbook of Labor Law]. Second edition. Moscow, 1939.

IA. L. Kiselev i S. E. Malkin, *Sbornik Vazneishikh Postanovlenii po Trudu* [Handbook of the Most Important Decrees on Labor]. Second edition, Moscow, 1931; third edition, Moscow, 1931; fourth edition, Moscow, 1932; fifth edition, Moscow, 1935; sixth edition, Moscow, 1936; tenth edition, Moscow, 1938.

Komissiia po Izucheniiu Istorii Professional'nogo Dvizheniia v SSSR [Commission on the Study of the History of the Trade Union Movement in the U.S.S.R.], *Professional'nye Soiuzy SSSR* [Trade Unions in the U.S.S.R.]. Moscow, 1927.

I. M. Koz'minykh-Lanin, *Zarabotki Fabrichno-Zavodskikh Rabochikh Rossii (Iiun' 1914 g. i Iiun' 1916 g.),* [Wages of Factory Workers in Russia, June 1914 and June 1916], part 1. Moscow, 1918.

M. Krivitskii, editor, *Trud v Pervoi Piatiletke* [Labor in the First Five Year Plan]. Moscow, 1934.

——, editor, *Ekonomika Truda* [Economics of Labor]. Second edition, Moscow, 1934.

V. P. Litvinov-Falinskii, *Novye Zakony o Strakhovanii Rabochikh* [New Laws on the Insurance of Workers]. St. Petersburg, 1912.

S. Livshits, *Kadry Spetsialistov* [Cadre of Specialists]. Moscow, 1931.

G. Melnichanskii, editor, *Sbornik Profrabotnika* [Handbook of the Trade Unionist]. Moscow, 1930.

G. IA. Neiman, *Vnutrenniaia Torgovlia SSSR* [Internal Trade of the U.S.S.R.]. Moscow, 1935.

A. IA. Podzemskii, compiler; I. D. Davydov i I. G. Klabunovskii, editors, *Direktivy VKP (b) po Voprosam Prosveshcheniia* [Directives of the Communist Party on Education]. Third edition, Moscow, 1931.

S. N. Prokopovich, *Biulleten'* [Bulletin]. November–December 1937. Prague, 1937.

S. L. Rabinovich-Zakharin, *Zarabotnaia Plata po Sovetskomu Pravu* [Wages according to Soviet Law]. Moscow, 1927.

A. G. Rashin, *Zarabotnaia Plata za Vosstanovitel'nyi Period Kho-ziaistva SSSR, 1922/23–1926/27 gg.* [Wages during the Restoration Period of the Economy of the U.S.S.R., 1922/23–1926/27]. Moscow, 1928.

V. V. Shmidt, *Osnovy Trudovogo Zakonodatel'stva* [Foundations of Labor Law]. Moscow, 1929.

I. Stalin, *Voprosy Leninizma* [Problems of Leninism]. Tenth edition, Moscow, 1934.

S. G. Strumilin, *Chernaia Metallurgiia v Rossii i v SSSR* [Ferrous Metallurgy in Russia and in the U.S.S.R.]. Moscow, 1935.

——, *Zarabotnaia Plata v Russkoi Promyshlennosti za 1913–1922 gg.* [Wages in Russian Industry during the Period 1913 to 1922], in the volume RSFSR STO, *Na Novykh Putiakh*, part iii. Moscow, 1923.

A. G. Titov, *Itogi Bor'by s Uravnilovkoi v Oplate Truda Rabotnikov Sviazi* [Results of the Struggle with Equalitarianism in the Remuneration of Communication Workers]. Moscow, 1933.

L. Trotskii, *Sochineniia* [Collected Works], vol. XII. Moscow, 1925.

V. I. Val'kov, *Perestroika Zarplaty v Lesopil'nom Proizvodstve* [Reconstruction of Wages in Saw-Milling]. Moscow, 1935.

B. M. Vinogradov, *Ordena i Pochetnye Zvaniia* [Orders and Honorary Titles]. Moscow, 1937.

I. S. Voitinskii, editor, *Azbuka Sovetskogo Trudovogo Prava* [Primer of Soviet Labor Law]. Fifth edition, Moscow, 1929.

Voprosy Zarabotnoi Platy i Zadachi Profsoiuzov [Problems of Wages and Tasks of the Trade Unions]. Moscow, 1934.

V. Zasetskii, *Progressivnaia Sdel'shchina* [The Progressive Piece System]. Moscow, 1936.

INDEX

DATE DUE